Solutions Manual

Options,
Futures
AND
Other
Derivatives

Solutions Manual

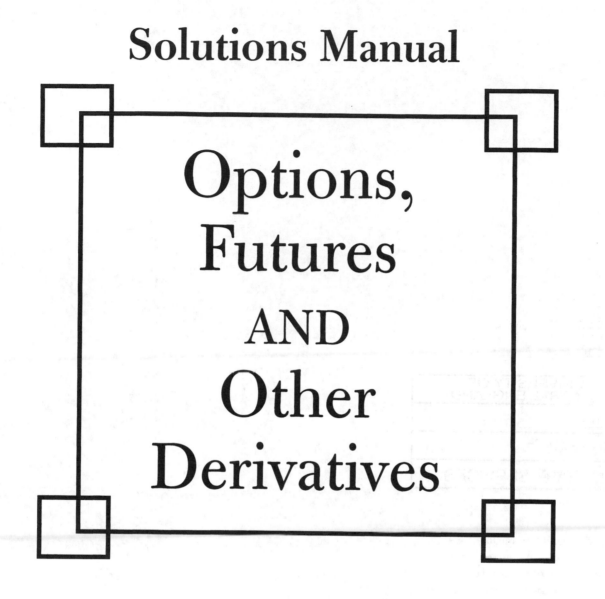

Options, Futures AND Other Derivatives

JOHN C. HULL

University of Toronto

Upper Saddle River, New Jersey 07458

Executive editor: Mickey Cox
Managing editor: Gladys Soto
Assistant editor: Beth Romph
Production editor: Wanda Rockwell
Manufacturer: VonHoffmann Graphics/MO

ISBN 0-13-009144-8

10 9 8 7 6 5

Contents

Preface

This book contains solutions to the questions and problems that appear at the ends of chapters in my book *Options, Futures, and Other Derivatives*, 5th edition. The questions and problems (about 550 in total) have been designed to help readers study on their own and test their understanding of the material. They range from quick checks on whether a key point is understood to much more challenging applications of analytical techniques. To maximize the benefits from this book readers are urged to sketch out their own solutions to the problems before consulting mine.

I welcome comments on either *Options, Futures, and Other Derivatives*, 5th edition or this book. My e-mail address is

hull@rotman.utoronto.ca

John C. Hull

CHAPTER 1
Introduction

1.1. When a trader enters into a long forward contract, she is agreeing to *buy* the underlying asset for a certain price at a certain time in the future. When a trader enters into a short forward contract, she is agreeing to *sell* the underlying asset for a certain price at a certain time in the future.

1.2. A trader is *hedging* when she has an exposure to the price of an asset and takes a position in a derivative to offset the exposure. In a *speculation* the trader has no exposure to offset. She is betting on the future movements in the price of the asset. *Arbitrage* involves taking a position in two or more different markets to lock in a profit.

1.3. In the first case the trader is obligated to buy the asset for $50. (The trader does not have a choice.) In the second case the trader has an option to buy the asset for $50. (The trader does not have to exercise the option.)

1.4. Writing a call option involves selling an option to someone else. It gives a payoff of

$$\min(K - S_T, 0)$$

Buying a put option involves buying an option from someone else. It gives a payoff of

$$\max(K - S_T, 0)$$

In both cases the potential payoff is $K - S_T$. When you write a call option, the payoff is negative or zero. (This is because the counterparty chooses whether to exercise.) When you buy a put option, the payoff is zero or positive. (This is because you choose whether to exercise.)

1.5. (a) The trader sells 100 million yen for $0.0080 per yen when the exchange rate is $0.0074 per yen. The gain is 100×0.0006 millions of dollars or $60,000.
(b) The trader sells 100 million yen for $0.0080 per yen when the exchange rate is $0.0091 per yen. The loss is 100×0.0011 millions of dollars or $110,000.

1.6. (a) The trader sells for 50 cents per pound something that is worth 48.20 cents per pound. Gain = $(\$0.5000 - \$0.4820) \times 50,000 = \$900$.
(b) The trader sells for 50 cents per pound something that is worth 51.30 cents per pound. Loss = $(\$0.5130 - \$0.5000) \times 50,000 = \$650$.

1.7. You have sold a put option. You have agreed to buy 100 AOL Time Warner shares for $40 per share if the party on the other side of the contract chooses to exercise his or her right to sell for this price. The option will be exercised only when the price of IBM is below \$40. If the counterparty exercises when the price is \$30, you have to buy at \$40 shares that are worth \$30. You lose \$10 per share or \$1,000 in total. If the counterparty exercises when the price is \$20, you lose \$20 per share or \$2,000 in total. The worst that can happen is that the price of AOL Time Warner declines to zero during the 3-month period. This highly unlikely event would cost you \$4,000. In return for the possible future losses you receive the price of the option from the purchaser.

1.8. One strategy would be to buy 200 shares. Another would be to buy 2,000 options. If the share price does well the second strategy will give rise to greater gains. For example, if the share price goes up to \$40 you gain $[2,000 \times (\$40 - \$30)] - \$5,800 = \$14,200$ from the second strategy and only $200 \times (\$40 - \$29) = \$2,200$ from the first strategy. However, if the share price does badly, the second strategy gives greater losses. For example, if the share price goes down to \$25, the first strategy leads to a loss of $200 \times (\$29 - \$25) = \$800$, whereas the second strategy leads to a loss of the whole \$5,800 investment. This example shows that options contain built in leverage.

1.9. You could buy 5,000 put options (or 50 contracts) with a strike price of \$25 and an expiration date in 4 months. This provides a type of insurance. If at the end of 4 months the stock price proves to be less than \$25 you can exercise the options and sell the shares for \$25 each. The cost of this strategy is the price you pay for the put options.

1.10. The trader makes a profit if the stock price is below \$37 at the maturity of the option. The option will be exercised if the stock price is below \$40. See Figure 1.1 for the variation of the profit with the stock price.

1.11. The trader makes a profit if the stock price is below \$54 at the maturity of the option. The option will be exercised by the counterparty if the stock price is above \$50. See Figure 1.2 for the variation of the profit with the stock price.

1.12. See Figure 1.3 for the variation of the trader's position with the asset price. We can divide the alternative asset prices into three ranges:
(a) When the asset price less than \$40, the put option provides a payoff of $40 - S_T$ and the call option provides no payoff. The options cost \$7 and so the total profit is $33 - S_T$.
(b) When the asset price is between \$40 and \$45, neither option provides a payoff. There is a net loss of \$7.
(c) When the asset price greater than \$45, the call option provides a payoff of $S_T - 45$ and the put option provides no payoff. Taking into account the \$7 cost of the options, the total profit is $S_T - 52$.
The trader makes a profit (ignoring the time value of money) if the stock price is less than \$33 or greater than \$52. This type of trading strategy is known as a strangle and is discussed in Chapter 9.

Figure 1.1   Profit from long put position in Problem 1.10

Figure 1.2   Profit from short call position in Problem 1.11

1.13. A stock option provides no funds for the company. It is a security sold by one trader to another. The company is not involved. By contrast, a stock when it is first issued is a claim sold by the company to investors and does provide funds for the company.

1.14. If a trader has an exposure to the price of an asset, she can hedge with a forward

3

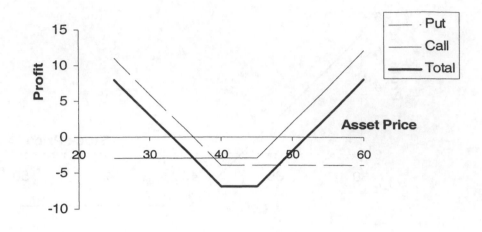

Figure 1.3 Profit from trading strategy in Problem 1.12

contract. If the exposure is such that the trader will gain when the price decreases and lose when the price increases, a long forward position will hedge the risk. If the exposure is such that the trader will lose when the price decreases and gain when the price increases, a short forward position will hedge the risk. Thus either a long or a short forward position can be entered into for hedging purposes. If the trader has no other exposure to the price of the underlying asset, entering into a forward contract is speculation.

1.15. Ignoring the time value of money, the holder of the option will make a profit if the stock price in March is greater than \$52.50. This is because the payoff to the holder of the option is, in these circumstances, greater than the \$2.50 paid for the option. The option will be exercised if the stock price at maturity is greater than \$50.00. Note that if the stock price is between \$50.00 and \$52.50 the option is exercised, but the holder of the option takes a loss overall. The profit from a long position is as shown in Figure 1.4.

1.16. Ignoring the time value of money, the seller of the option will make a profit if the stock price in June is greater than \$56.00. This is because the cost to the seller of the option is in these circumstances less than the price received for the option. The option will be exercised if the stock price at maturity is less than \$60.00. Note that if the stock price is between \$56.00 and \$60.00 the seller of the option makes a profit even though the option is exercised. The profit from the short position is as shown in Figure 1.5.

1.17. The trader receives an inflow of \$2 in May. Since the option is exercised, the trader

4

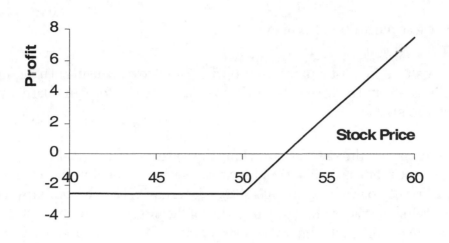

Figure 1.4   Profit from long position in Problem 1.15

Figure 1.5   Profit from short position In Problem 1.16

also has an outflow of $5 in September. The $2 is the cash received from the sale of the option. The $5 is the result of buying the stock for $25 in September and selling it to the purchaser of the option for $20.

1.18. The trader makes a gain if the price of the stock is above $26 in December. (This ignores the time value of money.)

1.19. A long position in a four-month put option can provide insurance against the exchange rate falling below the strike price. It ensures that the foreign currency can be sold for at least the strike price.

1.20. The company could enter into a long forward contract to buy 1 million Canadian dollars in six months. This would have the effect of locking in an exchange rate equal to the current forward exchange rate. Alternatively the company could buy a call option giving it the right (but not the obligation) to purchase 1 million Canadian dollar at a certain exchange rate in six months. This would provide insurance against a strong Canadian dollar in six months while still allowing the company to benefit from a weak Canadian dollar at that time.

1.21. Most traders who use the contract will wish to do one of the following:
(a) Hedge their exposure to long-term interest rates,
(b) Speculate on the future direction of long-term interest rates, and
(c) Arbitrage between cash and futures markets.
This contract is discussed in Chapter 5.

1.22. The statement means that the gain (loss) to the party with a short position in an option is always equal to the loss (gain) to the party with the long position. The sum of the gains is zero.

1.23. The terminal value of the long forward contract is:

$$S_T - F_0$$

where S_T is the price of the asset at maturity and F_0 is the forward price of the asset at the time the portfolio is set up. (The delivery price in the forward contract is F_0.) The terminal value of the put option is:

$$\max\left(F_0 - S_T,\, 0\right)$$

The terminal value of the portfolio is therefore

$$S_T - F_0 + \max\left(F_0 - S_T,\, 0\right)$$

$$= \max\left(0,\, S_T - F_0\right]$$

This is the same as the terminal value of a European call option with the same maturity as the forward contract and an exercise price equal to F_0. This result is illustrated

6

Figure 1.6   Payoff from portfolio in Problem 1.24

in the Figure 1.6. The profit equals the terminal value less the amount paid for the option.

1.24. Suppose that the yen exchange rate (yen per dollar) at maturity of the ICON is S_T. The payoff from the ICON is

$$1,000 \qquad \text{if} \qquad S_T > 169$$

$$1,000 - 1,000(\tfrac{169}{S_T} - 1) \quad \text{if} \quad 84.5 \leq S_T \leq 169$$

$$0 \qquad \text{if} \qquad S_T < 84.5$$

When $84.5 \leq S_T \leq 169$ the payoff can be written

$$2,000 - \frac{169,000}{S_T}$$

The payoff from an ICON is the payoff from:
(a) A regular bond
(b) A short position in call options to buy 169,000 yen with an exercise price of 1/169
(c) A long position in call options to buy 169,000 yen with an exercise price of 1/84.5
This is demonstrated by the following table

7

	Terminal Value of Regular Bond	Terminal Value of Short Calls	Terminal Value of Long Calls	Terminal Value of Whole Position
$S_T > 169$	1,000	0	0	1000
$84.5 \leq S_T \leq 169$	1000	$-169{,}000 \left(\frac{1}{S_T} - \frac{1}{169} \right)$	0	$2000 - \frac{169{,}000}{S_T}$
$S_T < 84.5$	1000	$-169{,}000 \left(\frac{1}{S_T} - \frac{1}{169} \right)$	$169{,}000 \left(\frac{1}{S_T} - \frac{1}{84.5} \right)$	0

1.25. Consider a range forward contract to buy one unit of a foreign currency. Suppose that S_T is the final exchange rate (value of one unit of the foreign currency) and the contract is structured so that
(a) If $S_T < K_1$, a price of K_1 is paid
(b) If $S_T > K_2$, a price of K_2 is paid
(c) If $K_1 \leq S_T \leq K_2$ the spot price is paid.
The range forward contract can be regarded as a short position in a put option with exercise price K_1 combined with a long position in a call option with exercise price K_2. This is demonstrated by the following table:

	Cost of Currency	Terminal Value of Put Position	Terminal Value of Call Position	Net Cost
$S_T < K_1$	$-S_T$	$-(K_1 - S_T)$	0	$-K_1$
$K_1 < S_T < K_2$	$-S_T$	0	0	$-S_T$
$K_2 < S_T$	$-S_T$	0	$S_T - K_2$	$-K_2$

The range forward contract is normally set up so that the initial value of the call equals the initial value of the put, that is, so that it costs nothing to set up the range forward contract. Note that when $K_1 = K_2$ a regular forward contract is obtained.

1.26. Suppose that the forward price for the contract entered into on July 1, 2002 is F_1 and that the forward price for the contract entered into on September 1, 2002 is F_2. If the value of one Japanese yen (measured in U.S. dollars) is S_T on January 1, 2003, then the value of the first contract (per yen bought) at that time is

$$S_T - F_1$$

while the value of the second contract (per yen sold) at that time is:

$$F_2 - S_T$$

The total payoff from the two contracts is therefore

$$S_T - F_1 + F_2 - S_T = F_2 - F_1$$

Thus if the forward price for delivery on January 1, 2003 increases between July 1, 2002 and September 1, 2002 the company will make a profit.

1.27. (a) The trader buys a 180-day call option and takes a short position in a 180 day forward contract. If S_T is the terminal spot rate, the profit from the call option is

$$\max\left(S_T - 1.57,\ 0\right) - 0.02$$

The profit from the short forward contract is

$$1.6018 - S_T$$

The profit from the strategy is therefore

$$\max\left(S_T - 1.57,\ 0\right) - 0.02 + 1.6018 - S_T$$

or

$$\max\left(S_T - 1.57,\ 0\right) + 1.5818 - S_T$$

This is

$$
\begin{array}{lll}
1.5818 - S_T & \text{when} & S_T < 1.57 \\
0.0118 & \text{when} & S_T > 1.57
\end{array}
$$

This shows that the profit is always positive. The time value of money has been ignored in these calculations. However, when it is taken into account the strategy is still likely to be profitable in all circumstances. (We would require an extremely high interest rate for $0.0118 interest to be required on an outlay of $0.02 over a 180-day period.)

(b) The trader buys 90-day put options and takes a long position in a 90 day forward contract. If S_T is the terminal spot rate, the profit from the put option is

$$\max\left(1.64 - S_T,\ 0\right) - 0.020$$

The profit from the long forward contract is

$$S_T - 1.6056$$

The profit from this strategy is therefore

$$\max\left(1.64 - S_T,\ 0\right) - 0.020 + S_T - 1.6056$$

or

$$\max\left(1.64 - S_T,\ 0\right) + S_T - 1.6256$$

This is

$$
\begin{array}{lll}
S_T - 1.6256 & \text{when} & S_T > 1.64 \\
0.0144 & \text{when} & S_T < 1.64
\end{array}
$$

The profit is therefore always positive. Again, the time value of money has been ignored but is unlikely to affect the overall profitability of the strategy. (We would require interest rates to be extremely high for $0.0144 interest to be required on an outlay of $0.02 over a 90-day period.)

CHAPTER 2
Mechanics of Futures Markets

2.1. The *open interest* of a futures contract at a particular time is the total number of long positions outstanding. (Equivalently, it is the total number of short positions outstanding.) The *trading volume* during a certain period of time is the number of contracts traded during this period.

2.2. A *commission broker* trades on behalf of a client and charges a commission. A *local* trades on his or her own behalf.

2.3. There will be a margin call when $1,000 has been lost from the margin account. This will occur when the price of silver increases by $1000/5000 = \$0.20$. The price of silver must therefore rise to $5.40 per ounce for there to be a margin call. If the margin call is not met, the position is closed out.

2.4. The total profit is $(\$20.50 - \$18.30) \times 1,000 = \$2,200$. Of this $(\$19.10 - \$18.30) \times 1,000 = \$800$ is realized on a day-by-day basis between September 2002 and December 31, 2002. A further $(\$20.50 - \$19.10) \times 1,000 = \$1,400$ is realized on a day-by-day basis between January 1, 2003, and March 2003. A hedger would be taxed on the whole profit of $2,200 in 2003. A speculator would be taxed on $800 in 2002 and $1,400 in 2003.

2.5. A *stop order* to sell at $2 is an order to sell at the best available price once a price of $2 or less is reached. It could be used to limit the losses from an existing long position. A *limit order* to sell at $2 is an order to sell at a price of $2 or more. It could be used to instruct a broker that a short position should be taken, providing it can be done at a price more favorable than $2.

2.6. The margin account administered by the clearinghouse is marked to market daily and the clearinghouse member is required to bring the account back up to the prescribed level daily. The margin account administered by the broker is also marked to market daily. However, it does not have to be brought up to the initial margin level on a daily basis. It has to be brought up to the initial margin level when the balance in the account falls below the maintenance margin level. The maintenance margin is about 75% of the initial margin.

2.7. In futures markets prices are quoted as the number of U.S. dollars per unit of foreign currency. Spot and forward rates are quoted in this way for the British pound, euro, Australian dollar, and New Zealand dollar. For other major currencies, spot and forward rates are quoted as the number of units of foreign currency per U.S. dollar.

2.8. These options make the contract less attractive to the party with the long position and more attractive to the party with the short position. They therefore tend to reduce the futures price.

2.9. The most important aspects of the design of a new futures contract are the specification of the underlying asset, the size of the contract, the delivery arrangements, and the delivery months.

2.10. A margin is a sum of money deposited by an investor with his or her broker. It acts as a guarantee that the investor can cover any losses on the futures contract. The balance in the margin account is adjusted daily to reflect gains and losses on the futures contract. If losses are above a certain level, the investor is required to deposit a further margin. This system makes it unlikely that the investor will default. A similar system of margins makes it unlikely that the investor's broker will default on the contract it has with the clearinghouse member and unlikely that the clearinghouse member will default with the clearinghouse.

2.11. There is a margin call if $1,500 is lost on one contract. This happens if the futures price of frozen orange juice falls by 10 cents to 150 cents per lb. $2,000 can be withdrawn from the margin account if there is a gain on one contract of $1,000. This will happen if the futures price rises by 6.67 cents to 166.67 cents per lb.

2.12. If the futures price is greater than the spot price during the delivery period, an arbitrageur buys the asset, shorts a futures contract, and makes delivery for an immediate profit. If the futures price is less than the spot price during the delivery period, there is no similar perfect arbitrage strategy. An arbitrageur can take a long futures position but cannot force immediate delivery of the asset. The decision on when delivery will be made is made by the party with the short position. Nevertheless companies interested in acquiring the asset will find it attractive to enter into a long futures contract and wait for delivery to be made.

2.13. A market-if-touched order is executed at the best available price after a trade occurs at a specified price or at a price more favorable than the specified price. A stop order is executed at the best available price after there is a bid or offer at the specified price or at a price less favorable than the specified price.

2.14. A stop-limit order to sell at 20.30 with a limit of 20.10 means that as soon as there is a bid at 20.30 the contract should be sold providing this can be done at 20.10 or a higher price.

2.15. The clearinghouse member is required to provide $20 \times \$2,000 = \$40,000$ as initial margin for the new contracts. There is a gain of $(50,200 - 50,000) \times 100 = \$20,000$ on the existing contracts. There is also a loss of $(51,000 - 50,200) \times 20 = \$16,000$ on the new contracts. The member must therefore add

$$40,000 - 20,000 + 16,000 = \$36,000$$

to the margin account.

2.16. Suppose F_1 and F_2 are the forward exchange rates for the contracts entered into July 1, 2002 and September 1, 2002, and S_T is the spot rate on January 1, 2003. The payoff from the first contract is $10(S_T - F_1)$ million yen and the payoff from the second contract is $10(F_2 - S_T)$ million yen. The total payoff is therefore $10(F_2 - F_1)$ million yen.

2.17. The 1.8204 forward quote is the number of Swiss francs per dollar. The 0.5479 futures quote is the number of dollars per Swiss franc. When quoted in the same way as the futures price the forward price is $1/1.8204 = 0.5493$. The Swiss franc is therefore more valuable in the forward market than in the futures market. The forward market is therefore more attractive for an investor wanting to sell Swiss francs.

2.18. Hog futures are traded on the Chicago Mercantile Exchange. (See Table 2.2). The broker will request some initial margin. The order will be relayed by telephone to your broker's trading desk on the floor of the exchange (or to the trading desk of another broker). It will be sent by messenger to a commission broker who will execute the trade according to your instructions. Confirmation of the trade eventually reaches you. If there are adverse movements in the futures price your broker may contact you to request additional margin.

2.19. Speculators are important market participants because they add liquidity to the market. However, contracts must have some useful economic purpose. Regulators generally only approve contracts when they are likely to be of interest to hedgers as well as speculators.

2.20. The contracts with the highest open interest are

Grains and Oilseeds:	Corn (CBT)
Livestock and Meat:	Cattle-Live (CME)
Food and Fiber:	Sugar–World (CSCE)
Metals and Petroleum:	Crude Oil (NYM)

2.21. The contract would not be a success. Parties with short positions would hold their contracts until delivery and then deliver the cheapest form of the asset. This might well be viewed by the party with the long position as garbage! Once news of the quality problem became widely known no one would be prepared to buy the contract. This shows that futures contracts are feasible only when there are rigorous standards within an industry for defining the quality of the asset. Many futures contracts have in practice failed because of the problem of defining quality.

2.22. If both sides of the transaction are entering into a new contract, the open interest increases by one. If both sides of the transaction are closing out existing positions, the open interest decreases by one. If one party is entering into a new contract while the other party is closing out an existing position, the open interest stays the same.

2.23. The total profit is

$$40,000 \times (0.6120 - 0.5830) = \$1,160$$

If you are a hedger this is all taxed in 2003. If you are a speculator

$$40,000 \times (0.6120 - 0.5880) = \$960$$

is taxed in 2002 and

$$40,000 \times (0.5880 - 0.5830) = \$200$$

is taxed in 2003.

2.24. The farmer can short 3 contracts which have 3 months to maturity. If the price of cattle falls, the gain on the futures contract will offset the loss on the sale of the cattle. If the price of cattle rises, the gain on the sale of the cattle will be offset by the loss on the futures contract. Using futures contracts to hedge has the advantage that it can at no cost reduce risk to almost zero. Its disadvantage is that the farmer no longer gains from favorable movements in cattle prices.

2.25. The mining company can estimate its production on a month-by-month basis. It can then short futures contracts to lock in the price received for the gold. For example, if 3000 ounces are expected to be produced in March 2003 and April 2003, the price received for this production can be hedged by shorting a total of 30 April 2003 contracts.

CHAPTER 3
Determination of Forward and Futures Prices

3.1. (a) The rate with continuous compounding is

$$4 \ln \left(1 + \frac{0.14}{4}\right) = 0.1376$$

or 13.76% per annum.

(b) The rate with annual compounding is

$$\left(1 + \frac{0.14}{4}\right)^4 - 1 = 0.1475$$

or 14.75% per annum.

3.2. The investor's broker borrows the shares from another client's account and sells them in the usual way. To close out the position the investor must purchase the shares. The broker then replaces them in the account of the client from whom they were borrowed. The party with the short position must remit to the broker dividends and other income paid on the shares. The broker transfers the funds to the account of the client from whom the shares were borrowed. Occasionally the broker runs out of places from which to borrow the shares. The investor is then short squeezed and has to close out the position immediately.

3.3. The forward price is
$$30e^{0.12 \times 0.5} = \$31.86$$

3.4. The futures price is
$$350e^{(0.08 - 0.04) \times 0.3333} = \$354.7$$

3.5. Gold is held for investment by some investors. If the futures price is too high, investors will find it profitable to increase their holdings of gold and short futures contracts. If the futures price is too low, they will find it profitable to decrease their holding of gold and go long in the futures market. Copper is a consumption asset. If the futures price is too high, a "buy copper and short futures" contract works. However, since investors do not in general hold the asset, the "sell copper and buy futures strategy" is not widely used when the futures price is low. There is therefore an upper bound but no lower bound to the futures price.

3.6. Convenience yield measures the extent to which there are benefits obtained from ownership of the physical asset that are not obtained by owners of long futures contracts. The cost of carry is the interest cost plus storage cost less the income earned. The futures price, F_0, and spot price, S_0, are related by

$$F_0 = S_0 e^{(c-y)T}$$

where c is the cost of carry, y is the convenience yield, and T is the time to maturity of the futures contract.

3.7. The futures price of a stock index is always less than the expected future value of the index. This follows from the arguments in Section 3.15 and the fact that the index has positive systematic risk. Let μ be the expected return required by investors on the index so that $E(S_T) = S_0 e^{(\mu-q)T}$ where E denotes expected value. Since $\mu > r$ and $F_0 = S_0 e^{(r-q)T}$, it follows that $E(S_T) > F_0$.

3.8. (a) With annual compounding the return is

$$\frac{1100}{1000} - 1 = 0.1$$

or 10% per annum.

(b) With semi-annual compounding the return is R where

$$1000 \left(1 + \frac{R}{2}\right)^2 = 1100$$

i.e.,

$$1 + \frac{R}{2} = \sqrt{1.1} = 1.0488$$

so that $R = 0.0976$. The percentage return is therefore 9.76% per annum.

(c) With monthly compounding the return is R where

$$1000 \left(1 + \frac{R}{12}\right)^{12} = 1100$$

i.e.,

$$\left(1 + \frac{R}{12}\right) = \sqrt[12]{1.1} = 1.00797$$

so that $R = 0.0957$ The percentage return is therefore 9.57% per annum.

(d) With continuous compounding the return is R where:

$$1000 e^R = 1100$$

i.e.,
$$e^R = 1.1$$
so that $R = \ln 1.1 = 0.0953$. The percentage return is therefore 9.53% per annum.

3.9. The rate of interest is R where:
$$e^R = \left(1 + \frac{0.15}{12}\right)^{12}$$

i.e.,
$$R = 12\ln\left(1 + \frac{0.15}{12}\right)$$
$$= 0.1491$$

The rate of interest is therefore 14.91% per annum.

3.10. The equivalent rate of interest with quarterly compounding is R where
$$e^{0.12} = \left(1 + \frac{R}{4}\right)^4$$

or
$$R = 4(e^{0.03} - 1) = 0.1218$$

The amount of interest paid each quarter is therefore:
$$10000 \times \frac{0.1218}{4} = 304.55$$

or $304.55.

3.11. (a) The forward price, F_0, is given by equation (3.5) as:
$$F_0 = 40e^{0.1} = 44.21$$

or $44.21. The initial value of the forward contract is zero.

(b) The delivery price K in the contract is $44.21. The value of the contract, f, after six months is given by equation (3.9) as:
$$f = 45 - 44.21e^{-0.1 \times 0.5}$$
$$= 2.95$$

i.e., it is $2.95. The forward price is given by:
$$45e^{0.1 \times 0.5} = 47.31$$

16

or $47.31.

3.12. Using equation (3.7) the six month futures price is

$$150e^{(0.07-0.032)\times0.5} = 152.88$$

or $152.88.

3.13. The futures contract lasts for five months. The dividend yield is 2% for three of the months and 5% for two of the months. The average dividend yield is therefore

$$\frac{1}{5}(3 \times 2 + 2 \times 5) = 3.2\%$$

The futures price is therefore

$$300e^{(0.09-0.032)\times0.4167} = 307.34$$

or $307.34.

3.14. The theoretical futures price is

$$400e^{(0.10-0.04)\times0.3333} = 408.08$$

The actual futures price is only 405. This shows that the index futures price is too low relative to the index. The correct arbitrage strategy is
(a) Go long futures contracts
(b) Short the shares underlying the index.

3.15. The settlement prices for the futures contracts are
   Mar   0.10403
   Sept   0.09815
The September 2001 price is about 5.65% below the March 2001 price. This suggests that the short-term interest rate in the Mexico exceeded short-term interest rates in the United States by about 5.65% per six months or about 11.3% per year.

3.16. The theoretical futures price is

$$0.65e^{0.1667\times(0.08-0.03)} = 0.6554$$

The actual futures price is too high. This suggests that an arbitrageur should borrow U.S. dollars, buy Swiss francs, and short Swiss franc futures.

3.17. The present value of the storage costs for nine months are

$$0.06 + 0.06e^{-0.25\times0.1} + 0.06e^{-0.5\times0.1} = 0.176$$

or $0.176. The futures price is from equation (3.15) given by F_0 where

$$F_0 = (9.000 + 0.176)e^{0.1 \times 0.75} = 9.89$$

i.e., it is $9.89 per ounce.

3.18. If

$$F_2 > (F_1 + U)e^{r(t_2 - t_1)}$$

an investor could make a riskless profit by
(a) taking a long position in a futures contract which matures at time t_1
(b) taking a short position in a futures contract which matures at time t_2
When the first futures contract matures, an amount $F_1 + U$ is borrowed at rate r
for time $t_2 - t_1$. The funds are used to purchase the asset for F_1 and store it until
time t_2. At time t_2 it is exchanged for F_2 under the second contract. An amount
$(F_1 + U)e^{r(t_2 - t_1)}$ is required to repay the loan. A positive profit of

$$F_2 - (F_1 + U)e^{r(t_2 - t_1)}$$

is, therefore, realized at time t_2. This type of arbitrage opportunity cannot exist for
long. Hence:

$$F_2 \leq (F_1 + U)e^{r(t_2 - t_1)}$$

3.19. In total the gain or loss under a futures contract is equal to the gain or loss under
the corresponding forward contract. However the timing of the cash flows is different.
When the time value of money is taken into account a futures contract may prove to
be more valuable or less valuable than a forward contract. Of course the company does
not know in advance which will work out better. The long forward contract provides
a perfect hedge. The long futures contract provides a slightly imperfect hedge.

(a) In this case, the forward contract leads to a slightly better outcome. The company
takes a loss on its hedge. If a forward contract is used, the whole of the loss is realized
at the end. If a futures contract is used, the loss is realized day by day throughout
the contract. On a present value basis the former is preferable.

(b) In this case the futures contract leads to a slightly better outcome. The company
makes a gain on the hedge. If a forward contract is used, the gain is realized at the
end. If a futures contract is used, the gain is realized day by day throughout the life
of the contract. On a present value basis the latter is preferable.

(c) In this case the futures contract leads to a slightly better outcome. This is because
it gives rise to positive cash flows early and negative cash flows later.

(d) In this case the forward contract leads to a slightly better outcome. This is
because, when a futures contract is used, the early cash flows are negative and the
later cash flows are positive.

3.20. From equation (3.25) the forward exchange rate is an unbiased predictor of the future exchange rate when $r - k$. This is the case when the exchange rate has no systematic risk.

3.21. Suppose that F_0 is the futures price at time zero for a contract maturing at time T and F_1 is the futures price for the same contract at time t_1. It follows that

$$F_0 = S_0 e^{(r-q)T}$$

$$F_1 = S_1 e^{(r-q)(T-t_1)}$$

where S_0 and S_1 are the spot price at times zero and t_1, r is the risk-free rate, and q is the dividend yield. These equations imply that

$$\frac{F_1}{F_0} = \frac{S_1}{S_0} e^{-(r-q)t_1}$$

Define the excess return of the index over the risk-free rate as x. The total return is $r + x$ and the return realized in the form of capital gains is $r + x - q$. It follows that $S_1 = S_0 e^{(r+x-q)t_1}$ and the equation for F_1/F_0 reduces to

$$\frac{F_1}{F_0} = e^{xt_1}$$

which is the required result.

3.22. Suppose we buy N units of the asset and invest the income from the asset in the asset. The income from the asset causes our holding in the asset to grow at a continuously compounded rate q. By time T our holding has grown to Ne^{qT} units of the asset. Analogously to footnotes 2 and 3, we therefore buy N units of the asset at time zero at a cost of S_0 per unit and enter into a forward contract to sell Ne^{qT} unit for F_0 per unit at time T. This generates the following cash flows:

Time 0: $-NS_0$

Time T: NF_0e^{qT}

Because there is no uncertainty about these cash flows, the present value of the time T inflow must equal the time zero outflow when we discount at the risk-free rate. This means that

$$NS_0 = (NF_0e^{qT})e^{-rT}$$

or

$$F_0 = S_0 e^{(r-q)T}$$

This is equation (3.7).

If $F_0 > S_0 e^{(r-q)T}$, an arbitrageur should borrow money at rate r and buy N units of the asset. At the same time the arbitrageur should enter into a forward contract to sell Ne^{qT} units of the asset at time T. As income is received, it is reinvested in the asset. At time T the loan is repaid and the arbitrageur makes a profit of $N(F_0e^{qT} - S_0e^{rT})$ at time T.

If $F_0 < S_0 e^{(r-q)T}$, an arbitrageur should short N units of the asset investing the proceeds at rate r. At the same time the arbitrageur should enter into a forward contract to buy Ne^{qT} units of the asset at time T. When income is paid on the asset, the arbitrageur owes money on the short position. The investor meets this obligation from the cash proceeds of shorting further units. The result is that the number of units shorted grows at rate q to Ne^{qT}. The cumulative short position is closed out at time T and the arbitrageur makes a profit of $N(S_0 e^{rT} - F_0 e^{qT})$.

3.23. When the geometric average of the price relatives is used, the changes in the value of the index do not correspond to changes in the value of a portfolio that is traded. Equation (3.12) is therefore no longer correct. The changes in the value of the portfolio is monitored by an index calculated from the arithmetic average of the prices of the stocks in the portfolio. Since the geometric average of a set of numbers is always less than the arithmetic average, equation (3.12) overstates the futures price. It is rumored that at one time (prior to 1988), equation (3.12) did hold for the Value Line Index. A major Wall Street firm was the first to recognize that this represented a trading opportunity. It made a financial killing by buying the stocks underlying the index and shorting the futures.

CHAPTER 4
Hedging Strategies Using Futures

4.1. A *short hedge* is appropriate when a company owns an asset and expects to sell that asset in the future. It can also be used when the company does not currently own the asset but expects to do so at some time in the future. A *long hedge* is appropriate when a company knows it will have to purchase an asset in the future. It can also be used to offset the risk from an existing short position.

4.2. *Basis risk* arises from the hedger's uncertainty as to the difference between the spot price and futures price at the expiration of the hedge.

4.3. A *perfect hedge* is one that completely eliminates the hedger's risk. A perfect hedge does not always lead to a better outcome than an imperfect hedge. It just leads to a more certain outcome. Consider a company that hedges its exposure to the price of an asset. Suppose the asset's price movements prove to be favorable to the company. A perfect hedge totally neutralizes the company's gain from these favorable price movements. An imperfect hedge, which only partially neutralizes the gains, might well give a better outcome.

4.4. A minimum variance hedge leads to no hedging at all when the coefficient of correlation between the futures price and the price of the asset being hedged is zero.

4.5. (a) If the company's competitors are not hedging, the treasurer might feel that the company will experience less risk if it does not hedge.
(b) The treasurer might feel that the company's shareholders have diversified the risk away.
(c) If there is a loss on the hedge and a gain from the company's exposure to the underlying asset, the treasurer might feel that he or she will have difficulty justifying the hedging to other executives within the organization.

4.6. The optimal hedge ratio is

$$0.8 \times \frac{0.65}{0.81} = 0.642$$

This means that the size of the futures position should be 64.2% of the size of the company's exposure in a three-month hedge.

4.7. The formula for the number of contracts that should be shorted gives

$$1.2 \times \frac{20,000,000}{1080 \times 250} = 88.9$$

Rounding to the nearest whole number, 89 contracts should be shorted. To reduce the beta to 0.6, half of this position, or a short position in 44 contracts, is required.

4.8. A good rule of thumb is to choose a futures contract that has a delivery month as close as possible to, but later than, the month containing the expiration of the hedge. The contracts that should be used are therefore
(a) July
(b) September
(c) March

4.9. No. Consider for example the use of a forward contract to hedge a known cash inflow in a foreign currency. The forward contract locks in the forward exchange rate — which is in general different from the spot exchange rate.

4.10. The basis is the amount by which the spot price exceeds the futures price. A short hedger is long the asset and short futures contracts. The value of his or her position therefore improves as the basis increases. Similarly it worsens as the basis decreases.

4.11. The simple answer to this question is that the treasurer should
1. Estimate the company's future cash flows in Japanese yen and U.S. dollars
2. Enter into forward and futures contracts to lock in the exchange rate for the U.S. dollar cash flows.
However, this is not the whole story. As the gold jewellery example in Table 4.1 shows, the company should examine whether the magnitudes of the foreign cash flows depend on the exchange rate. For example, will the company be able to raise the price of its product in U.S. dollars if the yen appreciates? If the company can do so its foreign exchange exposure may be quite low. The key estimates required are those showing the overall effect on the company's profitability of changes in the exchange rate at various times in the future. Once these estimates have been produced the company can choose between using futures and options to hedge its risk. The results of the analysis should be presented carefully to other executives. It should be explained that a hedge does not ensure that profits will be higher. It means that profit will be more certain. When futures/forwards are used both the downside and upside are eliminated. With options a premium is paid to eliminate only the downside.

4.12. If the hedge ratio is 0.8, the company takes a long position in 16 NYM December oil futures contracts on June 8 when the futures price is $18.00. It closes out its position on November 10. The spot price and futures price at this time are $20.00 and $19.10. The gain on the futures position is

$$(19.10 - 18.00) \times 16,000 = 17,600$$

The effective cost of the oil is therefore

$$20,000 \times 20 - 17,600 = 382,400$$

or $19.12 per barrel. (This compares with $18.90 per barrel when the company is fully hedged.)

4.13. The statement is not true. The minimum variance hedge ratio is

$$\rho \frac{\sigma_S}{\sigma_F}$$

It is 1.0 when $\rho = 0.5$ and $\sigma_S = 2\sigma_F$. Since $\rho < 1.0$ the hedge is clearly not perfect.

4.14. The statement is true. Using the notation in the text, if the hedge ratio is 1.0, the hedger locks in a price of $F_1 + b_2$. Since both F_1 and b_2 are known this has a variance of zero and must be the best hedge.

4.15. When the convenience yield is high the futures price is much less than the current spot price. A company that knows it will purchase a commodity in the future is able to lock in a price close to the futures price.

4.16. The optimal hedge ratio is

$$0.7 \times \frac{1.2}{1.4} = 0.6$$

The beef producer requires a long position in $200000 \times 0.6 = 120,000$ lbs of cattle. The beef producer should therefore take a long position in 3 December contracts closing out the position on November 15.

4.17. If weather creates a significant uncertainty about the volume of corn that will be harvested, the farmer should not enter into short forward contracts to hedge the price risk on his or her expected production. The reason is as follows. Suppose that the weather is bad and the farmer's production is lower than expected. Other farmers are likely to have been affected similarly. Corn production overall will be low and as a consequence the price of corn will be relatively high. The farmer's problems arising from the bad harvest will be made worse by losses on the short futures position. This problem emphasizes the importance of looking at the big picture when hedging. The farmer is correct to question whether hedging price risk while ignoring other risks is a good strategy.

4.18. A short position in

$$1.3 \times \frac{50,000 \times 30}{50 \times 1,500} = 26$$

contracts is required.

4.19. If the company uses a hedge ratio of 1.5 it would at each stage short 150 contracts. The gain from the futures contracts would be

$$1.50 \times 1.70 = \$2.55 \text{ per barrel}$$

and the company would be \$0.85 per barrel better off.

4.20. (a) The relationship between the futures price F_t and the spot price S_t at time t is

$$F_t = S_t e^{(r - r_f)(T - t)}$$

Suppose that the hedge ratio is h. The price obtained with hedging is

$$h(F_0 - F_t) + S_t$$

where F_0 is the initial futures price. This is

$$hF_0 + S_t - hS_t e^{(r-r_f)(T-t)}$$

If $h = e^{(r_f-r)(T-t)}$, this reduces to hF_0 and a zero variance hedge is obtained.

(b) When t is one day, h is approximately $e^{(r_f-r)T} = S_0/F_0$. The appropriate hedge ratio is therefore S_0/F_0.

(c) When a futures contract is used for hedging, the price movements in each day should in theory be hedged separately. This is because the daily settlement means that a futures contract is closed out and rewritten at the end of each day. From (b) the correct hedge ratio at any given time is, therefore, S/F where S is the spot price and F is the futures price. Suppose there is an exposure to N units of the foreign currency and M units of the foreign currency underlie one futures contract. With a hedge ratio of 1 we should trade N/M contracts. With a hedge ratio of S/F we should trade

$$\frac{SN}{FM}$$

contracts. In other words we should calculate the number of contracts that should be traded as the dollar value of our exposure divided by the dollar value of one futures contract (This is not the same as the dollar value of our exposure divided by the dollar value of the assets underlying one futures contract.) Since a futures contract is settled daily, we should in theory rebalance our hedge daily so that the outstanding number of futures contracts is always $(SN)/(FM)$. This is known as tailing the hedge.

4.21. What the airline executive says may be true. However, it can be argued that an airline is not in the business of forecasting the price of oil or of exposing its shareholders to the risk associated with the future price of oil. It should hedge and focus on its area of expertise.

CHAPTER 5
Interest Rate Markets

5.1. Forward rates (with continuous compounding) for years two, three, four, and five are 7.0%, 6.6%, 6.4%, and 6.5%, respectively.

5.2. When the term structure is upward sloping $c > a > b$. When it is downward sloping $b > a > c$.

5.3. Consider a bond with a face value of $100. Its price is obtained by discounting the cash flows at 10.4% per year or 5.2% per six months. The price is

$$\frac{4}{1.052} + \frac{4}{1.052^2} + \frac{104}{1.052^3} = 96.74$$

If the 18-month spot rate is R we must have

$$\frac{4}{1.05} + \frac{4}{1.05^2} + \frac{104}{(1 + R/2)^3} = 96.74$$

which gives $R = 10.42\%$.

5.4. There are 89 days between October 12 and January 9 and 182 days between October 12 and April 12. The cash price of the bond is obtained by adding the accrued interest to the quoted price. It is

$$102.21875 + \frac{89}{182} \times 6 = 105.15$$

5.5. Cash price of Treasury bill is

$$100 - \frac{1}{4} \times 10 = 97.5$$

Continuously compounded return on an actual/actual basis is

$$\frac{365}{90} \ln \frac{100}{97.5} = 10.27\%$$

5.6. A duration-based hedging scheme assumes that term structure movements are always parallel. In other words it assumes that interest rates of all maturities always change by the same amount in a given period of time.

5.7. Value of a contract is $108.46875 \times 1,000 = 108,468.75$. The number of contracts that should be shorted is

$$\frac{6,000,000}{108,468.75} \times \frac{8.2}{7.6} = 59.7$$

Rounding to the nearest whole number, 60 contracts should be shorted.

5.8. The bond pays \$2 in 6, 12, 18, and 24 months, and \$102 in 30 months. The cash price is

$$2e^{-0.04 \times 0.5} + 2e^{-0.042 \times 1.0} + 2e^{-0.044 \times 1.5} + 2e^{-0.046 \times 2} + 102e^{-0.048 \times 2.5} = 98.04$$

5.9. The bond pays \$4 in 6, 12, 18, 24, and 30 months, and \$104 in 36 months. The bond yield is the value of y that solves

$$4e^{-0.5y} + 4e^{-1.0y} + 4e^{-1.5y} + 4e^{-2.0y} + 4e^{-2.5y} + 104e^{-3.0y} = 104$$

Using the Goal Seek tool in Excel $y = 0.06407$ or 6.407%.

5.10. Using the notation in the text, $m = 2$, $d = e^{-0.07 \times 2} = 0.8694$. Also

$$A = e^{-0.05 \times 0.5} + e^{-0.06 \times 1.0} + e^{-0.065 \times 1.5} + e^{-0.07 \times 2.0} = 3.6935$$

The formula in the text gives the par yield as

$$\frac{(100 - 100 \times 0.8694) \times 2}{3.6935} = 7.072$$

To verify that this is correct we calculate the value of a bond that pays a coupon of 7.072% per year (that is 3.05365 every six months). The value is

$$3.536e^{-0.05 \times 0.5} + 3.5365e^{-0.06 \times 1.0} + 3.536e^{-0.065 \times 1.5} + 103.536e^{-0.07 \times 2.0} = 100$$

verifying that 7.072% is the par yield.

5.11. The 6-month rate (with continuous compounding) is $2\ln(1 + 6/94) = 12.38\%$. The 12-month rate is $\ln(1 + 11/89) = 11.65\%$.
For the 1.5-year bond we must have

$$4e^{-0.1238 \times 0.5} + 4e^{-0.1165 \times 1.0} + 104e^{-1.5R} = 94.84$$

where R is the 1.5-year spot rate. It follows that

$$3.76 + 3.56 + 104e^{-1.5R} = 94.84$$

$$e^{-1.5R} = 0.8415$$

$$R = 0.115$$

or 11.5%. For the 2-year bond we must have

$$5e^{-0.1238 \times 0.5} + 5e^{-0.1165 \times 1.0} + 5e^{-0.115 \times 1.5} + 105e^{-2R} = 97.12$$

where R is the 2-year spot rate. It follows that

$$e^{-2R} = 0.7977$$
$$R = 0.113$$

or 11.3%.

5.12. The forward rates are as follows:

Year 2:	14.0%
Year 3:	15.1%
Year 4:	15.7%
Year 5:	15.7%

5.13. The forward rates are as follows

Qtr 2:	8.4%
Qtr 3:	8.8%
Qtr 4:	8.8%
Qtr 5:	9.0%
Qtr 6:	9.2%

5.14 A long position in two of the 4% coupon bonds combined with a short position in one of the 8% coupon bonds leads to the following cash flows

$$\text{Year } 0 : 90 - 2 \times 80 = -70$$
$$\text{Year } 10 : 200 - 100 = 100$$

since the coupons cancel out. The 10-year spot rate is therefore

$$\frac{1}{10} \ln \frac{100}{70} = 0.0357$$

or 3.57% per annum.

5.15. If long-term rates were simply a reflection of expected future short-term rates, we would expect the term structure to be downward sloping as often as it is upward sloping. (This is based on the assumption that half of the time investors expect rates to increase and half of the time investors expect rates to decrease). Liquidity preference theory argues that long-term rates are high relative to expected future short-term rates. This means that the term structure should be upward sloping more often than it is downward sloping.

5.16. The number of days between January 27, 2003 and May 5, 2003 is 98. The number of days between January 27, 2003 and July 27, 2003 is 181. The accrued interest is therefore

$$6 \times \frac{98}{181} = 3.2486$$

The quoted price is 110.5312. The cash price is therefore

$$110.5312 + 3.2486 = 113.7798$$

or $113.78.

5.17. The cheapest-to-deliver bond is the one for which

$$\text{Quoted Price} - \text{Futures Price} \times \text{Conversion Factor}$$

is least. Calculating this factor for each of the 4 bonds we get

$$\text{Bond 1: } 125.15625 - 101.375 \times 1.2131 = 2.178$$
$$\text{Bond 2: } 142.46875 - 101.375 \times 1.3792 = 2.652$$
$$\text{Bond 3: } 115.96875 - 101.375 \times 1.1149 = 2.946$$
$$\text{Bond 4: } 144.06250 - 101.375 \times 1.4026 = 1.874$$

Bond 4 is therefore the cheapest to deliver.

5.18. There are 176 days between February 4 and July 30 and 181 days between February 4 and August 4. The cash price of the bond is, therefore:

$$110 + \frac{176}{181} \times 6.5 = 116.32$$

The rate of interest with continuous compounding is $2 \ln 1.06 = 0.1165$ or 11.65% per annum. A coupon of 6.5 will be received in 5 days ($= 0.01366$ years) time. The present value of the coupon is

$$6.5 e^{-0.01366 \times 0.1165} = 6.490$$

The futures contract lasts for 62 days ($= 0.1694$ years). The cash futures price if the contract were written on the 13% bond would be

$$(116.32 - 6.490) e^{0.1694 \times 0.1165} = 112.02$$

At delivery there are 57 days of accrued interest. The quoted futures price if the contract were written on the 13% bond would therefore be

$$112.02 - 6.5 \times \frac{57}{184} = 110.01$$

Taking the conversion factor into account the quoted futures price should be:

$$\frac{110.01}{1.5} = 73.34$$

5.19. If the bond to be delivered and the time of delivery were known, arbitrage would be straightforward. When the futures price is too high, the arbitrageur buys bonds and shorts an equivalent number of bond futures contracts. When the futures price is too low, the arbitrageur sells bonds and goes long an equivalent number of bond futures contracts.

Uncertainty as to which bond will be delivered introduces complications. The bond that appears cheapest to deliver now may not in fact be cheapest-to-deliver at maturity. In the case where the futures price is too high, this is not a major problem since the party with the short position (i.e., the arbitrageur) determines which bond is to be delivered. In the case where the futures price is too low, the arbitrageur's position is far more difficult since he or she does not know which bond to buy; it is unlikely that a profit can be locked in for all possible outcomes.

5.20. The forward rate is 9.0% with continuous compounding or 9.102% with quarterly compounding. The value of the FRA is therefore

$$[1,000,000 \times 0.25 \times (0.095 - 0.09102)]e^{-0.086 \times 1.25} = 893.56$$

or $893.56.

5.21. The forward interest rate for the time period between months 6 and 9 is 9% per annum. This is because 9% per annum for three months when combined with $7\frac{1}{2}$% per annum for six months gives an average interest rate of 8% per annum for the nine-month period.

For there to be no arbitrage the Eurodollar futures contract should lock an interest rate of 9% per annum for the period between 6 months and 9 months. When expressed with quarterly compounding this is:

$$4[e^{0.09 \times 0.25} - 1] = 0.09102$$

When expressed on an actual/360 basis it is $0.09102 \times 360/365 = 0.08977$. Its price should therefore be $100 - 8.977 = 91.023$ This analysis assumes no difference between forward and futures prices.

5.22. (a) The bond's price is

$$8e^{-0.11} + 8e^{-0.11 \times 2} + 8e^{-0.11 \times 3} + 8e^{-0.11 \times 4} + 108e^{-0.11 \times 5} = 86.80$$

(b) The bond's duration is

$$\frac{1}{86.80}\left[8e^{-0.11} + 2 \times 8e^{-0.11 \times 2} + 3 \times 8e^{-0.11 \times 3} + 4 \times 8e^{-0.11 \times 4} + 5 \times 108e^{-0.11 \times 5}\right]$$

$$= 4.256 \text{ years}$$

(c) Since, with the notation in the chapter

$$\delta B = -BD\delta y$$

the effect on the bond's price of a 0.2% decrease in its yield is

$$86.80 \times 4.256 \times 0.002 = 0.74$$

The bond's price should increase from 86.80 to 87.54.

(d) With a 10.8% yield the bond's price is

$$8e^{-0.108} + 8e^{-0.108 \times 2} + 8e^{-0.108 \times 3} + 8e^{-0.108 \times 4} + 108e^{-0.108 \times 5} = 87.54$$

This is consistent with the answer in (c).

5.23. Duration-based hedging schemes assume parallel shifts in the yield curve. Since the 12-year rate moves by less than the 4-year rate, the portfolio manager is likely to be over-hedged.

5.24. The company treasurer can hedge the company's exposure by shorting Eurodollar futures contracts. The Eurodollar futures position leads to a profit if rates rise and a loss if they fall.
The duration of the commercial paper (180 days) is twice that of the Eurodollar deposit underlying the Eurodollar futures contract (90 days). From equation (5.6) the contract price of a Eurodollar futures contract is 980,000. The number of contracts that should be shorted is, therefore,

$$\frac{4,820,000}{980,000} \times 2 = 9.84$$

Rounding to the nearest whole number 10 contracts should be shorted.

5.25. The treasurer should short Treasury bond futures contract. If bond prices go down, this futures position will provide offsetting gains. The number of contracts that should be shorted is
$$\frac{10,000,000 \times 7.1}{91,375 \times 8.8} = 88.30$$

Rounding to the nearest whole number 88 contracts should be shorted.

5.26. The answer in Problem 5.25 is designed to reduce the duration to zero. To reduce the duration from 7.1 to 3.0 instead of from 7.1 to 0, the treasurer should short

$$\frac{4.1}{7.1} \times 88.30 = 50.99$$

or 51 contracts.

5.27. You would prefer to own the corporate bond. Under the 30/360 daycount convention there are 3 days between February 28, 2002 and March 1, 2002. Under the actual/actual (in period) day count convention, there is only one day. Therefore you would earn approximately three times as much interest by holding the corporate bond!

5.28. The Eurodollar futures contract price of 88 means that the Eurodollar futures rate is 12% per annum with quarterly compounding. This is the forward rate for the 60- to 150-day period with quarterly compounding and an actual/360 day count convention.

5.29. The par yield is the yield on a coupon-bearing bond that is worth par. The zero rate is the yield on a zero-coupon bond. When the yield curve is upward sloping, the yield on an N-year coupon-bearing bond is less than the yield on an N-year zero-coupon bond. This is because the coupons are discounted at a lower rate than the N-year rate and drag the yield down below this rate. Similarly, when the yield curve is downward sloping, the yield on an N-year coupon bearing bond is higher than the yield on an N-year zero-coupon bond.

5.30. Using the notation of Section 5.11, $\sigma = 0.011$, $t_1 = 6$, and $t_2 = 6.25$. The convexity adjustment is

$$\frac{1}{2} \times 0.011^2 \times 6 \times 6.25 = 0.002269$$

or about 23 basis points. The futures rate is 4.8% with quarterly compounding and an actual/360 day count. This becomes $4.8 \times 365/360 = 4.867\%$ with an actual/actual day count. It is $4\ln(1 + .04867/4) = 4.84\%$ with continuous compounding. The forward rate is therefore $4.84 - 0.23 = 4.61\%$ with continuous compounding.

5.31. When the yield, y is expressed with a compounding frequency of m times per year, equation (5.8) becomes

$$B = \sum_{i=1}^{n} \frac{c_i}{(1 + y/m)^{mt_i}}$$

so that

$$\frac{\partial B}{\partial y} = -\sum_{i=1}^{n} \frac{c_i t_i}{(1 + y/m)^{mt_i + 1}}$$

The bond's duration is

$$D = \frac{1}{B} \sum_{i=1}^{n} \frac{t_i c_i}{(1 + y/m)^{mt_i}}$$

It follows that

$$\frac{\partial B}{\partial y} = -\frac{BD}{1 + y/m}$$

so that for small δy

$$\delta B = -\frac{BD\delta y}{1 + y/m}$$

Note that as m tends to infinity, so that y is expressed with continuous compounding, this becomes the result in equation (5.12).

5.32. Section 3.9 shows that when the the underlying asset in a futures contract is positively correlated with interest rates we expect the futures price of the asset to be higher than the forward price. In this case the underlying variable is a three-month interest rate. It is highly positively correlated to other short-term interest rates. The arguments in Section 3.9 therefore show that the futures interest rate is higher than the forward interest rate.

31

CHAPTER 6
Swaps

6.1. A has an apparent comparative advantage in fixed-rate markets but wants to borrow floating. B has an apparent comparative advantage in floating-rate markets but wants to borrow fixed. This provides the basis for the swap. There is a 1.4% per annum differential between the fixed rates offered to the two companies and a 0.5% per annum differential between the floating rates offered to the two companies. The total gain to all parties from the swap is therefore $1.4 - 0.5 = 0.9\%$ per annum. Because the bank gets 0.1% per annum of this gain, the swap should make each of A and B 0.4% per annum better off. This means that it should lead to A borrowing at LIBOR -0.3% and to B borrowing at 13%. The appropriate arrangement is therefore as shown in Figure 6.1.

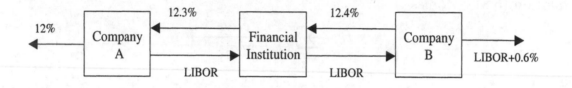

Figure 6.1 Swap for Problem 6.1

6.2. In four months $6 million ($= 0.5 \times 0.12 \times \$100$ million) will be received and $4.8 million ($= 0.5 \times 0.096 \times \$100$ million) will be paid. (We ignore day count issues.) In 10 months $6 million will be received, and the LIBOR rate prevailing in four months' time will be paid. The value of the fixed-rate bond underlying the swap is

$$6e^{-0.1 \times 4/12} + 106e^{-0.1 \times 10/12} = \$103.328 \text{ million}$$

The value of the floating-rate bond underlying the swap is

$$(100 + 4.8)e^{-0.1 \times 4/12} = \$101.364 \text{ million}$$

The value of the swap to the party paying floating is $103.328 - \$101.364 = \$1.964$ million. The value of the swap to the party paying fixed is $-\$1.964$ million. These results can also be derived by decomposing the swap into forward contracts. Consider the party paying floating. The first forward contract involves paying $4.8 million and receiving $6 million in four months. It has a value of $1.2e^{-0.1 \times 4/12} = \$1.161$ million. To value the second forward contract, we note that the forward interest rate is 10% per annum with continuous compounding, or 10.254% per annum with semiannual compounding. The value of the forward contract is

$$100 \times (0.12 \times 0.5 - 0.10254 \times 0.5)e^{-0.1 \times 10/12} = \$0.803 \text{ million}$$

The total value of the forward contract is therefore $1.161 + $0.803 = $1.964 million.

6.3. X has a comparative advantage in yen markets but wants to borrow dollars. Y has a comparative advantage in dollar markets but wants to borrow yen. This provides the basis for the swap. There is a 1.5% per annum differential between the yen rates and a 0.4% per annum differential between the dollar rates. The total gain to all parties from the swap is therefore $1.5 - 0.4 = 1.1\%$ per annum. The bank requires 0.5% per annum, leaving 0.3% per annum for each of X and Y. The swap should lead to X borrowing dollars at $9.6 - 0.3 = 9.3\%$ per annum and to Y borrowing yen at $6.5 - 0.3 = 6.2\%$ per annum. The appropriate arrangement is therefore as shown in Figure 6.2. All foreign exchange risk is borne by the bank.

Figure 6.2   Swap for Problem 6.3

6.4. A swap rate for a particular maturity is the average of the bid and offer fixed rates that a market maker is prepared to exchange for LIBOR in a standard plain vanilla swap with that maturity. The frequency of payments and day count conventions in the standard swap that is considered vary from country to country. In the United States, payments on a standard swap are semiannual and the day count convention for quoting LIBOR is actual/360. The day count convention for quoting the fixed rate is usually actual/365. The swap rate for a particular maturity is the LIBOR par yield for that maturity.

6.5. The swap involves exchanging the sterling interest of $20 \times 0.14 = 2.8$ million for the dollar interest of $30 \times 0.1 = \$3$ million. The principal amounts are also exchanged at the end of the life of the swap. The value of the sterling bond underlying the swap is

$$\frac{2.8}{(1.11)^{1/4}} + \frac{22.8}{(1.11)^{5/4}} = 22.739 \text{ million pounds}$$

The value of the dollar bond underlying the swap is

$$\frac{3}{(1.08)^{1/4}} + \frac{33}{(1.08)^{5/4}} = \$32.916 \text{ million}$$

The value of the swap to the party paying sterling is therefore

$$32.916 - (22.739 \times 1.65) = -\$4.604 \text{ million}$$

The value of the swap to the party paying dollars is +$4.604 million. The results can also be obtained by viewing the swap as a portfolio of forward contracts. The continuously compounded interest rates in sterling and dollars are 10.436% per annum and 7.696% per annum. The 3-month and 15-month forward exchange rates are $1.65e^{-(0.10436-0.07696)\times0.25} = 1.6387$ and $1.65e^{-(0.10436-0.07696)\times1.25} = 1.5944$. The values of the two forward contracts corresponding to the exchange of interest for the party paying sterling are therefore

$$(3 - 2.8 \times 1.6387)e^{-0.07696\times0.25} = -\$1.558 \text{ million}$$

$$(3 - 2.8 \times 1.5944)e^{-0.07696\times1.25} = -\$1.330 \text{ million}$$

The value of the forward contract corresponding to the exchange of principals is

$$(30 - 20 \times 1.5944)e^{-0.07696\times1.25} = -\$1.716 \text{ million}$$

The total value of the swap is $-\$1.558 - \$1.330 - \$1.716 = -\$4.604$ million.

6.6. Credit risk arises from the possibility of a default by the counterparty. Market risk arises from movements in market variables such as interest rates and exchange rates. A complication is that the credit risk in a swap is contingent on the values of market variables. A company's position in a swap has credit risk only when the value of the swap to the company is positive.

6.7. At the start of the swap, both contracts have a value of approximately zero. As time passes, it is likely that the swap values will change, so that one swap has a positive value to the bank and the other has a negative value to the bank. If the counterparty on the other side of the positive-value swap defaults, the bank still has to honor its contract with the other counterparty. It is liable to lose an amount equal to the positive value of the swap.

6.8. This is an example of apparent comparative advantage. The spread between the interest rates offered to X and Y is 0.8% per annum on fixed rate investments and 0.0% per annum on floating rate investments. This means that the total apparent benefit to all parties from the swap is 0.8% per annum. Of this 0.2% per annum will go to the bank. This leaves 0.3% per annum for each of X and Y. In other words, company X should be able to get a fixed-rate return of 8.3% per annum while company Y should be able to get a floating-rate return LIBOR + 0.3% per annum. The required swap is shown in Figure 6.3. Company X has a net borrowing costs of LIBOR + 0.2% (or 0.3% per annum less than it would have if it went directly to floating rate markets).

Figure 6.3 Swap for Problem 6.8

6.9. At the end of year 3 the financial institution was due to receive $500,000 $(= 0.5 \times 10\%$ of \$10 million) and pay \$450,000 $(- 0.5 \times 9\%$ of \$10 million). The immediate loss is therefore \$50,000. To value the remaining swap we assume than forward rates are realized. All forward rates are 8% per annum. The remaining cash flows are therefore valued on the assumption that the floating payment is $0.5 \times 0.08 \times 10,000,000 = 400,000$ and the net payment that would be received is $500,000 - 400,000 = \$100,000$. The total cost of default is therefore the cost of foregoing the following cash flows:

year 3:	\$50,000
year $3\frac{1}{2}$:	\$100,000
year 4:	\$100,000
year $4\frac{1}{2}$:	\$100,000
year 5:	\$100,000

Discounting these cash flows to year 3 at 4% per six months we obtain the cost of the default as \$413,000.

6.10. When interest rates are compounded annually

$$F_0 = S_0 \left(\frac{1+r}{1+r_f} \right)^T$$

where F_0 is the T-year forward rate, S_0 is the spot rate, r is the domestic risk-free rate, and r_f is the foreign risk free rate. As $r - 0.08$ and $r_f = 0.03$, the spot and forward exchange rates at the end of year 6 are

spot:	0.8000
1 year forward:	0.8388
2 year forward:	0.8796
3 year forward:	0.9223
4 year forward:	0.9670

The value of the swap at the time of the default can be calculated on the assumption that forward rates are realized. The cash flows lost as a result of the default are therefore as follows:

Year	Dollar due to be Paid	Sw. Fr. due to be Received	Forward Rate	Dollar Equivalent of Sw. Fr. Amount	Cash Flow Lost
6	560,000	300,000	0.8000	240,000	(320,000)
7	560,000	300,000	0.8388	251,600	(308,400)
8	560,000	300,000	0.8796	263,900	(296,100)
9	560,000	300,000	0.9223	276,700	(283,300)
10	7,560,000	10,300,000	0.9670	9,960,100	2,400,100

Discounting the numbers in the final column to the end of year 6 at 8% per annum, the cost of the default is \$679,800.

Note that, if this were the only contract entered into by company Y, it would make no sense for the company to default at the end of year six as the exchange of payments at that time has a positive value to company Y. In practice company Y is likely to be defaulting and declaring bankruptcy for reasons unrelated to this particular contract and payments on the contract are likely to stop when bankruptcy is declared.

6.11. Company A has a comparative advantage in the Canadian dollar fixed-rate market. Company B has a comparative advantage in the U.S. dollar floating-rate market. (This may be because of their tax positions.) However, company A wants to borrow in the U.S. dollar floating-rate market and company B wants to borrow in the Canadian dollar fixed-rate market. This gives rise to the swap opportunity.

The differential between the U.S. dollar floating rates is 0.5% per annum, and the differential between the Canadian dollar fixed rates is 1.5% per annum. The difference between the differentials is 1% per annum. The total potential gain to all parties from the swap is therefore 1% per annum, or 100 basis points. If the financial intermediary requires 50 basis points, each of A and B can be made 25 basis points better off. Thus a swap can be designed so that it provides A with U.S. dollars at LIBOR + 0.25% per annum, and B with Canadian dollars at 6.25% per annum. The swap is shown in Figure 6.4.

Figure 6.4   Swap for Problem 6.11

Principal payments flow in the opposite direction to the arrows at the start of the life of the swap and in the same direction as the arrows at the end of the life of the swap. The financial institution would be exposed to some foreign exchange risk which could be hedged using forward contracts.

6.12. The financial institution will have to buy 1.1% of the AUD principal in the forward market for each year of the life of the swap. Since AUD interest rates are higher than dollar interest rates, AUD is at a discount in forward markets. This means that the AUD purchased for year 2 is less expensive than that purchased for year 1; the AUD purchased for year 3 is less expensive than that purchased for year 2; and so on. This works in favor of the financial institution and means that its spread increases with time. The spread is always above 20 basis points.

6.13. Consider a plain-vanilla interest rate swap involving two companies X and Y. We suppose that X is paying fixed and receiving floating while Y is paying floating and receiving fixed.

The quote suggests that company X will usually be less creditworthy than company Y. (Company X might be a BBB-rated company that has difficulty in accessing fixed-rate markets directly; company Y might be a AAA-rated company that has no difficulty accessing fixed or floating rate markets.) Presumably company X wants fixed-rate funds and company Y wants floating-rate funds.

The financial institution will realize a loss if company Y defaults when rates are high or if company X defaults when rates are low. These events are relatively unlikely since (a) Y is unlikely to default in any circumstances and (b) defaults are less likely to happen when rates are low. For the purposes of illustration, suppose that the probabilities of various events are as follows:

Default by Y:	0.001
Default by X:	0.010
Rates high when default occurs:	0.7
Rates low when default occurs:	0.3

The probability of a loss is

$$0.001 \times 0.7 + 0.010 \times 0.3 = 0.0037$$

If the roles of X and Y in the swap had been reversed the probability of a loss would be

$$0.001 \times 0.3 + 0.010 \times 0.7 = 0.0073$$

Assuming companies are more likely to default when interest rates are high, the above argument shows that the observation in quotes has the effect of decreasing the risk of a financial institution's swap portfolio. It is worth noting that the assumption that defaults are more likely when interest rates are high is open to question. The assumption is motivated by the thought that high interest rates often lead to financial difficulties for corporations. However, there is often a time lag between interest rates being high and the resultant default. When the default actually happens interest rates may be relatively low.

6.14. In an interest-rate swap a financial institution's exposure depends on the difference between a fixed-rate of interest and a floating-rate of interest. It has no exposure to the notional principal. In a loan the whole principal can be lost.

6.15. The bank is paying a floating-rate on the deposits and receiving a fixed-rate on the loans. It can offset its risk by entering into interest rate swaps (with other financial institutions or corporations) in which it contracts to pay fixed and receive floating.

6.16. The floating payments can be valued in currency A by (i) assuming that the forward rates are realized, and (ii) discounting the resulting cash flows at appropriate currency A discount rates. Suppose that the value is V_A. The fixed payments can be valued in currency B by discounting them at the appropriate currency B discount rates. Suppose that the value is V_B. If Q is the current exchange rate (number of units of currency A per unit of currency B), the value of the swap in currency A is $V_A - QV_B$. Alternatively, it is $V_A/Q - V_B$ in currency B.

6.17. The two-year swap rate is 5.4%. This means that a two-year LIBOR bond paying a semiannual coupon at the rate of 5.4% per annum sells for par. If R_2 is the two-year LIBOR zero rate

$$2.7e^{-0.05 \times 0.5} + 2.7e^{-0.05 \times 1.0} + 2.7e^{-0.05 \times 1.5} + 102.7e^{-R_2 \times 2.0} = 100$$

Solving this gives $R_2 = 0.05342$. The 2.5-year swap rate is assumed to be 5.5%. This means that a 2.5-year LIBOR bond paying a semiannual coupon at the rate of 5.5% per annum sells for par. If $R_{2.5}$ is the 2.5-year LIBOR zero rate

$$2.75e^{-0.05 \times 0.5} + 2.75e^{-0.05 \times 1.0} + 2.75e^{-0.05 \times 1.5} + 2.75e^{-0.05342 \times 2.0} + 102.75e^{-R_{2.5} \times 2.5} = 100$$

Solving this gives $R_{2.5} = 0.05442$. The 3-year swap rate is 5.6%. This means that a 3-year LIBOR bond paying a semiannual coupon at the rate of 5.6% per annum sells for par. If R_3 is the three-year LIBOR zero rate

$$2.8e^{-0.05 \times 0.5} + 2.8e^{-0.05 \times 1.0} + 2.8e^{-0.05 \times 1.5} + 2.8e^{-0.05342 \times 2.0} + 2.8e^{-0.05442 \times 2.5}$$

$$+ 102.8e^{-R_3 \times 3.0} = 100$$

Solving this gives $R_3 = 0.05544$. The zero rates for maturities 2.0, 2.5, and 3.0 years are therefore 5.342%, 5.442%, and 5.544%, respectively.

CHAPTER 7
Mechanics of Options Markets

7.1. When a trader buys an option, she must pay cash up front. There is no possibility of future liabilities and therefore no need for a margin account. When a trader sells an option, there are potential future liabilities. To protect against the risk of a default, margins are required.

7.2. On April 1, options trade with expiration months of April, May, August, and November. On May 30, options trade with expiration months of June, July, August and November. Longer maturity options are also sometimes traded.

7.3. The strike price is reduced to $20 and the option gives the holder the right to purchase 300 instead of 100 shares.

7.4. Writing a put gives a payoff of $\min(S_T - K, 0)$. Buying a call gives a payoff of $\max(S_T - K, 0)$. In both cases the potential payoff is $S_T - K$. The difference is that for a written put the counterparty chooses whether you get the payoff (and will allow you to get it only when it is negative). For a long put you decide whether you get the payoff and you choose to get it when it is positive.

7.5. The Philadelpia Exchange offers European and American options with standard strike prices and times to maturity. Options in the over-the-counter market have the advantage that they can be tailored to meet the precise needs of the treasurer. Their disadvantage is that they expose the treasurer to some credit risk. Exchanges organize their trading so that there is virtually no credit risk.

7.6. The holder of an American option has all the same rights as the holder of a European option and more. It must therefore be worth at least as much. If it were not, an arbitrageur could short the European option and take a long position in the American option.

7.7. The holder of an American option has the right to exercise it immediately. The American option must therefore be worth at least as much as its intrinsic value. If it were not an arbitrageur could lock in a sure profit by buying the option and exercising it immediately.

7.8. Forward contracts lock in the exchange rate that will apply to a particular transaction in the future. Options provide insurance that the exchange rate will not be worse than some level. The advantage of a forward contract is that uncertainty is eliminated as far as possible. The disadvantage is that the outcome with hedging can be significantly worse than the outcome with no hedging. This disadvantage is not as marked with options. However, unlike forward contracts, options involve an up-front cost.

7.9. (a) The option contract becomes one to by $500 \times 1.1 = 550$ shares with an exercise price $40/1.1 = 36.36$.

(b) There is no effect. The terms of an options contract are not normally adjusted for cash dividends.

(c) The option contract becomes one to buy $500 \times 4 = 2,000$ shares with an exercise price of $40/4 = \$10$.

7.10. The exchange has certain rules governing when trading in a new option is initiated. These mean that the option is fairly close to being at-the-money when it is first traded. If all call options are in the money it is therefore likely that the stock price has risen since trading in the option began.

7.11. An unexpected cash dividend will reduce the stock price more than was expected. This will in turn reduce the value of a call option and increase the value of a put option.

7.12. (a) March, April, June and September
(b) July, August, September, December
(c) August, September, December, March
Longer dated options may also trade.

7.13. A "fair" price for the option can reasonably be assumed to be half way between the bid and the ask price. An investor typically buys at the ask and sells at the bid. Each time she does this there is a hidden cost equal to half the bid-ask spread.

7.14. The two calculations are necessary to determine the initial margin. The first gives

$$500 \times (3.5 + 0.2 \times 57 - 3) = 5,950$$

The second gives

$$500 \times (3.5 + 0.1 \times 57) = 4,600$$

The initial margin is the greater of these, or $5,950. Part of this can be provided by the initial amount of $500 \times 3.5 = \$1,750$ received for the options.

CHAPTER 8
Properties of Stock Options

8.1. The six factors affecting stock option prices are the stock price, strike price, risk-free interest rate, volatility, time to maturity, and dividends.

8.2. The lower bound is

$$28 - 25e^{-0.08 \times 0.3333} = \$3.66$$

8.3. The lower bound is

$$15e^{-0.06 \times 0.08333} - 12 = \$2.93$$

8.4. Delaying exercise delays the payment of the strike price. This means that the option holder is able to earn interest on the strike price for a longer period of time. Delaying exercise also provides insurance against the stock price falling below the strike price by the expiration date. Assume that the option holder has an amount of cash K and interest rates are zero. Exercising early means that the option holder's position will be worth S_T at expiration. Delaying exercise means that it will be worth $\max(K, S_T)$ at expiration.

8.5. An American put when held in conjunction with the underlying stock provides insurance. It guarantees that the stock can be sold for the strike price, K. If the put is exercised early, the insurance ceases. However, the option holder receives the strike price immediately. He or she is able to earn interest on K between the time of the early exercise and the expiration date.

8.6. An American call option can be exercised at any time. If it is exercised its holder gets the intrinsic value. It follows that an American call option must be worth at least its intrinsic value. A European call option can be worth less than its intrinsic value. Consider, for example, the situation where a stock is expected to provide a very high dividend during the life of an option. The price of the stock will decline as a result of the dividend. Because the European option can be exercised only after the dividend has been paid, its value may be less than the intrinsic value today.

8.7. When early exercise is not possible we can argue that two portfolios that are worth the same at time T must be worth the same at earlier times. When early exercise is possible, the argument falls down. Suppose that $P + S_0 > C + Ke^{-rT}$. This does not lead to an arbitrage opportunity. If we buy the call, short the put, and short the stock, we cannot be sure of the result since we cannot be sure when the put will be exercised.

8.8. The lower bound is

$$80 - 75e^{-0.1 \times 0.5} = \$8.66$$

8.9. The lower bound is

$$65e^{-0.1667 \times 0.05} - 58 = \$6.46$$

8.10. The present value of the strike price is $60e^{-0.3333 \times 0.12} = \$57.65$. The present value of the dividend is $0.80e^{-0.08333 \times 0.12} = 0.79$. Since

$$5 < 64 - 57.65 - 0.79$$

the condition in equation (8.5) is violated. An arbitrageur should buy the option and short the stock. Regardless of what happens a profit will materialize. If the stock price declines below \$60, the arbitrageur loses the \$5 spent on the option but gains at least $64 - 57.65 - 0.79 = \$5.56$ in present value terms from the short position. If the stock price is above \$60 at the expiration of the option, the arbitrageur gains in present value terms exactly $5.56 - 5.00 = \$0.56$.

8.11. In this case the present value of the strike price is $50e^{-0.08333 \times 0.06} = 49.75$ Since

$$2.5 < 49.75 - 47.00$$

the condition in equation (8.2) is violated. An arbitrageur can lock in a profit of at least \$0.25 by buying the put option and buying the stock.

8.12. The early exercise of an American put is attractive when the interest earned on the strike price is greater than the insurance element lost. When interest rates increase, the interest earned on the strike price increases making early exercise more attractive. When volatility decreases, the insurance element is less valuable. Again this makes early exercise more attractive.

8.13. Using the notation in the chapter, put-call parity gives [see equation (8.3)]

$$c + Ke^{-rT} + D = p + S_0$$

or

$$p = c + Ke^{-rT} + D - S_0$$

In this case

$$p = 2 + 30e^{-0.5 \times 0.1} + 0.5e^{-0.1667 \times 0.1} + 0.5e^{-0.4167 \times 0.1} - 29 = 2.51$$

In other words the put price is \$2.51.

8.14. If the put price is \$3.00, it is too high relative to the call price. An arbitrageur should buy the call, short the put and short the stock. Regardless of what happens this locks in a profit which has a present value of $3.00 - 2.51 = \$0.49$.

8.15. From equation (8.4)

$$S_0 - K < C - P < S_0 - Ke^{-rT}$$

42

In this case

$$31 - 30 < 4 - P < 31 - 30e^{-0.08 \times 0.25}$$

or

$$1.00 < 4.00 - P < 1.59$$

or

$$2.41 < P < 3.00$$

Upper and lower bounds for the price of an American put are therefore $2.41 and $3.00.

8.16. If the American put price is greater than $3.00 an arbitrageur can sell the American put, short the stock, and buy the American call. This realizes at least $3 + 31 - 4 = \$30$ which can be invested at the risk-free interest rate. At some stage during the 3-month period either the American put or the American call will be exercised. The arbitrageur then pays $30, receives the stock and closes out the short position for a profit.

8.17. As in the text we use c and p to denote the European call and put option price, and C and P to denote the American call and put option prices. Since $P > p$, it follows from put–call parity that

$$P > c + Ke^{-rT} - S_0$$

and since $c = C$,

$$P > C + Ke^{-rT} - S_0$$

or

$$C - P < S_0 - Ke^{-rT}$$

For a further relationship between C and P, consider

Portfolio I: One European call option plus an amount of cash equal to K.
Portfolio J: One American put option plus one share.
Both options have the same exercise price and expiration date. Assume that the cash in portfolio I is invested at the risk-free interest rate. If the put option is not exercised early portfolio J is worth

$$\max(S_T, K)$$

at time T. Portfolio I is worth

$$\max(S_T - K, 0) + Ke^{rT} = \max(S_T, K) - K + Ke^{rT}$$

at this time. Portfolio I is therefore worth more than portfolio J. Suppose next that the put option in portfolio J is exercised early, say, at time τ. This means that portfolio J is worth K at time τ. However, even if the call option were worthless, portfolio I would be worth $Ke^{r\tau}$ at time τ. It follows that portfolio I is worth more than portfolio J in all circumstances. Hence

$$c + K > P + S_0$$

Since $c = C$,

$$C + K > P + S_0$$

43

or
$$C - P > S_0 - K$$

Combining this with the other inequality derived above for $C - P$, we obtain

$$S_0 - K < C - P < S_0 - Ke^{-rT}$$

8.18. As in the text we use c and p to denote the European call and put option price, and C and P to denote the American call and put option prices. The present value of the dividends will be denoted by D. As shown in the answer to Problem 8.17, when there are no dividends

$$C - P < S_0 - Ke^{-rT}$$

Dividends reduce C and increase P. Hence this relationship must also be true when there are dividends.

For a further relationship between C and P, consider

  Portfolio I: one European call option plus an amount of cash equal to $D + K$
  Portfolio J: one American put option plus one share

Both options have the same exercise price and expiration date. Assume that the cash in portfolio I is invested at the risk-free interest rate. If the put option is not exercised early, portfolio J is worth

$$\max{(S_T, \, K)} + De^{rT}$$

at time T. Portfolio I is worth

$$\max{(S_T, \, 0)} + (D + K)e^{rT} = \max{(S_T, \, K)} + De^{rT} + Ke^{rT} - K$$

at this time. Portfolio I is therefore worth more than portfolio J. Suppose next that the put option in portfolio J is exercised early, say, at time τ. This means that portfolio J is worth at most $K + De^{r\tau}$ at time τ. However, even if the call option were worthless, portfolio I would be worth $(D + K)e^{r\tau}$ at time τ. It follows that portfolio I is worth more than portfolio J in all circumstances. Hence

$$c + D + K > P + S_0$$

8.19. Executive stock options may be exercised early because the executive needs the cash or because she is uncertain about the company's future prospects. Regular call options can be sold in the market in either of these two situations, but executive stock options cannot be sold. In theory an executive can short the company's stock as an alternative to exercising. In practice this is not usually encouraged and may even be illegal.

8.20. The graphs can be produced from the first worksheet in DerivaGem. Select Equity as the Underlying Type. Select Analytic European as the Option Type. Input stock price as 50, volatility as 30%, risk-free rate as 5%, time to exercise as 1 year, and exercise price as 50. Leave the dividend table blank because we are assuming no dividends. Select the button corresponding to call. Do not select the implied volatility button.

44

Hit the *Enter* key and click on calculate. DerivaGem will show the price of the option as 7.15562248. Move to the Graph Results on the right hand side of the worksheet. Enter Option Price for the vertical axis and Asset price for the horizontal axis. Choose the minimum K value as 10 (software will not accept 0) and the maximum K value as 100. Hit enter and click on *Draw Graph*. This will produce Figure 8.1a. Figures 8.1c, 8.1e, 8.2a, and 8.2c can be produced similarly by changing the horizontal axis. By selecting put instead of call and recalculating the rest of the figures can be produced. You are encouraged to experiment with this worksheet. Try different parameter values and different types of options.

CHAPTER 9
Trading Strategies Involving Options

9.1. A protective put consists of a long position in a put option combined with a long position in the underlying shares. It is equivalent to a long position in a call option plus a certain amount of cash. This follows from put-call parity:

$$p + S_0 = c + Ke^{-rT} + D$$

9.2. A bear spread can be created using two call options with the same maturity and different strike prices. The investor shorts the call option with the lower strike price and buys the call option with the higher strike price. A bear spread can also be created using two put options with the same maturity and different strike prices. In this case the investor shorts the put option with the lower strike price and buys the put option with the higher strike price.

9.3. A butterfly spread involves a position in options with three different strike prices $(K_1, K_2, \text{and } K_3)$. An investor should purchase a butterfly spread when it is considered that the price of the underlying stock is likely to stay close to the central strike price, K_2.

9.4. An investor can create a butterfly spread by buying call options with strike prices of \$15 and \$20, and selling two call options with strike prices of \$$17\frac{1}{2}$. The initial investment is $4 + \frac{1}{2} - 2 \times 2 = \$\frac{1}{2}$. The following table shows the variation of profit with the final stock price:

Stock Price S_T	Profit
$S_T < 15$	$-\frac{1}{2}$
$15 < S_T < 17\frac{1}{2}$	$S_T - 15\frac{1}{2}$
$17\frac{1}{2} < S_T < 20$	$19\frac{1}{2} - S_T$
$S_T > 20$	$-\frac{1}{2}$

9.5. A reverse calendar spread is created by buying a short-maturity option and selling a long-maturity option, both with the same strike price.

9.6. Both a straddle and a strangle are created by combining a call and a put. In a straddle they have the same strike price and expiration date. In a strangle they have different strike prices and the same expiration date.

9.7. A strangle is created by buying both options. The pattern of profits is as follows:

Stock Price S_T	Profit
$S_T < 45$	$40 - S_T$
$45 < S_T < 50$	-5
$S_T > 50$	$S_T - 55$

9.8. A bull spread using calls provides a profit pattern with the same general shape as a bull spread using puts (see Figures 9.2 and 9.3 in the text). Define p_1 and c_1 as the prices of put and call with strike price K_1 and p_2 and c_2 as the prices of a put and call with strike price K_2. From put-call parity

$$p_1 + S_0 = c_1 + K_1 e^{-rT}$$

$$p_2 + S_0 = c_2 + K_2 e^{-rT}$$

Hence:

$$p_1 - p_2 = c_1 - c_2 - (K_2 - K_1)e^{-rT}$$

This shows that the initial investment when the spread is created from puts is less than the initial investment when it is created from calls by an amount $(K_2 - K_1)e^{-rT}$. In fact as mentioned in the text the initial investment when the bull spread is created from puts is negative, while the initial investment when it is created from calls is positive.

The profit when calls are used to create the bull spread is higher than when puts are used by $(K_2 - K_1)(1 - e^{-rT})$. This reflects the fact that the call strategy involves an additional risk-free investment of $(K_2 - K_1)e^{-rT}$ over the put strategy. This earns interest of $(K_2 - K_1)(1 - e^{-rT})$.

9.9. An aggressive bull spread using call options is discussed in the text. Both of the options used have relatively high strike prices. Similarly, an aggressive bear spread can be created using put options. Both of the options should be out of the money (that is, they should have relatively low strike prices). The spread then costs very little to set up since both of the puts are worth close to zero. In most circumstances the spread will be worth zero. However, there is a small chance that the stock price will fall fast so that on expiration both options will be in the money. The spread is then worth the difference between the two strike prices $K_2 - K_1$.

9.10. A bull spread is created by buying the \$30 put and selling the \$35 put. This strategy gives rise to an initial cash inflow of \$3. The outcome is as follows:

Stock Price	Payoff	Profit
$S_T \geq 35$	0	3
$30 \leq S_T < 35$	$S_T - 35$	$S_T - 32$
$S_T < 30$	-5	-2

A bear spread is created by selling the $30 put and buying the $35 put. This strategy costs $3 initially. The outcome is as follows:

Stock Price	Payoff	Profit
$S_T \geq 35$	0	-3
$30 \leq S_T < 35$	$35 - S_T$	$32 - S_T$
$S_T < 30$	5	2

9.11. Define c_1, c_2, and c_3 as the prices of calls with strike prices K_1, K_2 and K_3. Define p_1, p_2 and p_3 as the prices of puts with strike prices K_1, K_2 and K_3. With the usual notation

$$c_1 + K_1 e^{-rT} = p_1 + S_0$$

$$c_2 + K_2 e^{-rT} = p_2 + S_0$$

$$c_3 + K_3 e^{-rT} = p_3 + S_0$$

Hence

$$c_1 + c_3 - 2c_2 + (K_1 + K_3 - 2K_2)e^{-rT} = p_1 + p_3 - 2p_2$$

Since $K_2 - K_1 = K_3 - K_2$, it follows that $K_1 + K_3 - 2K_2 = 0$ and

$$c_1 + c_3 - 2c_2 = p_1 + p_3 - 2p_2$$

The cost of a butterfly spread created using European calls is therefore exactly the same as the cost of a butterfly spread created using European puts.

9.12. A straddle is created by buying both the call and the put. This strategy costs $10. The profit/loss is shown in the following table:

Stock Price	Payoff	Profit
$S_T > 60$	$S_T - 60$	$S_T - 70$
$S_T \leq 60$	$60 - S_T$	$50 - S_T$

This shows that the straddle will lead to a loss if the final stock price is between $50 and $70.

9.13. The bull spread is created by buying a put with strike price K_1 and selling a put with strike price K_2. The payoff is calculated as follows:

Stock Price Range	Payoff from Long Put Option	Payoff from Short Put Option	Total Payoff
$S_T \geq K_2$	0	0	0
$K_1 < S_T < K_2$	0	$S_T - K_2$	$-(K_2 - S_T)$
$S_T \leq K_1$	$K_1 - S_T$	$S_T - K_2$	$-(K_2 - K_1)$

9.14. Possible strategies are:

    Strangle
    Straddle
    Strip
    Strap
    Reverse calendar spread
    Reverse butterfly spread

The strategies all provide positive profits when there are large stock price moves. A strangle is less expensive than a straddle, but requires a bigger move in the stock price in order to provide a positive profit. Strips and straps are more expensive than straddles but provide bigger profits in certain circumstances. A strip will provide a bigger profit when there is a large downward stock price move. A strap will provide a bigger profit when there is a large upward stock price move. In the case of strangles, straddles, strips and straps, the profit increases as the size of the stock price movement increases. By contrast in a reverse calendar spread and a reverse butterfly spread there is a maximum potential profit regardless of the size of the stock price movement.

9.15. Suppose that the delivery price is K and the delivery date is T. The forward contract is created by buying a European call and selling a European put when both options have strike price K and exercise date T. It is easy to see that this portfolio provides a payoff of $S_T - K$ under all circumstances where S_T is the stock price at time T. Suppose that F_0 is the forward price. If $K = F_0$, the forward contract that is created has zero value. This shows that the price of a call equals the price of a put when the strike price is K.

9.16. The bull spread involves buying a European call with strike price K_1 and selling a European call with strike price K_2. The bear spread involves buying a European put with strike price K_2 and selling a European put with strike price K_1. The payoff from a box spread is shown in the following table:

Stock Price Range	Bull Call Spread	Bear Put Spread	Total
$S_T \geq K_2$	$K_2 - K_1$	0	$K_2 - K_1$
$K_1 < K_T < K_2$	$S_T - K_1$	$K_2 - S_T$	$K_2 - K_1$
$S_T \leq K_1$	0	$K_2 - K_1$	$K_2 - K_1$

It can be seen that under all circumstances the box spread pays off $K_2 - K_1$. If there are to be no arbitrage opportunities, the value of the box spread today must be the present value of $K_2 - K_1$.

9.17. The result is shown in Figure 9.1. The initial investment required is much higher but the profit pattern is very similar.

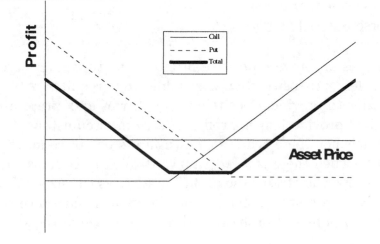

Figure 9.1   Profit Pattern in Problem 9.17

9.18. DerivaGem shows that the values of calls with strike prices of 0.60, 0.65, and 0.70 are 0.0618, 0.0352, and 0.0181. The values of puts with these three strike prices are 0.0176, 0.0386, and 0.0690. The cost of setting up the butterfly spread when calls are used is therefore

$$0.0618 + 0.0181 - 2 \times 0.0352 = 0.0095$$

The cost of setting up the butterfly spread when puts are used is

$$0.0176 + 0.0690 - 2 \times 0.0386 = 0.0094$$

Allowing for rounding errors these two are the same.

CHAPTER 10
Introduction To Binomial Trees

10.1. Consider a portfolio consisting of

$-1:$ call option

$+\Delta:$ shares

If the stock price rises to $42, this is worth $42\Delta - 3$. If the stock price falls to $38, it is worth 38Δ. These are the same when

$$42\Delta - 3 = 38\Delta$$

or $\Delta = 0.75$. The value of the portfolio in one month is $28.5 for both stock prices. Its value today must be the present value of 28.5 or $28.5e^{-0.08 \times 0.08333} = 28.31$. This means that

$$-f + 40\Delta = 28.31$$

where f is the call price. Since $\Delta = 0.75$, the call price is $40 \times 0.75 - 28.31$ or $1.69. As an alternative approach, we can calculate the probability, p, of an up movement in a risk-neutral world. This must satisfy:

$$42p + 38(1 - p) = 40e^{0.08 \times 0.08333}$$

so that

$$4p = 40e^{0.08 \times 0.08333} - 38$$

or $p = 0.5669$. The value of the option is then its expected payoff discounted at the risk-free rate or

$$(3 \times 0.5669 + 0 \times 0.4331)e^{-0.08 \times 0.08333} = 1.69$$

This agrees with the previous calculation.

10.2. In the no-arbitrage approach, we set up a riskless portfolio consisting of a position in the option and a position in the stock. By setting the return on the portfolio equal to the risk-free interest rate, we are able to value the option. When we use risk-neutral valuation, we first choose probabilities for the branches of the tree so that the expected return on the stock equals the risk-free interest rate. We then value the option by calculating its expected payoff and discounting this expected payoff at the risk-free interest rate.

10.3. The delta of a stock option measures the sensitivity of the option price to the price of the stock when small changes are considered. Specifically, it is the ratio of the change in the price of the stock option to the change in the price of the underlying stock.

10.4. Consider a portfolio consisting of

$$-1 : \qquad \text{put option}$$
$$+\Delta : \qquad \text{shares}$$

If the stock price rises to $55, this is worth 55Δ. If the stock price falls to $45, it is worth $45\Delta - 5$. These are the same when

$$45\Delta - 5 = 55\Delta$$

or $\Delta = -0.50$. The value of the portfolio in one month is -27.5 for both stock prices. Its value today must be the present value of -27.5 or $-27.5e^{-0.1\times0.5} = -26.16$. This means that

$$-pp + 50\Delta = -26.16$$

where pp is the put price. Since $\Delta = -0.50$, the put price is $1.16. As an alternative approach we can calculate the probability, p, of an up movement in a risk-neutral world. This must satisfy:

$$55p + 45(1 - p) = 50e^{0.1\times0.5}$$

so that

$$10p = 50e^{0.1\times0.5} - 45$$

or $p = 0.7564$. The value of the option is then its expected payoff discounted at the risk-free rate or

$$(0 \times 0.7564 + 5 \times 0.2436)e^{-0.1\times0.5} = 1.16$$

This agrees with the previous calculation.

10.5. In this case $u = 1.10$, $d = 0.90$, and $r = 0.08$ so that

$$p = \frac{e^{0.08\times0.5} - 0.90}{1.10 - 0.90} = 0.7041$$

The tree for stock price movements is shown in Figure 10.1. We can work back from the end of the tree to the beginning as indicated in the diagram to give the value of the option as $9.61. The option value can also be calculated directly from Equation (10.8):

$$e^{-2\times0.08\times0.5}(0.7041^2 \times 21 + 2 \times 0.7041 \times 0.2959 \times 0 + 0.2959^2 \times 0) = 9.61$$

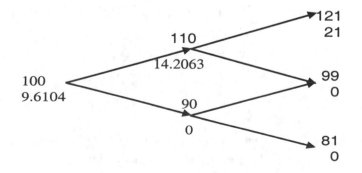

Figure 10.1   Tree for Problem 10.5

10.6. Figure 10.2 shows how we can value the put option using the same tree as in Figure 10.1. The value of the option is $1.92. The option value can also be calculated directly from Equation (10.8):

$$e^{-2 \times 0.5 \times 0.08}[0.7041^2 \times 0 + 2 \times 0.7041 \times 0.2959 \times 1 + 0.2959^2 \times 19] = 1.92$$

The stock price plus the put price is $100 + 1.92 = 101.92$. The present value of the strike price plus the call price is $100e^{-0.08} + 9.61 = 101.92$. These are the same, verifying that put–call parity holds.

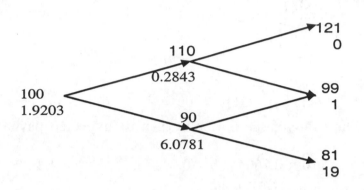

Figure 10.2   Tree for Problem 10.6

10.7. The riskless portfolio consists of a short position in the option and a long position in Δ shares. Since Δ changes during the life of the option, this riskless portfolio must also change.

10.8. At the end of two months the value of the option will be either $4 (if the stock price is $53) or $0 (if the stock price is $48). Consider a portfolio consisting of:

$$+\Delta \quad : \quad \text{shares}$$
$$-1 \quad : \quad \text{option}$$

The value of the portfolio is either 48Δ or $53\Delta - 4$ in two months. If

$$48\Delta = 53\Delta - 4$$

i.e.,

$$\Delta = 0.8$$

the value of the portfolio is certain to be 38.4. For this value of Δ the portfolio is therefore riskless. The current value of the portfolio is:

$$0.8 \times 50 - f$$

where f is the value of the option. Since the portfolio must earn the risk-free rate of interest

$$(0.8 \times 50 - f)e^{0.10 \times 0.16667} = 38.4$$

i.e.,

$$f = 2.23$$

The value of the option is therefore \$2.23.
This can also be calculated directly from equations (10.2) and (10.3). $u = 1.06$, $d = 0.96$ so that

$$p = \frac{e^{0.10 \times 0.16667} - 0.96}{1.06 - 0.96} = 0.5681$$

and

$$f = e^{-0.10 \times 0.16667} \times 0.5681 \times 4 = 2.23$$

10.9. At the end of four months the value of the option will be either \$5 (if the stock price is \$75) or \$0 (if the stock price is \$85). Consider a portfolio consisting of:

$$-\Delta \quad : \quad \text{shares}$$
$$+1 \quad : \quad \text{option}$$

(Note: The delta, Δ of a put option is negative. We have constructed the portfolio so that it is $+1$ option and $-\Delta$ shares rather than -1 option and $+\Delta$ shares so that the initial investment is positive.)
The value of the portfolio is either -85Δ or $-75\Delta + 5$ in four months. If

$$-85\Delta = -75\Delta + 5$$

i.e.,

$$\Delta = -0.5$$

the value of the portfolio is certain to be 42.5. For this value of Δ the portfolio is therefore riskless. The current value of the portfolio is:

$$0.5 \times 80 + f$$

where f is the value of the option. Since the portfolio is riskless

$$(0.5 \times 80 + f)e^{0.05 \times 0.3333} = 42.5$$

i.e.,

$$f = 1.80$$

The value of the option is therefore \$1.80.
This can also be calculated directly from equations (10.2) and (10.3). $u = 1.0625$, $d = 0.9375$ so that

$$p = \frac{e^{0.05 \times 0.3333} - 0.9375}{1.0625 - 0.9375} = 0.6345$$

$1 - p = 0.3655$ and

$$f = e^{-0.05 \times 0.33333} \times 0.3655 \times 5 = 1.80$$

10.10. At the end of three months the value of the option is either $5 (if the stock price is $35) or $0 (if the stock price is $45).
Consider a portfolio consisting of:

$$
\begin{aligned}
-\Delta \quad &: \quad \text{shares} \\
+1 \quad &: \quad \text{option}
\end{aligned}
$$

(Note: The delta, Δ, of a put option is negative. We have constructed the portfolio so that it is $+1$ option and $-\Delta$ shares rather than -1 option and $+\Delta$ shares so that the initial investment is positive.)
The value of the portfolio is either $-35\Delta + 5$ or -45Δ. If:

$$-35\Delta + 5 = -45\Delta$$

i.e.,

$$\Delta = -0.5$$

the value of the portfolio is certain to be 22.5. For this value of Δ the portfolio is therefore riskless. The current value of the portfolio is

$$-40\Delta + f$$

where f is the value of the option. Since the portfolio must earn the risk-free rate of interest

$$(40 \times 0.5 + f) \times 1.02 = 22.5$$

Hence

$$f = 2.06$$

i.e., the value of the option is $2.06.
This can also be calculated using risk-neutral valuation. Suppose that p is the probability of an upward stock price movement in a risk-neutral world. We must have

$$45p + 35(1 - p) = 40 \times 1.02$$

i.e.,

$$10p = 5.8$$

or:

$$p = 0.58$$

The expected value of the option in a risk-neutral world is:

$$0 \times 0.58 + 5 \times 0.42 = 2.10$$

This has a present value of

$$\frac{2.10}{1.02} = 2.06$$

This is consistent with the no-arbitrage answer.

10.11. A tree describing the behavior of the stock price is shown in Figure 10.3. The risk-neutral probability of an up move, p, is given by

$$p = \frac{e^{0.25 \times 0.05} - 0.95}{1.06 - 0.95} = 0.5689$$

There is a payoff from the option of $56.18 - 51 = 5.18$ for the highest final node (which corresponds to two up moves) zero in all other cases. The value of the option is therefore

$$5.18 \times 0.5689^2 \times e^{-0.05 \times 0.5} = 1.635$$

This can also be calculated by working back through the tree. The value of the call option is the lower number at each node in the diagram.

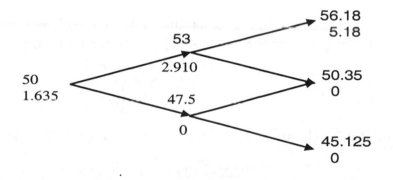

Figure 10.3   Tree for Problem 10.11

10.12. The tree for valuing the put option is shown in Figure 10.4. We get a payoff of $51 - 50.35 = 0.65$ if the middle final node is reached and a payoff of $51 - 45.125 = 5.875$ if the lowest final node is reached. The value of the option is therefore

$$(0.65 \times 2 \times 0.5689 \times 0.4311 + 5.875 \times 0.4311^2)e^{-0.05 \times 0.5} = 1.376$$

This can also be calculated by working back through the tree.
The value of the put plus the stock price is

$$1.376 + 50 = 51.376$$

The value of the call plus the present value of the strike price is

$$1.635 + 51e^{-0.05 \times 0.5} = 51.376$$

This verifies that put–call parity holds

To test whether it worth exercising the option early we compare the value calculated for the option at each node with the payoff from immediate exercise. At node C the payoff from immediate exercise is $51 - 47.5 = 3.5$. Since this is greater than 2.8664, the option should be exercised at this node. The option should not be exercised at either node A or node B.

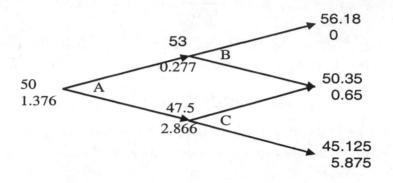

Figure 10.4   Tree for Problem 10.12

10.13. At the end of two months the value of the derivative will be either 529 (if the stock price is 23) or 729 (if the stock price is 27). Consider a portfolio consisting of:

$$+\Delta \quad : \quad \text{shares}$$
$$-1 \quad : \quad \text{derivative}$$

The value of the portfolio is either $27\Delta - 729$ or $23\Delta - 529$ in two months. If

$$27\Delta - 729 = 23\Delta - 529$$

i.e.,

$$\Delta = 50$$

the value of the portfolio is certain to be 621. For this value of Δ the portfolio is therefore riskless. The current value of the portfolio is:

$$50 \times 25 - f$$

where f is the value of the derivative. Since the portfolio must earn the risk-free rate of interest

$$(50 \times 25 - f)e^{0.10 \times 0.16667} = 621$$

i.e.,

$$f = 639.3$$

The value of the option is therefore \$639.3.

This can also be calculated directly from equations (10.2) and (10.3). $u = 1.08$, $d = 0.92$ so that

$$p = \frac{e^{0.10 \times 0.16667} - 0.92}{1.08 - 0.92} = 0.6050$$

and

$$f = e^{-0.10 \times 0.16667}(0.6050 \times 729 + 0.3950 \times 529) = 639.3$$

CHAPTER 11
Model of the Behavior of Stock Prices

11.1. Imagine that you have to forecast the future temperature from a) the current temperature, b) the history of the temperature in the last week, and c) a knowledge of seasonal averages and seasonal trends. If temperature followed a Markov process, the history of the temperature in thr last week would be irrelevant.
To answer the second part of the question you might like to consider the following scenario for the first week in May:
  (i) Monday to Thursday are warm days; today, Friday, is a very cold day.
  (ii) Monday to Friday are all very cold days.
What is your forecast for the weekend? If you are more pessimistic in the case of the second scenario, temperatures do not follow a Markov process.

11.2. The first point to make is that any trading strategy can, just because of good luck, produce above average returns. The key question is whether a trading strategy *consistently* outperforms the market when adjustments are made for risk. It is certainly possible that a trading strategy could do this. However, when enough investors know about the strategy and trade on the basis of the strategy, the profit will disappear.
As an illustration of this, consider a phenomenon known as the small firm effect. Portfolios of stocks in small firms appear to have outperformed portfolios of stocks in large firms when appropriate adjustments are made for risk. Papers were published about this in the early 1980s and mutual funds were set up to take advantage of the phenomenon. There is some evidence that this has resulted in the phenomenon disappearing.

11.3. Suppose that the company's initial cash position is x. The probability distribution of the cash position at the end of one year is

$$\phi(x + 4 \times 0.5, \sqrt{4} \times \sqrt{4}) = \phi(x + 2.0,\ 4)$$

where $\phi(m, s)$ is a normal probability distribution with mean m and standard deviation s. The probability of a negative cash position at the end of one year is

$$N\left(-\frac{x + 2.0}{4}\right)$$

where $N(x)$ is the cumulative probability that a standardized normal variable (with mean zero and standard deviation 1.0) is less than x. From normal distribution tables

$$N\left(-\frac{x + 2.0}{4}\right) = 0.05$$

when:
$$\frac{x + 2.0}{4} = -1.6449$$

i.e., when $x = 4.5796$. The initial cash position must therefore be \$4.56 million.

11.4. (a) Suppose that X_1 and X_2 equal a_1 and a_2 initially. After a time period of length T, X_1 has the probability distribution

$$\phi(a_1 + \mu_1 T,\ \sigma_1 \sqrt{T})$$

and X_2 has a probability distribution

$$\phi(a_2 + \mu_2 T,\ \sigma_2 \sqrt{T})$$

From the property of sums of independent normally distributed variables, $X_1 + X_2$ has the probability distribution

$$\phi\left(a_1 + \mu_1 T + a_2 + \mu_2 T,\ \sqrt{\sigma_1^2 T + \sigma_2^2 T}\right)$$

i.e.,

$$\phi\left[a_1 + a_2 + (\mu_1 + \mu_2)T,\ \sqrt{(\sigma_1^2 + \sigma_2^2)T}\right]$$

This shows that $X_1 + X_2$ follows a generalized Wiener process with drift rate $\mu_1 + \mu_2$ and variance rate $\sigma_1^2 + \sigma_2^2$.

(b) In this case the change in the value of $X_1 + X_2$ in a short interval of time δt has the probability distribution:

$$\phi\left[(\mu_1 + \mu_2)\delta t,\ \sqrt{(\sigma_1^2 + \sigma_2^2 + 2\rho\sigma_1\sigma_2)\delta t}\right]$$

If μ_1, μ_2, σ_1, σ_2 and ρ are all constant, arguments similar to those in Section 11.2 show that the change in a longer period of time T is

$$\phi\left[(\mu_1 + \mu_2)T,\ \sqrt{(\sigma_1^2 + \sigma_2^2 + 2\rho\sigma_1\sigma_2)T}\right]$$

The variable, $X_1 + X_2$, therefore follows a generalized Wiener process with drift rate $\mu_1 + \mu_2$ and variance rate $\sigma_1^2 + \sigma_2^2 + 2\rho\sigma_1\sigma_2$.

11.5. The change in S during the first three years has the probability distribution

$$\phi(2 \times 3,\ 3 \times \sqrt{3}) = \phi(6,\ 5.20)$$

The change during the next three years has the probability distribution

$$\phi(3 \times 3,\ 4 \times \sqrt{3}) = \phi(9,\ 6.93)$$

61

The change during the six years is the sum of a variable with probability distribution $\phi(6, 5.20)$ and a variable with probability distribution $\phi(9, 6.93)$. The probability distribution of the change is therefore

$$\phi(6 + 9, \sqrt{5.20^2 + 6.93^2})$$

$$= \phi(15, 8.66)$$

Since the initial value of the variable is 5, the probability distribution of the value of the variable at the end of year six is

$$\phi(20, 8.66)$$

11.6. From Ito's lemma

$$\sigma_G G = \frac{\partial G}{\partial S} \sigma_S S$$

Also the drift of G is

$$\frac{\partial G}{\partial S} \mu S + \frac{\partial G}{\partial t} + \frac{1}{2} \frac{\partial^2 G}{\partial S^2} \sigma^2 S^2$$

where μ is the expected return on the stock. When μ increases by $\lambda \sigma_S$, the drift of G increases by

$$\frac{\partial G}{\partial S} \lambda \sigma_S S$$

or

$$\lambda \sigma_G G$$

The growth rate of G, therefore, increases by $\lambda \sigma_G$.

11.7. Define S_A, μ_A and σ_A as the stock price, expected return and volatility for stock A. Define S_B, μ_B and σ_B as the stock price, expected return and volatility for stock B. Define δS_A and δS_B as the change in S_A and S_B in time δt. Since each of the two stocks follows geometric Brownian motion,

$$\delta S_A = \mu_A S_A \delta t + \sigma_A S_A \epsilon_A \sqrt{\delta t}$$

$$\delta S_B = \mu_B S_B \delta t + \sigma_B S_B \epsilon_B \sqrt{\delta t}$$

where ϵ_A and ϵ_B are independent random samples from a normal distribution.

$$\delta S_A + \delta S_B = (\mu_A S_A + \mu_B S_B)\delta t + (\sigma_A S_A \epsilon_A + \sigma_B S_B \epsilon_B)\sqrt{\delta t}$$

This *cannot* be written as

$$\delta S_A + \delta S_B = \mu(S_A + S_B)\delta t + \sigma(S_A + S_B)\epsilon\sqrt{\delta t}$$

for any constants μ and σ. (Neither the drift term nor the stochastic term correspond.) Hence the value of the portfolio does not follow geometric Brownian motion.

11.8. In:

$$\delta S = \mu S \delta t + \sigma S \epsilon \sqrt{\delta t}$$

the expected increase in the stock price and the variability of the stock price are constant when both are expressed as a proportion (or as a percentage) of the stock price
In:

$$\delta S = \mu \delta t + \sigma \epsilon \sqrt{\delta t}$$

the expected increase in the stock price and the variability of the stock price are constant in absolute terms. For example, if the expected growth rate is $5 per annum when the stock price is $25, it is also $5 per annum when it is $100. If the standard deviation of weekly stock price movements is $1 when the price is $25, it is also $1 when the price is $100.
In:

$$\delta S = \mu S \delta t + \sigma \epsilon \sqrt{\delta t}$$

the expected increase in the stock price is a constant proportion of the stock price while the variability is constant in absolute terms.
In:

$$\delta S = \mu \delta t + \sigma S \epsilon \sqrt{\delta t}$$

the expected increase in the stock price is constant in absolute terms while the variability of the proportional stock price change is constant.
The model:

$$\delta S = \mu S \delta t + \sigma S \epsilon \sqrt{\delta t}$$

is the most appropriate one since it is most realistic to assume that the expected *percentage return* and the variability of the *percentage return* in a short interval is constant.

11.9. The drift rate is $a(b - r)$. Thus, when the interest rate is above b the drift rate is negative and, when the interest rate is below b, the drift rate is positive. The interest rate is therefore continually pulled towards the level b. The rate at which it is pulled toward this level is a. A volatility equal to c is superimposed upon the "pull" or the drift.

Suppose $a = 0.4$, $b = 0.1$ and $c = 0.15$ and the current interest rate is 20% per annum. The interest rate is pulled towards the level of 10% per annum. This can be regarded as a long run average. The current drift is −4% per annum so that the expected rate at the end of one year is about 16% per annum. (In fact it is slightly greater than this, because as the interest rate decreases, the "pull" decreases.) Superimposed upon the drift is a volatility of 15% per annum.

11.10. If $G(S,t) = S^n$ then $\partial G/\partial t = 0$, $\partial G/\partial S = nS^{n-1}$, and $\partial^2 G/\partial S^2 = n(n-1)S^{n-2}$. Using Ito's lemma:

$$dG = \left[\mu n G + \frac{1}{2}n(n-1)\sigma^2 G\right] dt + \sigma n G\, dz$$

This shows that $G = S^n$ follows geometric Brownian motion where the expected return is

$$\mu n + \frac{1}{2}n(n-1)\sigma^2$$

and the volatility is $n\sigma$. The stock price S has an expected return of μ and the expected value of S_T is $S_0 e^{\mu T}$. The expected value of S_T^n is

$$S_0^n e^{[\mu n + \frac{1}{2}n(n-1)\sigma^2]T}$$

11.11. The process followed by B, the bond price, is from Ito's lemma:

$$dB = \left[\frac{\partial B}{\partial x}a(x_0 - x) + \frac{\partial B}{\partial t} + \frac{1}{2}\frac{\partial^2 B}{\partial x^2}s^2 x^2\right] dt + \frac{\partial B}{\partial x}sx\,dz$$

Since:

$$B = e^{-x(T-t)}$$

the required partial derivatives are

$$\frac{\partial B}{\partial t} = xe^{-x(T-t)} = xB$$

$$\frac{\partial B}{\partial x} = -(T-t)e^{-x(T-t)} = -(T-t)B$$

$$\frac{\partial^2 B}{\partial x^2} = (T-t)^2 e^{-x(T-t)} = (T-t)^2 B$$

Hence:

$$dB = \left[-a(x_0 - x)(T-t) + x + \frac{1}{2}s^2 x^2(T-t)^2\right] B\,dt - sx(T-t)B\,dz$$

CHAPTER 12
The Black–Scholes Model

12.1. The Black–Scholes option pricing model assumes that the probability distribution of the stock price in 1 year (or at any other future time) is lognormal. It assumes that the continuously compounded rate of return on the stock during the year is normally distributed.

12.2. The standard deviation of the percentage price change in time δt is $\sigma\sqrt{\delta t}$ where σ is the volatility. In this problem $\sigma = 0.3$ and, assuming 252 trading days in one year, $\delta t = 1/252 = 0.004$ so that $\sigma\sqrt{\delta t} = 0.3\sqrt{0.004} = 0.019$ or 1.9%.

12.3. The price of an option or other derivative when expressed in terms of the price of the underlying stock is independent of risk preferences. Options therefore have the same value in a risk-neutral world as they do in the real world. We may therefore assume that the world is risk neutral for the purposes of valuing options. This simplifies the analysis. In a risk-neutral world all securities have an expected return equal to risk-free interest rate. Also, in a risk-neutral world, the appropriate discount rate to use for expected future cash flows is the risk-free interest rate.

12.4. In this case $S_0 = 50$, $K = 50$, $r = 0.1$, $\sigma = 0.3$, $T = 0.25$, and

$$d_1 = \frac{\ln(50/50) + (0.1 + 0.09/2)0.25}{0.3\sqrt{0.25}} = 0.2417$$

$$d_2 = d_1 - 0.3\sqrt{0.25} = 0.0917$$

The European put price is

$$50N(-0.0917)e^{-0.1\times0.25} - 50N(-0.2417)$$

$$= 50 \times 0.4634e^{-0.1\times0.25} - 50 \times 0.4045 = 2.37$$

or \$2.37.

12.5. In this case we must subtract the present value of the dividend from the stock price before using Black–Scholes. Hence the appropriate value of S_0 is

$$S_0 = 50 - 1.50e^{-0.1667\times0.1} = 48.52$$

As before $K = 50$, $r = 0.1$, $\sigma = 0.3$, and $T = 0.25$. In this case

$$d_1 = \frac{\ln(48.52/50) + (0.1 + 0.09/2)0.25}{0.3\sqrt{0.25}} = 0.0414$$

$$d_2 = d_1 - 0.3\sqrt{0.25} = -0.1086$$

The European put price is

$$50N(0.1086)e^{-0.1 \times 0.25} - 48.52N(-0.0414)$$

$$= 50 \times 0.5432e^{-0.1 \times 0.25} - 48.52 \times 0.4835 = 3.03$$

or $3.03.

12.6. The implied volatility is the volatility that makes the Black–Scholes price of an option equal to its market price. It is calculated using an iterative procedure.

12.7. In this case $\mu = 0.15$ and $\sigma = 0.25$. From equation (12.7) the probability distribution for the rate of return over a 2-year period with continuous compounding is:

$$\phi\left(0.15 - \frac{0.25^2}{2}, \frac{0.25}{\sqrt{2}}\right)$$

i.e.,

$$\phi(0.11875, 0.1768)$$

The expected value of the return is 11.875% per annum and the standard deviation is 17.68% per annum.

12.8. (a) The required probability is the probability of the stock price being above $40 in six months' time. Suppose that the stock price in six months is S_T

$$\ln S_T \sim \phi(\ln 38 + (0.16 - \frac{0.35^2}{2})0.5, \ 0.35\sqrt{0.5})$$

i.e.,

$$\ln S_T \sim \phi(3.687, 0.247)$$

Since $\ln 40 = 3.689$, the required probability is

$$1 - N\left(\frac{3.689 - 3.687}{0.247}\right) = 1 - N(0.008)$$

From normal distribution tables $N(0.008) = 0.5032$ so that the required probability is 0.4968. In general the required probability is $N(d_2)$. (See Problem 12.22).
(b) In this case the required probability is the probability of the stock price being less than $40 in six months' time. It is

$$1 - 0.4968 = 0.5032$$

12.9. From equation 12.2:

$$\ln S_T \sim \phi[\ln S_0 + (\mu - \frac{\sigma^2}{2})T, \sigma\sqrt{T}]$$

95% confidence intervals for $\ln S_T$ are therefore

$$\ln S_0 + (\mu - \frac{\sigma^2}{2})T - 1.96\sigma\sqrt{T}$$

and

$$\ln S_0 + (\mu - \frac{\sigma^2}{2})T + 1.96\sigma\sqrt{T}$$

95% confidence intervals for S_T are therefore

$$e^{\ln S_0 + (\mu - \sigma^2/2)T - 1.96\sigma\sqrt{T}}$$

and

$$e^{\ln S_0 + (\mu - \sigma^2/2)T + 1.96\sigma\sqrt{T}}$$

i.e.

$$S_0 e^{(\mu - \sigma^2/2)T - 1.96\sigma\sqrt{T}}$$

and

$$S_0 e^{(\mu - \sigma^2/2)T + 1.96\sigma\sqrt{T}}$$

12.10. The statement is misleading in that a certain sum of money, say $1000, when invested for 10 years in the fund would have realized a return (with annual compounding) of less than 20% per annum.

The average of the returns realized in each year is always greater than the return per annum (with annual compounding) realized over 10 years. The first is an arithmetic average of the returns in each year; the second is a geometric average of these returns.

12.11. (a) At time t, the expected value of $\ln S_T$ is, from equation (12.2)

$$\ln S + (\mu - \frac{\sigma^2}{2})(T - t)$$

In a risk-neutral world the expected value of $\ln S_T$ is therefore:

$$\ln S + (r - \frac{\sigma^2}{2})(T - t)$$

Using risk-neutral valuation the value of the security at time t is:

$$e^{-r(T-t)} \left[\ln S + (r - \frac{\sigma^2}{2})(T - t) \right]$$

(b) If:

$$f = e^{-r(T-t)} \left[\ln S + (r - \frac{\sigma^2}{2})(T - t) \right]$$

$$\frac{\partial f}{\partial t} = re^{-r(T-t)} \left[\ln S + (r - \frac{\sigma^2}{2})(T - t) \right] - e^{-r(T-t)}(r - \frac{\sigma^2}{2})$$

$$\frac{\partial f}{\partial S} = \frac{e^{-r(T-t)}}{S}$$

$$\frac{\partial^2 f}{\partial S^2} = -\frac{e^{-r(T-t)}}{S^2}$$

The left-hand side of the Black Scholes differential equation is

$$e^{-r(T-t)} \left[r \ln S + r(r - \frac{\sigma^2}{2})(T - t) - (r - \frac{\sigma^2}{2}) + r - \frac{\sigma^2}{2} \right]$$

$$= re^{-r(T-t)} \left[\ln S + (r - \frac{\sigma^2}{2})(T - t) \right]$$

$$= rf$$

Hence equation (12.15) is satisfied.

12.12. This problem is related to Problem 11.10.

(a) If $G(S,t) = h(t,T)S^n$ then $\partial G/\partial t = h_t S^n$, $\partial G/\partial S = hnS^{n-1}$, and $\partial^2 G/\partial S^2 = hn(n-1)S^{n-2}$ where $h_t = \partial h/\partial t$. Substituting into the Black–Scholes differential equation we obtain

$$h_t + rhn + \frac{1}{2}\sigma^2 hn(n-1) = rh$$

(b) The derivative is worth S^n when $t = T$. The boundary condition for this differential equation is therefore $h(T,T) = 1$

(c) The equation

$$h(t,T) = e^{[0.5\sigma^2 n(n-1)+r(n-1)](T-t)}$$

satisfies the boundary condition since it collapses to $h = 1$ when $t = T$. It can also be shown that it satisfies the differential equation in (a). Alternatively we can solve the differential equation in (a) directly. The differential equation can be written

$$\frac{h_t}{h} = -r(n-1) - \frac{1}{2}\sigma^2 n(n-1)$$

The solution to this is

$$\ln h = [-r(n-1) - \frac{1}{2}\sigma^2 n(n-1)]t + k$$

where k is a constant. Since $\ln h = 0$ when $t = T$ it follows that

$$k = [r(n-1) + \frac{1}{2}\sigma^2 n(n-1)]T$$

so that

$$\ln h = [r(n-1) + \frac{1}{2}\sigma^2 n(n-1)](T-t)$$

or

$$h(t,T) = e^{[0.5\sigma^2 n(n-1) + r(n-1)](T-t)}$$

12.13. In this case $S_0 = 52$, $K = 50$, $r = 0.12$, $\sigma = 0.30$ and $T = 0.25$.

$$d_1 = \frac{\ln(52/50) + (0.12 + 0.3^2/2)0.25}{0.30\sqrt{0.25}} = 0.5365$$
$$d_2 = d_1 - 0.30\sqrt{0.25} = 0.3865$$

The price of the European call is

$$52N(0.5365) - 50e^{-0.12 \times 0.25}N(0.3865)$$

$$= 52 \times 0.7042 - 50e^{-0.03} \times 0.6504$$

$$= 5.06$$

or $5.06.

12.14. In this case $S_0 - 69$, $K = 70$, $r = 0.05$, $\sigma = 0.35$ and $T = 0.5$.

$$d_1 = \frac{\ln(69/70) + (0.05 + 0.35^2/2) \times 0.5}{0.35\sqrt{0.5}} = 0.1666$$
$$d_2 = d_1 - 0.35\sqrt{0.5} = -0.0809$$

The price of the European put is

$$70e^{-0.05 \times 0.5}N(0.0809) - 69N(-0.1666)$$

$$= 70e^{-0.025} \times 0.5323 - 69 \times 0.4338$$

$$= 6.40$$

or $6.40.

12.15. Using the notation of Section 12.13, $D_1 = D_2 = 1$, $K(1 - e^{-r(T-t_2)}) = 65(1 - e^{-0.1 \times 0.1667}) = 1.07$, and $K(1 - e^{-r(t_2-t_1)}) = 65(1 - e^{-0.1 \times 0.25}) = 1.60$. Since

$$D_1 < K(1 - e^{-r(T-t_2)})$$

and

$$D_2 < K(1 - e^{-r(t_2-t_1)})$$

It is never optimal to exercise the call option early. DerivaGem shows that the value of the option is 10.94.

12.16. In the case $c = 2.5$, $S_0 = 15$, $K = 13$, $T = 0.25$, $r = 0.05$. The implied volatility must be calculated using an iterative procedure.
A volatility of 0.2 (or 20% per annum) gives $c = 2.20$. A volatility of 0.3 gives $c = 2.32$. A volatility of 0.4 gives $c = 2.507$. A volatility of 0.39 gives $c = 2.487$. By interpolation the implied volatility is about 0.397 or 39.7% per annum.

12.17. (a) Since $N(x)$ is the cumulative probability that a variable with a standardized normal distribution will be less than x, $N'(x)$ is the probability density function for a standardized normal distribution, that is,

$$N'(x) = \frac{1}{\sqrt{2\pi}} e^{-\frac{x^2}{2}}$$

(b)

$$N'(d_1) = N'(d_2 + \sigma\sqrt{T-t})$$

$$= \frac{1}{\sqrt{2\pi}} \exp\left[-\frac{d_2^2}{2} - \sigma d_2\sqrt{T-t} - \frac{1}{2}\sigma^2(T-t)\right]$$

$$= N'(d_2) \exp\left[-\sigma d_2\sqrt{T-t} - \frac{1}{2}\sigma^2(T-t)\right]$$

Because

$$d_2 = \frac{\ln(S/K) + (r - \sigma^2/2)(T-t)}{\sigma\sqrt{T-t}}$$

it follows that

$$\exp\left[-\sigma d_2\sqrt{T-t} - \frac{1}{2}\sigma^2(T-t)\right] = \frac{Ke^{-r(T-t)}}{S}$$

As a result

$$SN'(d_1) = Ke^{-r(T-t)}N'(d_2)$$

which is the required result.

(c)

$$d_1 = \frac{\ln\frac{S}{K} + (r + \frac{\sigma^2}{2})(T-t)}{\sigma\sqrt{T-t}}$$

$$= \frac{\ln S - \ln K + (r + \frac{\sigma^2}{2})(T-t)}{\sigma\sqrt{T-t}}$$

Hence

$$\frac{\partial d_1}{\partial S} = \frac{1}{S\sigma\sqrt{T-t}}$$

Similarly

$$d_2 = \frac{\ln S - \ln K + (r - \frac{\sigma^2}{2})(T \quad t)}{\sigma\sqrt{T - t}}$$

and

$$\frac{\partial d_2}{\partial S} = \frac{1}{S\sigma\sqrt{T - t}}$$

Therefore:

$$\frac{\partial d_1}{\partial S} = \frac{\partial d_2}{\partial S}$$

(d)

$$c = SN(d_1) - Ke^{-r(T-t)}N(d_2)$$

$$\frac{\partial c}{\partial t} = SN'(d_1)\frac{\partial d_1}{\partial t} - rKe^{-r(T-t)}N(d_2) - Ke^{-r(T-t)}N'(d_2)\frac{\partial d_2}{\partial t}$$

From (b):

$$SN'(d_1) = Ke^{-r(T-t)}N'(d_2)$$

Hence

$$\frac{\partial c}{\partial t} = -rKe^{-r(T-t)}N(d_2) + SN'(d_1)\left(\frac{\partial d_1}{\partial t} - \frac{\partial d_2}{\partial t}\right)$$

Since

$$d_1 - d_2 = \sigma\sqrt{T - t}$$

$$\frac{\partial d_1}{\partial t} - \frac{\partial d_2}{\partial t} = \frac{\partial}{\partial t}(\sigma\sqrt{T - t})$$

$$= -\frac{\sigma}{2\sqrt{T - t}}$$

Hence

$$\frac{\partial c}{\partial t} = -rKe^{-r(T-t)}N(d_2) - SN'(d_1)\frac{\sigma}{2\sqrt{T - t}}$$

(e) From differentiating the Black–Scholes formula for a call price we obtain

$$\frac{\partial c}{\partial S} = N(d_1) + SN'(d_1)\frac{\partial d_1}{\partial S} - Ke^{-r(T-t)}N'(d_2)\frac{\partial d_2}{dS}$$

From the results in (b) and (c) it follows that

$$\frac{\partial c}{\partial S} = N(d_1)$$

71

(f) Differentiating the result in (e) and using the result in (c), we obtain

$$\frac{\partial^2 c}{\partial S^2} = N'(d_1)\frac{\partial d_1}{\partial S}$$

$$= N'(d_1)\frac{1}{S\sigma\sqrt{T-t}}$$

From the results in d) and e)

$$\frac{\partial c}{\partial t} + rS\frac{\partial c}{\partial S} + \frac{1}{2}\sigma^2 S^2\frac{\partial^2 c}{\partial S^2} = -rKe^{-r(T-t)}N(d_2) - SN'(d_1)\frac{\sigma}{2\sqrt{T-t}}$$

$$+ rSN(d_1) + \frac{1}{2}\sigma^2 S^2 N'(d_1)\frac{1}{S\sigma\sqrt{T-t}}$$

$$= r[SN(d_1) - Ke^{-r(T-t)}N(d_2)]$$

$$= rc$$

This shows that the Black–Scholes formula for a call option does indeed satisfy the Black–Scholes differential equation

12.18. From the Black–Scholes equations

$$p + S_0 = Ke^{-rT}N(-d_2) - S_0N(-d_1) + S_0$$

Because $1 - N(-d_1) = N(d_1)$ this is

$$Ke^{-rT}N(-d_2) + S_0N(d_1)$$

Also:

$$c + Ke^{-rT} = S_0N(d_1) - Ke^{-rT}N(d_2) + Ke^{-rT}$$

Because $1 - N(d_2) = N(-d_2)$, this is also

$$Ke^{-rT}N(-d_2) + S_0N(d_1)$$

The Black–Scholes equations are therefore consistent with put–call parity.

12.19. This problem naturally leads on to the material in Chapter 15 on volatility smiles. Using DerivaGem we obtain the following table of implied volatilities:

	Maturity (months)		
Strike Price ($)	3	6	12
45	37.78	34.99	34.02
50	34.15	32.78	32.03
55	31.98	30.77	30.45

The option prices are not exactly consistent with Black–Scholes. If they were, the implied volatilities would be all the same. We usually find in practice that low strike price options on a stock have significantly higher implied volatilities than high strike price options on the same stock.

12.20. Black's approach in effect assumes that the holder of option must decide at time zero whether it is a European option maturing at time t_n (the final ex-dividend date) or a European option maturing at time T. In fact the holder of the option has more flexibility than this. The holder can choose to exercise at time t_n if the stock price at that time is above some level but not otherwise. Furthermore, if the option is not exercised at time t_n, it can still be exercised at time T.

It appears that Black's approach understates the true option value. This is because the holder of the option has more alternative strategies for deciding when to exercise the option than the two alternatives implicitly assumed by the approach. These alternatives add value to the option. In fact Black's approach sometimes gives a higher value than the approach in Appendix 12B. This is because Appendix 12B applies the volatility to the stock price less the present value of the dividend whereas Black's approach when considering exercise just prior to the dividend date applies the volatility to the stock price itself. Thus part of the Black calculation assumes more stock price variability than Roll–Geske–Whaley. This issue is also discussed in Example 12.9.

12.21. With the notation in the text

$$D_1 = D_2 = 1.50, \quad t_1 = 0.3333, \quad t_2 = 0.8333, \quad T = 1.25, \quad r = 0.08 \quad \text{and} \quad K = 55$$

$$K\left[1 - e^{-r(T-t_2)}\right] = 55(1 - e^{-0.08 \times 0.4167}) = 1.80$$

Hence

$$D_2 < K\left[1 - e^{-r(T-t_2)}\right]$$

Also:

$$K\left[1 - e^{-r(t_2-t_1)}\right] = 55(1 - e^{-0.08 \times 0.5}) = 2.16$$

Hence:

$$D_1 < K\left[1 - e^{-r(t_2-t_1)}\right]$$

It follows from the conditions established in Section 12.13 that the option should never be exercised early.

The present value of the dividends is

$$1.5e^{-0.3333 \times 0.08} + 1.5e^{-0.8333 \times 0.08} = 2.864$$

The option can be valued using the European pricing formula with:

$$S_0 = 50 - 2.864 = 47.136, \quad K = 55, \quad \sigma = 0.25, \quad r = 0.08, \quad T = 1.25$$

$$d_1 = \frac{\ln(47.136/55) + (0.08 + 0.25^2/2)1.25}{0.25\sqrt{1.25}} = -0.0545$$

$$d_2 = d_1 - 0.25\sqrt{1.25} = -0.3340$$

$$N(d_1) = 0.4783, \quad N(d_2) = 0.3692$$

and the call price is

$$47.136 \times 0.4783 - 55e^{-0.08 \times 1.25} \times 0.3692 = 4.17$$

or \$4.17.

12.22. The probability that the call option will be exercised is the probability that $S_T > K$ where S_T is the stock price at time T. In a risk neutral world

$$\ln S_T \sim \phi[\ln S_0 + (r - \sigma^2/2)T, \sigma\sqrt{T}]$$

The probability that $S_T > K$ is the same as the probability that $\ln S_T > \ln K$. This is

$$1 - N\left[\frac{\ln K - \ln S_0 - (r - \sigma^2/2)T}{\sigma\sqrt{T}}\right]$$

$$= N\left[\frac{\ln(S_0/K) + (r - \sigma^2/2)T}{\sigma\sqrt{T}}\right]$$

$$= N(d_2)$$

The expected value at time T in a risk neutral world of a derivative security which pays off \$100 when $S_T > K$ is therefore

$$100N(d_2)$$

From risk neutral valuation the value of the security at time t is

$$100e^{-rT}N(d_2)$$

12.23. If $f = S^{-2r/\sigma^2}$ then

$$\frac{\partial f}{\partial S} = -\frac{2r}{\sigma^2}S^{-2r/\sigma^2 - 1}$$

$$\frac{\partial^2 f}{\partial S^2} = \left(\frac{2r}{\sigma^2}\right)\left(\frac{2r}{\sigma^2}+1\right) S^{-2r/\sigma^2-2}$$

$$\frac{\partial f}{\partial t} = 0$$

$$\frac{\partial f}{\partial t} + rS\frac{\partial f}{\partial S} + \frac{1}{2}\sigma^2 S^2 \frac{\partial^2 f}{\partial S^2} = rS^{-2r/\sigma^2} = rf$$

This shows that the Black–Scholes equation is satisfied. S^{-2r/σ^2} could therefore be the price of a traded security.

CHAPTER 13
Options on Stock Indices,
Currencies, and Futures

13.1. When the S&P 100 goes down to 480, the value of the portfolio can be expected to be $10 \times (480/500) = \$9.6$ million. (This assumes that the dividend yield on the portfolio equals the dividend yield on the index.) Buying put options on $10,000,000/500 = 20,000$ times the index with a strike of 480 therefore provides protection against a drop in the value of the portfolio below $9.6 million. Since each contract is on 100 times the index a total of 200 contracts would be required.

13.2. A stock index is analogous to a stock paying a continuous dividend yield, the dividend yield being the dividend yield on the index. A currency is analogous to a stock paying a continuous dividend yield, the dividend yield being the foreign risk-free interest rate. A futures contract is analogous to a stock paying a continuous dividend yield, the dividend yield being the domestic risk-free interest rate.

13.3. The lower bound is given by Equation 13.1 as
$$300e^{-0.03 \times 0.5} - 290e^{-0.08 \times 0.5} = 16.90$$

13.4. The tree of exchange-rate movements is shown in Figure 13.1. In this case $u = 1.02$ and $d = 0.98$. The probability of an up movement is
$$p = \frac{e^{(0.06-0.08) \times 0.08333} - 0.98}{1.02 - 0.98} = 0.4584$$

The tree shows that the value of an option to purchase one unit of the currency is $0.0067.

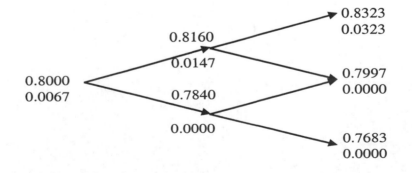

Figure 13.1   Tree for Problem 13.4

76

13.5. A call option on yen gives the holder the right to buy yen in the spot market at an exchange rate equal to the strike price. A call option on yen futures gives the holder the right to receive the amount by which the futures price exceeds the strike price. If the yen futures option is exercised, the holder also obtains a long position in the yen futures contract.

13.6. A company that knows it is due to receive a foreign currency at a certain time in the future can buy a put option. This guarantees that the price at which the currency will be sold will be at or above a certain level. A company that knows it is due to pay a foreign currency a certain time in the future can buy a call option. This guarantees that the price at which the currency will be purchased will be at or below a certain level.

13.7. In this case, $S_0 = 250$, $K = 250$, $r = 0.10$, $\sigma = 0.18$, $T = 0.25$, $q = 0.03$ and

$$d_1 = \frac{\ln(250/250) + (0.10 - 0.03 + 0.18^2/2)0.25}{0.18\sqrt{0.25}} = 0.2394$$

$$d_2 = d_1 - 0.18\sqrt{0.25} = 0.1494$$

and the call price is

$$250N(0.2394)e^{-0.03\times0.25} - 250N(0.1494)e^{-0.10\times0.25}$$

$$= 250 \times 0.5946e^{-0.03\times0.25} - 250 \times 0.5594e^{-0.10\times0.25}$$

or 11.15.

13.8. The American futures option is worth more than the corresponding American option on the underlying asset when the futures price is greater than the spot price prior to the maturity of the futures contract. This is the case when the cost of carry net of the convenience yield is positive.

13.9. In this case $S_0 = 0.52$, $K = 0.50$, $r = 0.04$, $r_f = 0.08$, $\sigma = 0.12$, $T = 0.6667$, and

$$d_1 = \frac{\ln(0.52/0.50) + (0.04 - 0.08 + 0.12^2/2)0.6667}{0.12\sqrt{0.6667}} = 0.1771$$

$$d_2 = d_1 - 0.12\sqrt{0.6667} = 0.0791$$

and the put price is

$$0.50N(-0.0791)e^{-0.04\times0.6667} - 0.52N(-0.1771)e^{-0.08\times0.6667}$$

$$= 0.50 \times 0.4685e^{-0.04\times0.6667} - 0.52 \times 0.4297e^{-0.08\times0.6667}$$

$$= 0.0162$$

13.10. The main reason is that a bond futures contract is a more liquid instrument than a bond. The price of a Treasury bond futures contract is known immediately from trading on CBOT. The price of a bond can be obtained only by contacting dealers.

13.11. A futures price behaves like a stock paying a continuous dividend yield at the risk-free interest rate.

13.12. In this case $u = 1.12$ and $d = 0.92$. The probability of an up movement in a risk-neutral world is

$$\frac{1 - 0.92}{1.12 - 0.92} = 0.4$$

From risk-neutral valuation, the value of the call is

$$e^{-0.06 \times 0.5}(0.4 \times 6 + 0.6 \times 0) = 2.33$$

13.13. In this case $F_0 = 19$, $K = 20$, $r = 0.12$, $\sigma = 0.20$, and $T = 0.4167$. The value of the European put futures option is

$$20N(-d_2)e^{-0.12 \times 0.4167} - 19N(-d_1)e^{-0.12 \times 0.4167}$$

where

$$d_1 = \frac{\ln(19/20) + (0.04/2)0.4167}{0.2\sqrt{0.4167}} = -0.3327$$
$$d_2 = d_1 - 0.2\sqrt{0.4167} = -0.4618$$

This is

$$e^{-0.12 \times 0.4167}[20N(0.4618) - 19N(0.3327)]$$
$$= e^{-0.12 \times 0.4167}(20 \times 0.6778 - 19 \times 0.6303)$$
$$= 1.50$$

or $1.50.

13.14. A total return index behaves like a stock paying no dividends. In a risk-neutral world it can be expected to grow on average at the risk-free rate. Forward contracts and options on total return indices should be valued in the same way as forward contracts and options on non-dividend-paying stocks.

13.15. In this case $S_0 = 696$, $K = 700$, $r = 0.07$, $\sigma = 0.3$, $T = 0.25$ and $q = 0.04$. The option can be valued using equation (13.5).

$$d_1 = \frac{\ln(696/700) + (0.07 - 0.04 + 0.09/2) \times 0.25}{0.3\sqrt{0.25}} = 0.0868$$
$$d_2 = d_1 - 0.3\sqrt{0.25} = -0.0632$$

and
$$N(-d_1) = 0.4654, \quad N(-d_2) = 0.5252$$

The value of the put, p, is given by:

$$p = 700e^{-0.07 \times 0.25} \times 0.5252 - 696e^{-0.04 \times 0.25} \times 0.4654 = 40.6$$

i.e., it is \$40.6.

13.16. The put–call parity relationship for European currency options is

$$c + Ke^{-rT} = p + Se^{-r_f T}$$

To prove this result, the two portfolios to consider are:

Portfolio A: one call option plus one discount bond which will be worth K at time T

Portfolio B: one put option plus $e^{-r_f T}$ of foreign currency invested at the foreign risk-free interest rate.

Both portfolios are worth $\max(S_T, K)$ at time T. They must therefore be worth the same today. The result follows.

13.17. Lower bound for European option is

$$S_0 e^{-r_f T} - Ke^{-rT} = 1.5e^{-0.09 \times 0.5} - 1.4e^{-0.05 \times 0.5} = 0.069$$

Lower bound for American option is

$$S_0 - K = 0.10$$

13.18. In this case $S_0 = 250$, $q = 0.04$, $r = 0.06$, $T = 0.25$, $K = 245$, and $c = 10$. Using put–call parity
$$c + Ke^{-rT} = p + S_0 e^{-qT}$$

or

$$p = c + Ke^{-rT} - S_0 e^{-qT}$$

Substituting:
$$p = 10 + 245e^{-0.25 \times 0.06} - 250e^{-0.25 \times 0.04} = 3.84$$

The put price is 3.84.

13.19. Following the hint, we first consider

Portfolio A: A European call option plus an amount K invested at the risk-free rate

Portfolio B: An American put option plus e^{-qT} of stock with dividends being reinvested in the stock.

79

Portfolio A is worth $c + K$ while portfolio B is worth $P + S_0 e^{-qT}$. If the put option is exercised at time $\tau (0 \le \tau \le T)$, portfolio B becomes:

$$K - S_\tau + S_\tau e^{-q(T-\tau)} \le K$$

where S_τ is the stock price at time τ. Portfolio A is worth

$$c + K e^{r\tau} > K$$

Hence portfolio A is worth more than portfolio B. If both portfolios are held to maturity (time T), portfolio A is worth

$$\max(S_T - K, 0) + K e^{rT}$$
$$= \max(S_T, K) + K[e^{rT} - 1]$$

Portfolio B is worth $\max(S_T, K)$. Hence portfolio A is worth more than portfolio B. Since portfolio A is worth more than portfolio B in all circumstances so that

$$P + S_0 e^{-qT} < c + K$$

Since $c \le C$:

$$P + S_0 e^{-qT} < C + K$$

or

$$S_0 e^{-qT} - K < C - P$$

This proves the first part of the inequality.

For the second part consider:

Portfolio C: An American call option plus an amount $K e^{-rT}$ invested at the risk-free rate

Portfolio D: A European put option plus one stock with dividends being reinvested in the stock.

Portfolio C is worth $C + K e^{-rT}$ while portfolio D is worth $p + S_0$. If the call option is exercised at time $\tau (0 \le \tau < T)$ portfolio C becomes:

$$S_\tau - K + K e^{-r(T-\tau)} < S_\tau$$

while portfolio D is worth

$$p + S_\tau e^{q(\tau - t)} > S_\tau$$

Hence portfolio D is worth more than portfolio C. If both portfolios are held to maturity (time T), portfolio C is worth $\max(S_T, K)$ while portfolio D is worth

$$\max(K - S_T, 0) + S_T e^{qT}$$
$$= \max(S_T, K) + S_T[e^{qT} - 1]$$

Hence portfolio D is worth more than portfolio C.

Since portfolio D is worth more than portfolio C in all circumstances:

$$C + Ke^{-rT} < p + S_0$$

Since $p < P$:

$$C + Ke^{-rT} < P + S_0$$

or

$$C - P < S_0 - Ke^{-rT}$$

This proves the second part of the inequality. Hence:

$$S_0 e^{-qT} - K < C - P < S_0 - Ke^{-rT}$$

13.20. In this case we consider

> *Portfolio A*: A European call option on futures plus an amount K invested at the risk-free interest rate
>
> *Portfolio B*: An American put option on futures plus an amount $F_0 e^{-rT}$ invested at the risk-free interest rate plus a long futures contract maturing at time T.

Following the arguments in Chapter 3 we will treat all futures contracts as forward contracts. Portfolio A is worth $c + K$ while portfolio B is worth $P + F_0 e^{-rT}$. If the put option is exercised at time τ ($0 \leq \tau \leq T$), portfolio B becomes:

$$K - F_\tau + F_0 e^{-r(T-\tau)} + F_\tau - F_0$$
$$= K + F_0 e^{-r(T-\tau)} - F_0 < K$$

where F_τ is the futures price at time τ. Portfolio A is worth

$$c + Ke^{r\tau} > K$$

Hence portfolio A is worth more than portfolio B. If both portfolios are held to maturity (time T) portfolio A is worth

$$\max(F_T - K, 0) + Ke^{rT}$$
$$= \max(F_T, K) + K[e^{rT} - 1]$$

Portfolio B is worth

$$\max(K - F_T, 0) + F_0 + F_T - F_0 = \max(F_T, K)$$

Hence portfolio A is worth more than portfolio B.
Since portfolio A is worth more than portfolio B in all circumstances:

$$P + F_0 e^{-r(T-t)} < c + K$$

Since $c < C$ it follows that

$$P + F_0 e^{-rT} < C + K$$

or

$$F_0 e^{-rT} - K < C - P$$

This proves the first part of the inequality.

For the second part of the inequality consider:

Portfolio C: An American call futures option plus an amount Ke^{-rT} invested at the risk-free interest rate

Portfolio D: A European put futures option plus an amount F_0 invested at the risk-free interest rate plus a long futures contract.

Portfolio C is worth $C + Ke^{-rT}$ while portfolio D is worth $p + F_0$. If the call option is exercised at time $\tau (0 \leq \tau < T)$ portfolio C becomes:

$$F_\tau - K + Ke^{-r(T-\tau)} < F_\tau$$

while portfolio D is worth

$$p + F_0 e^{r\tau} + F_\tau - F_0$$
$$= p + F_0[e^{r\tau} - 1] + F_\tau > F_\tau$$

Hence portfolio D is worth more than portfolio C. If both portfolios are held to maturity (time T), portfolio C is worth $\max(F_T, K)$ while portfolio D is worth

$$\max(K - F_T, 0) + F_0 e^{rT} + F_T - F_0$$
$$= \max(K, F_T) + F_0[e^{rT} - 1]$$
$$> \max(K, F_T)$$

Hence portfolio D is worth more than portfolio C.

Since portfolio D is worth more than portfolio C in all circumstances

$$C + Ke^{-rT} < p + F_0$$

Since $p < P$ it follows that

$$C + Ke^{-rT} < P + F_0$$

or

$$C - P < F_0 - Ke^{-rT}$$

This proves the second part of the inequality. The result:

$$F_0 e^{-rT} - K < C - P < F_0 - Ke^{-rT}$$

has therefore been proved.

13.21. The risk-neutral process for the price of currency A in terms of the price of currency B is

$$dS = (r_B - r_A)Sdt + \sigma S dz$$

The price of currency B expressed in terms of currency A is $1/S$. Define

$$G = \frac{1}{S}$$

then:

$$\frac{\partial G}{\partial t} = 0; \quad \frac{\partial G}{\partial S} = -\frac{1}{S^2}; \quad \frac{\partial^2 G}{\partial S^2} = \frac{2}{S^3}$$

Applying Ito's lemma:

$$dG = \left(-\frac{1}{S^2}\mu S + \frac{1}{2}\frac{2}{S^3}\sigma^2 S^2\right) dt - \frac{1}{S^2}\sigma S dz$$

$$= \frac{1}{S}\left(-\mu + \sigma^2\right) dt - \frac{1}{S}\sigma dz$$

$$= (-\mu + \sigma^2)G dt - \sigma G dz$$

We can define a process dz^* by:

$$dz^* = -dz$$

This is also a Wiener process and:

$$dG = (r_A - r_B + \sigma^2)G dt + \sigma G dz^*$$

This shows that $G = 1/S$ follows geometric Brownian motion. The expected growth rate might be expected to be $r_A - r_B$ rather than $r_A - r_B + \sigma^2$. This result is sometimes referred to as Siegel's paradox and is discussed in Chapter 21.

13.22. The volatility of a stock index can be expected to be less than the volatility of a typical stock. This is because some risk (i.e., return uncertainty) is diversified away when a portfolio of stocks is created. In capital asset pricing model terminology, there exists systematic and unsystematic risk in the returns from an individual stock. However, in a stock index, unsystematic risk has been largely diversified away and only the systematic risk contributes to volatility.

13.23. The cost of portfolio insurance increases as the beta of the portfolio increases. This is because portfolio insurance involves the purchase of a put option on a portfolio. As beta increases, the volatility of the portfolio increases and the strike price required also increases.

13.24. If the value of the portfolio mirrors the value of the index, the index can be expected to have dropped by 10% when the value of the portfolio drops by 10%. Hence when the value of the portfolio drops to $54 million the value of the index can be expected to be 1080. This indicates that put options with an exercise price of 1080 should be purchased. The options should be on:

$$\frac{60,000,000}{1200} = \$50,000$$

times the index. Each option contract is for $100 times the index. Hence 500 contracts should be purchased.

13.25. When the value of the portfolio falls to $54 million the holder of the portfolio makes a capital loss of 10%. After dividends are taken into account the loss is 7% during the year. This is 12% below the risk-free interest rate. According to the capital asset pricing model:

$$\text{Excess expected return of portfolio above riskless interest rate} = \beta \times \text{Excess return of market above riskless interest rate}$$

Therefore, when the portfolio provides a return 12% below the risk-free interest rate, the market's expected return is 6% below the risk-free interest rate. As the index can be assumed to have a beta of 1.0, this is also the excess expected return (including dividends) from the index. The expected return from the index is therefore −1% per annum. Since the index provides a 3% per annum dividend yield, the expected movement in the index is −4%. Thus when the portfolio's value is $54 million the expected value of the index $0.96 \times 1200 = 1152$. Hence European put options should be purchased with an exercise price of 1152. Their maturity date should be in one year.

The number of options required is twice the number required in Problem 13.24. This is because we wish to protect a portfolio which is twice as sensitive to changes in market conditions as the portfolio in Problem 13.24. Hence options on $100,000 (or 1,000 contracts) should be purchased. To check that the answer is correct consider what happens when the value of the portfolio declines by 20% to $48 million. The return including dividends is −17%. This is 22% less than the risk-free interest rate. The index can be expected to provide a return (including dividends) which is 11% less than the risk-free interest rate, i.e. a return of −6%. The index can therefore be expected to drop by 9% to 1092. The payoff from the put options is $(1152 - 1092) \times 100,000 = \$6$ million. This is exactly what is required to restore the value of the portfolio to $54 million.

13.26. Consider the following two portfolios

Portfolio A: one call option plus one zero-coupon bond which will be worth K at time T

Portfolio B: one put option plus e^{-qT} of the stock portfolio underlying the index

We assume that the dividends on the stock portfolio are reinvested in the stock portfolio. This means that at maturity portfolio B equals one put option plus one unit of the stock portfolio underlying the index. It is worth $\max(S_T, K)$. Similarly portfolio

A is worth $\max(S_T, K)$. As the two portfolios are worth the same at time T, they must be worth the same today.

Hence

$$c + Ke^{-rT} = p + S_0 e^{-qT}$$

13.27. An amount $(400 - 380) \times 100 = \$2,000$ is added to your margin account and you acquire a short futures position giving you the right to sell 100 ounces of gold in October. This position is marked to market at the end of each day in the usual way until you choose to close it out.

13.28. In this case an amount $(0.75 - 0.70) \times 40,000 = \$2,000$ is subtracted from your margin account and you acquire a short position in a live cattle futures contract to sell 40,000 pounds of cattle in April. This position is marked to marked at the end of each day in the usual way until you choose to close it out.

13.29. Lower bound if option is European is

$$(F_0 - K)e^{-rT} = (47 - 40)e^{-0.1 \times 0.1667} = 6.88$$

Lower bound if option is American is

$$F_0 - K = 7$$

13.30. Lower bound if option is European is

$$(K - F_0)e^{-rT} = (50 - 47)e^{-0.1 \times 0.3333} = 2.90$$

Lower bound if option is American is

$$K - F_0 = 3$$

13.31 In this case the risk-neutral probability of an up move is

$$\frac{1 - 0.9}{1.1 - 0.9} = 0.5$$

In the tree shown in Figure 13.2 the middle number at each node is the price of the European option and the lower number is the price of the American option. The tree shows that the price of both the European and the American option is 3.0265. The American option should never be exercised early.

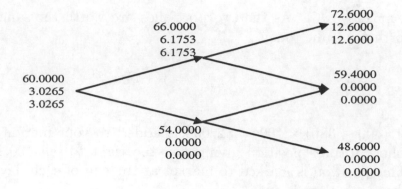

Figure 13.2   Tree to evaluate European and American call options in Problem 13.31.

13.32. In this case the risk-neutral probability of an up move is

$$\frac{1 - 0.9}{1.1 - 0.9} = 0.5$$

The tree in Figure 13.3 shows that the price of the European option is 3.0265 while the price of the American option is 3.0847.

Using the result in the previous problem

$$c + Ke^{-rT} = 3.0265 + 60e^{-0.04} = 60.6739$$

From this problem

$$p + F_0 e^{-rT} = 3.0265 + 60e^{-0.04} = 60.6739$$

This verifies that the put–call parity relationship in equation (13.13) holds for the European option prices. For the American option prices we have:

$$C - P = -0.0582; \qquad F_0 e^{-rT} - K = -2.353; \qquad F_0 - Ke^{-rT} = 2.353$$

The put–call inequalities for American options are therefore satisfied

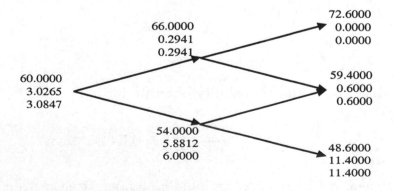

Figure 13.3   Tree to evaluate European and American call options in Problem 13.32.

13.33. In this case $F_0 = 25$, $K = 26$, $\sigma = 0.3$, $r = 0.1$, $T = 0.75$

$$d_1 = \frac{\ln(F_0/K) + \sigma^2 T/2}{\sigma\sqrt{T}} = -0.0211$$

$$d_2 = \frac{\ln(F_0/K) - \sigma^2 T/2}{\sigma\sqrt{T}} = -0.2809$$

$$c = e^{-0.075}[25N(-0.0211) - 26N(-0.2809)]$$

$$= e^{-0.075}[25 \times 0.4916 - 26 \times 0.3894] = 2.01$$

13.34. In this case $F_0 = 70$, $K = 65$, $\sigma = 0.2$, $r = 0.06$, $T = 0.4167$

$$d_1 = \frac{\ln(F_0/K) + \sigma^2 T/2}{\sigma\sqrt{T}} = 0.6386$$

$$d_2 = \frac{\ln(F_0/K) - \sigma^2 T/2}{\sigma\sqrt{T}} = 0.5095$$

$$p = e^{-0.025}[65N(-0.5095) - 70N(-0.6386)]$$

$$= e^{-0.025}[65 \times 0.3052 - 70 \times 0.2615] = 1.495$$

13.35. In this case

$$c + Ke^{-rT} = 2 + 34e^{-0.1 \times 1} = 30.76$$

$$p + F_0 e^{-rT} = 2 + 35e^{-0.1 \times 1} = 31.67$$

Put-call parity shows that the put is overpriced relative to the call. We should buy one call, short one put and short $e^{-0.1} = 0.90$ of the stock.

13.36. The put price is

$$e^{-rT}[KN(-d_2) - F_0 N(-d_1)]$$

Since $N(-x) = 1 - N(x)$ for all x the put price can also be written

$$e^{-rT}[K - KN(d_2) - F_0 + F_0 N(d_1)]$$

Since $F_0 = K$ this is the same as the call price:

$$e^{-rT}[F_0 N(d_1) - KN(d_2)]$$

This result can also be proved from put-call parity showing that it is not model dependent.

13.37. From the result at the end of Section 13.5, $C - P$ must lie between

$$30 - 28e^{-0.05 \times 0.25} = 2.35$$

and

$$30e^{-0.05 \times 0.25} - 28 = 1.63$$

Since $C = 4$ we must have

$$1.65 < P < 2.37$$

13.38. There is no way of doing this. A natural idea is to create an option to exchange K euros for one yen from an option to exchange Y dollars for 1 yen and an option to exchange K euros for Y dollars. The problem with this is that it assumes that either both options are exercised or that neither option is exercised. There are always some circumstances where the first option is in-the-money at expiration while the second is not and vice versa.

13.39. The appropriate contract is a three-month Eurodollar call futures option contract with a strike price of 93.00. This provides protection against LIBOR falling below 7%, or LIBOR minus 50 basis points falling below 6.5%. If the 90-day rate in three months is X basis points below 7%, one contract will pay off $25X$ dollars. The corporation requires a payoff of $5,000,000 \times 0.0001 = 500X$ when the 90-day rate is X basis points below 7%. A total of 20 contracts should therefore be purchased.

13.40. In portfolio A, the cash, if it is invested at the risk-free interest rate, will grow to K at time T. If $S_T > K$, the call option is exercised at time T and portfolio A is worth S_T. If $S_T < K$, the call option expires worthless and the portfolio is worth K. Hence, at time T, portfolio A is worth

$$\max(S_T, K)$$

Because of the reinvestment of dividends, portfolio B becomes one share at time T. It is, therefore, worth S_T at this time. It follows that portfolio A is always worth as much as, and is sometimes worth more than, portfolio B at time T. In the absence of arbitrage opportunities, this must also be true today. Hence,

$$c + Ke^{-rT} \geq S_0 e^{-qT}$$

or

$$c \geq S_0 e^{-qT} - Ke^{-rT}$$

This proves equation (13.1)

In portfolio C, the reinvestment of dividends means that the portfolio is one put option plus one share at time T. If $S_T < K$, the put option is exercised at time T and portfolio C is worth K. If $S_T > K$, the put option expires worthless and the portfolio is worth S_T. Hence, at time T, portfolio C is worth

$$\max(S_T, K)$$

Portfolio D is worth K at time T. It follows that portfolio C is always worth as much as, and is sometimes worth more than, portfolio D at time T. In the absence of arbitrage opportunities, this must also be true today. Hence,

$$p + S_0 e^{-qT} \geq K e^{-rT}$$

or

$$p \geq K e^{-rT} - S_0 e^{-qT}$$

This proves equation (13.2)

Portfolios A and C are both worth $\max(S_T, K)$ at time T. They must, therefore, be worth the same today, and the put–call parity result in equation (13.3) follows.

CHAPTER 14
The Greek Letters

14.1. Suppose the strike price is 10.00. The option writer aims to be fully covered whenever the option is in the money and naked whenever it is out of the money. The option writer attempts to achieve this by buying the assets underlying the option as soon as the asset price reaches 10.00 from below and selling as soon as the asset price reaches 10.00 from above. The trouble with this scheme is that it assumes that when the asset price moves from 9.99 to 10.00, the next move will be to a price above 10.00. (In practice the next move might back to 9.99.) Similarly it assumes that when the asset price moves from 10.01 to 10.00, the next move will be to a price below 10.00. (In practice the next move might be back to 10.01.) The scheme can be implemented by buying at 10.01 and selling at 9.99. However, it is not a good hedge. The cost of the trading strategy is zero if the asset price never reaches 10.00 and can be quite high if it reaches 10.00 many times. A good hedge has the property that its cost is always very close the value of the option.

14.2. A delta of 0.7 means that, when the price of the stock increases by a small amount, the price of the option increases by 70% of this amount. Similarly, when the price of the stock decreases by a small amount, the price of the option decreases by 70% of this amount. A short position in 1,000 options has a delta of -700 and can be made delta neutral with the purchase of 700 shares.

14.3. In this case $S_0 = K$, $r = 0.1$, $\sigma = 0.25$, and $T = 0.5$. Also,

$$d_1 = \frac{\ln(S_0/K) + (0.1 + 0.25^2/2)0.5}{0.25\sqrt{0.5}} = 0.3712$$

The delta of the option is $N(d_1)$ or 0.64.

14.4. A theta of -0.1 means that if δt years pass with no change in either the stock price or its volatility, the value of the option declines by $0.1\delta t$. If a trader feels that neither the stock price nor its implied volatility will change, he or she should write an option with as high a theta as possible. Relatively short-life at-the-money options have the highest theta.

14.5. The gamma of an option position is the rate of change of the delta of the position with respect to the asset price. For example, a gamma of 0.1 would indicate that when the asset price increases by a certain small amount delta increases by 0.1 of this amount. When the gamma of an option writer's position is large and negative and the delta is zero, the option writer will lose significant amounts of money if there is a large movement (either an increase or a decrease) in the asset price.

14.6. To hedge an option position it is necessary to create the opposite option position synthetically. For example, to hedge a long position in a put it is necessary to create

90

a short position in a put synthetically. It follows that the procedure for creating an option position synthetically is the reverse of the procedure for hedging the option position.

14.7. Portfolio insurance involves creating a put option synthetically. It assumes that as soon as a portfolio's value declines by a small amount the portfolio manager's position is rebalanced by either (a) selling part of the portfolio, or (b) selling index futures. On October 19, 1987, the market declined so quickly that the sort of rebalancing anticipated in portfolio insurance schemes could not be accomplished.

14.8. The strategy costs the trader $0.20 each time the stock is bought and sold. The total expected cost of the strategy, in present value terms, must be $4. This means that the expected number of times the stock will be bought and sold is approximately 20. The expected number of times it will be bought is approximately 20 and the expected number of times it will be sold is also approximately 20. The buy and sell transactions can take place at any time during the life of the option. The above numbers are therefore only approximately correct because of the effects of discounting. Also they assume a risk-neutral world.

14.9. The holding of the stock at any given time must be $N(d_1)$. Hence the stock is bought just after the price has risen and sold just after the price has fallen. (This is the buy high sell low strategy referred to in the text.) In the first scenario the stock is continually bought. In second scenario the stock is bought, sold, bought again, sold again, etc. The final holding is the same in both scenarios. The buy, sell, buy, sell... situation clearly leads to higher costs than the buy, buy, buy... situation. This problem emphasizes one disadvantage of creating options synthetically. Whereas the cost of an option that is purchased is known up front and depends on the forecasted volatility, the cost of an option that is created synthetically is not known up front and depends on the volatility actually encountered.

14.10. The delta of a European futures option is usually defined as the rate of change of the option price with respect to the futures price (not the spot price). It is

$$e^{-rT} N(d_1)$$

In this case $F_0 = 8$, $K = 8$, $r = 0.12$, $\sigma = 0.18$, $T = 0.6667$

$$d_1 = \frac{\ln(8/8) + (0.18^2/2) \times 0.6667}{0.18\sqrt{0.6667}} = 0.0735$$

$N(d_1) = 0.5293$ and the delta of the option is

$$e^{-0.12 \times 0.6667} \times 0.5293 = 0.4886$$

The delta of a short position in 1000 futures options is therefore -488.6.

14.11. In order to answer this problem it is important to distinguish between the rate of change of the price of a derivative security with respect to the futures price and the rate of change of the price of the derivative security with respect to the spot price.

The former will be referred to as the futures delta; the latter will be referred to as the spot delta. The futures delta of a nine-month futures contract to buy one ounce of silver is by definition 1.0. Hence, from the answer to Problem 14.10, a long position in nine-month futures on 488.6 ounces is necessary to hedge the option position. The spot delta of a nine-month futures contract is $e^{0.12 \times 0.75} = 1.094$ assuming no storage costs. (This is because silver can be treated in the same way as a non-dividend-paying stock when there are no storage costs.) Hence the spot delta of the option position is $-488.6 \times 1.094 = -534.6$. Thus a long position in 534.6 ounces of silver is necessary to hedge the option position.

The spot delta of a one-year silver futures contract to buy one ounce of silver is $e^{0.12} = 1.1275$. Hence a long position in $e^{-0.12} \times 534.6 = 474.1$ ounces of one-year silver futures is necessary to hedge the option position.

14.12. A long position in either a put or a call option has a positive gamma. From Figure 14.8, when gamma is positive the hedger gains from a large change in the stock price and loses from a small change in the stock price. Hence the hedger will fare better in case (b).

14.13. A short position in either a put or a call option has a negative gamma. From Figure 14.8, when gamma is negative the hedger gains from a small change in the stock price and loses from a large change in the stock price. Hence the hedger will fare better in case (a).

14.14. In this case $S_0 = 0.80$, $K = 0.81$, $r = 0.08$, $r_f = 0.05$, $\sigma = 0.15$, $T = 0.5833$

$$d_1 = \frac{\ln(0.80/0.81) + (0.08 - 0.05 + 0.15^2/2) \times 0.5833}{0.15\sqrt{0.5833}} = 0.1016$$

$$d_2 = d_1 - 0.15\sqrt{0.5833} = -0.0130$$

$$N(d_1) = 0.5405; \quad N(d_2) = 0.4998$$

The delta of one call option is $e^{-r_f T} N(d_1) = e^{-0.05 \times 0.5833} \times 0.5405 = 0.5250$.

$$N'(d_1) = \frac{1}{\sqrt{2\pi}} e^{-d_1^2/2} = \frac{1}{\sqrt{2\pi}} e^{-0.00516} = 0.3969$$

so that the gamma of one call option is

$$\frac{N'(d_1)e^{-r_f T}}{S\sigma\sqrt{T}} = \frac{0.3969 \times 0.9713}{0.80 \times 0.15 \times \sqrt{0.5833}} = 4.206$$

The vega of one call option is

$$S_0\sqrt{T}N'(d_1)e^{-r_f T} = 0.80\sqrt{0.5833} \times 0.3969 \times 0.9713 = 0.2355$$

The theta of one call option is

$$-\frac{S_0 N'(d_1)\sigma e^{-r_f T}}{2\sqrt{T}} + r_f S_0 N(d_1)e^{-r_f T} - rKe^{-rT}N(d_2)$$

$$= -\frac{0.8 \times 0.3969 \times 0.15 \times 0.9713}{2\sqrt{0.5833}}$$

$$+ 0.05 \times 0.8 \times 0.5405 \times 0.9713 - 0.08 \times 0.81 \times 0.9544 \times 0.4948$$

$$= -0.0399$$

The rho of one call option is

$$KTe^{-rT}N(d_2)$$

$$= 0.81 \times 0.5833 \times 0.9544 \times 0.4948$$

$$= 0.2231$$

Delta can be interpreted as meaning that, when the spot price increases by a small amount (measured in cents), the value of an option to buy one yen increases by 0.525 times that amount. Gamma can be interpreted as meaning that, when the spot price increases by a small amount (measured in cents), the delta increases by 4.206 times that amount. Vega can be interpreted as meaning that, when the volatility (measured in decimal form) increases by a small amount, the option's value increases by 0.2355 times that amount. Theta can be interpreted as meaning that, when a small amount of time (measured in years) passes, the option's value decreases by 0.0399 times that amount. Finally, rho can be interpreted as meaning that, when the interest rate (measured in decimal form) increases by a small amount the option's value increases by 0.2231 times that amount.

14.15. Assume that S_0, K, r, σ, T, q are the parameters for the over-the-counter option and S_0, K^*, r, σ, T^*, q are the parameters for the traded option. Suppose that d_1 has its usual meaning and is calculated on the basis of the first set of parameters while d_1^* is the value of d_1 calculated on the basis of the second set of parameters. Suppose further that w traded options are held for each over-the-counter option. The gamma of the portfolio is:

$$\alpha \left[\frac{N'(d_1)e^{-qT}}{S_0\sigma\sqrt{T}} + w\frac{N'(d_1^*)e^{-qT^*}}{S_0\sigma\sqrt{T^*}} \right]$$

where α is the number of over-the-counter options held.
Since we require gamma to be zero:

$$w = -\frac{N'(d_1)e^{-q(T-T^*)}}{N'(d_1^*)}\sqrt{\frac{T^*}{T}}$$

The vega of the portfolio is:

$$\alpha \left[S_0\sqrt{T}N'(d_1)e^{-q(T)} + wS_0\sqrt{T^*}N'(d_1^*)e^{-q(T^*)} \right]$$

Since we require vega to be zero:

$$w = -\sqrt{\frac{T}{T^*}} \frac{N'(d_1)e^{-q(T-T^*)}}{N'(d_1^*)}$$

Equating the two expressions for w

$$T^* = T$$

Hence the maturity of the over-the-counter option must equal the maturity of the traded option.

14.16. The fund is worth \$300,000 times the value of the index. When the value of the portfolio falls by 5% (to \$342 million), the value of the S&P 500 also falls by 5% to 1140. The fund manager therefore requires European put options on 300,000 times the S&P 500 with exercise price 1140.
(a) $S_0 = 1200$, $K = 1140$, $r = 0.06$, $\sigma = 0.30$, $T = 0.50$ and $q = 0.03$. Hence:

$$d_1 = \frac{\ln(1200/1140) + \left(0.06 - 0.03 + 0.3^2/2\right) \times 0.5}{0.3\sqrt{0.5}} = 0.4186$$

$$d_2 = d_1 - 0.3\sqrt{0.5} = 0.2064$$

$$N(d_1) = 0.6622; \quad N(d_2) = 0.5818$$

$$N(-d_1) = 0.3378; \quad N(-d_2) = 0.4182$$

The value of one put option is

$$1140e^{-rT}N(-d_2) - 1200e^{-qT}N(-d_1)$$
$$=1140e^{-0.06 \times 0.5} \times 0.4182 - 1200e^{-0.03 \times 0.5} \times 0.3378$$
$$=63.40$$

The total cost of the insurance is therefore

$$300,000 \times 63.40 = \$19,020,000$$

(b) From put–call parity
$$S_0e^{-qT} + p = c + Ke^{-rT}$$

or:
$$p = c - S_0e^{-qT} + Ke^{-rT}$$

This shows that a put option can be created by selling (or shorting) e^{-qT} of the index, buying a call option and investing the remainder at the risk-free rate of interest. Applying this to the situation under consideration, the fund manager should:
1) Sell $360e^{-0.03 \times 0.5} = \$354.64$ million of stock

2) Buy call options on 300,000 times the S&P 500 with exercise price 1140 and maturity in six months.

3) Invest the remaining cash at the risk-free interest rate of 6% per annum.

This strategy gives the same result as buying put options directly.

(c) The delta of one put option is

$$e^{-qT}[N(d_1) - 1]$$
$$= e^{-0.03 \times 0.5}(0.6622 - 1)$$
$$- 0.3327$$

This indicates that 33.27% of the portfolio (i.e., $119.77 million) should be initially sold and invested in risk-free securities.

(d) The delta of a nine-month index futures contract is

$$e^{(r-q)T} = e^{0.03 \times 0.75} = 1.023$$

The spot short position required is

$$\frac{119,770,000}{1200} = 99,808$$

times the index. Hence a short position in

$$\frac{99,808}{1.023 \times 250} = 390$$

futures contracts is required.

14.17. When the value of the portfolio goes down 5% in six months, the total return from the portfolio, including dividends, in the six months is

$$-5 + 2 = -3\%$$

i.e., -6% per annum. This is 12% per annum less than the risk-free interest rate. Since the portfolio has a beta of 1.5 we would expect the market to provide a return of 8% per annum less than the risk-free interest rate, i.e., we would expect the market to provide a return of -2% per annum. Since dividends on the market index are 3% per annum, we would expect the market index to have dropped at the rate of 5% per annum or 2.5% per six months; i.e., we would expect the market to have dropped to 1170. A total of $450,000 = (1.5 \times 300,000)$ put options on the S&P 500 with exercise price 1170 and exercise date in six months are therefore required.

(a) $S_0 = 1200$, $K = 1170$, $r = 0.06$, $\sigma = 0.3$, $T = 0.5$ and $q = 0.03$. Hence

$$d_1 = \frac{\ln(1200/1170) + (0.06 - 0.03 + 0.09/2) \times 0.5}{0.3\sqrt{0.5}} = 0.2961$$

$$d_2 = d_1 - 0.3\sqrt{0.5} = 0.0840$$

$$N(d_1) = 0.6164; \quad N(d_2) = 0.5335$$
$$N(-d_1) = 0.3836; \quad N(-d_2) = 0.4665$$

The value of one put option is

$$Ke^{-rT}N(-d_2) - S_0 e^{-qT}N(-d_1)$$
$$= 1170e^{-0.06 \times 0.5} \times 0.4665 - 1200e^{-0.03 \times 0.5} \times 0.3836$$
$$= 76.28$$

The total cost of the insurance is therefore

$$450,000 \times 76.28 = \$34,326,000$$

Note that this is significantly greater than the cost of the insurance in Problem 14.16.

(b) As in Problem 14.16 the fund manager can 1) sell \$354.64 million of stock, 2) buy call options on 450,000 times the S&P 500 with exercise price 1170 and exercise date in six months and 3) invest the remaining cash at the risk-free interest rate.

(c) The portfolio is 50% more volatile than the S&P 500. When the insurance is considered as an option on the portfolio the parameters are as follows: $S_0 = 360$, $K = 342$, $r = 0.06$, $\sigma = 0.45$, $T = 0.5$ and $q = 0.04$

$$d_1 = \frac{\ln(360/342) + \left(0.06 - 0.04 + 0.45^2/2\right) \times 0.5}{0.45\sqrt{0.5}} = 0.3517$$

$$N(d_1) = 0.6374$$

The delta of the option is

$$e^{-qT}[N(d_1) - 1]$$
$$= e^{-0.03 \times 0.5}(0.6474 - 1)$$
$$= -0.355$$

This indicates that 35.5% of the portfolio (i.e., \$127.8 million) should be sold and invested in riskless securities.

(d) We now return to the situation considered in (a) where put options on the index are required. The delta of each put option is

$$e^{-qT}(N(d_1) - 1)$$
$$= e^{-0.03 \times 0.5}(0.6164 - 1)$$
$$= -0.3779$$

The delta of the total position required in put options is $-450,000 \times 0.3779 = -170,000$. The delta of a nine month index futures is (see Problem 14.16) 1.023. Hence a short position in

$$\frac{170,000}{1.023 \times 250} = 665$$

index futures contracts.

14.18. (a) For a call option on a non-dividend-paying stock

$$\Delta = N(d_1)$$

$$\Gamma = \frac{N'(d_1)}{S_0 \sigma \sqrt{T}}$$

$$\Theta = -\frac{S_0 N'(d_1)\sigma}{2\sqrt{T}} - rKe^{-rT}N(d_2)$$

Hence the left-hand side of equation (14.7) is:

$$= -\frac{S_0 N'(d_1)\sigma}{2\sqrt{T}} - rKe^{-rT}N(d_2) + rS_0 N(d_1) + \frac{1}{2}\sigma S_0 \frac{N'(d_1)}{\sqrt{T}}$$

$$= r[S_0 N(d_1) - Ke^{-rT}N(d_2)]$$

$$= r\Pi$$

(b) For a put option on a non-dividend-paying stock

$$\Delta = N(d_1) - 1 = -N(-d_1)$$

$$\Gamma = \frac{N'(d_1)}{S_0 \sigma \sqrt{T}}$$

$$\Theta = -\frac{S_0 N'(d_1)\sigma}{2\sqrt{T}} + rKe^{-rT}N(-d_2)$$

Hence the left-hand side of equation (14.7) is:

$$-\frac{S_0 N'(d_1)\sigma}{2\sqrt{T}} + rKe^{-rT}N(-d_2) - rS_0 N(-d_1) + \frac{1}{2}\sigma S_0 \frac{N'(d_1)}{\sqrt{T}}$$

$$= r[Ke^{-rT}N(-d_2) - S_0 N(-d_1)]$$

$$= r\Pi$$

(c) For a portfolio of options, Π, Δ, Θ and Γ are the sums of their values for the individual options in the portfolio. It follows that equation (14.7) is true for any portfolio of European put and call options.

14.19. A currency is analogous to a stock paying a continuous dividend yield at rate r_f. The differential equation for a portfolio of derivatives dependent on a currency is (see Appendix 13A)

$$\frac{\partial \Pi}{\partial t} + (r - r_f)S\frac{\partial \Pi}{\partial S} + \frac{1}{2}\sigma^2 S^2 \frac{\partial^2 \Pi}{\partial S^2} = r\Pi$$

Hence

$$\Theta + (r - r_f)S\Delta + \frac{1}{2}\sigma^2 S^2 \Gamma = r\Pi$$

Similarly, for a portfolio of derivatives dependent on a futures price (see Appendix 13B)

$$\Theta + \frac{1}{2}\sigma^2 S^2 \Gamma = r\Pi$$

14.20. We can regard the position of all portfolio insurers taken together as a single put option. The three known parameters of the option, before the 23% decline, are $S_0 = 70$, $K = 66.5$, $T = 1$. Other parameters can be estimated as $r = 0.06$, $\sigma = 0.25$ and $q = 0.03$. Then:

$$d_1 = \frac{\ln(70/66.5) + (0.06 - 0.03 + 0.25^2/2)}{0.25} = 0.4502$$

$$N(d_1) = 0.6737$$

The delta of the option is

$$e^{-qT}[N(d_1) - 1]$$
$$= e^{-0.03 \times 0.5}(0.6737 - 1)$$
$$= -0.3167$$

This shows that 31.67% or \$22.17 billion of assets should have been sold before the decline.

After the decline, $S_0 = 53.9$, $K = 66.5$, $T = 1$, $r = 0.06$, $\sigma = 0.25$ and $q = 0.03$.

$$d_1 = \frac{\ln(53.9/66.5) + (0.06 - 0.03 + 0.25^2/2)}{0.25} = -0.5953$$

$$N(d_1) = 0.2758$$

The delta of the option has dropped to

$$e^{-0.03 \times 0.5}(0.2758 - 1)$$
$$= -0.7028$$

This shows that cumulatively 70.28% or \$49.20 billion of assets (measured at their pre-crash prices) should be sold. In other words about \$27 billion of additional assets should be sold as a result of the decline.

14.21. With our usual notation the value of a forward contract on the asset is $S_0 e^{-qT} - K e^{-rT}$. When there is a small change, δS, in S_0 the value of the forward contract changes by $e^{-qT}\delta S$. The delta of the forward contract is therefore e^{-qT}. The futures price is $S_0 e^{(r-q)T}$. When there is a small change, δS, in S_0 the futures price changes by $\delta S e^{(r-q)T}$. Given the daily settlement procedures in futures contracts, this is also the immediate change in the wealth of the holder of the futures contract. The delta of the futures contract is therefore $e^{(r-q)T}$. We conclude that the deltas of a futures and forward contract are not the same. The delta of the futures is greater than the delta of the corresponding forward by a factor of e^{rT}.

14.22. The delta indicates that when the value of the euro exchange rate increases by $0.01, the value of the bank's position increases by $0.01 \times 30,000 = \$300$. The gamma indicates that when the euro exchange rate increases by $0.01 the delta of the portfolio decreases by $0.01 \times 80,000 = 800$. For delta neutrality 30,000 euros should be shorted. When the exchange rate moves up to 0.93, we expect the delta of the portfolio to decrease by $(0.93 - 0.90) \times 80,000 = 2,400$ so that it becomes 27,600. To maintain delta neutrality, it is therefore necessary for the bank to unwind its short position 2,400 euros so that a net 27,600 have been shorted. As shown in the text (see Figure 14.8), when a portfolio is delta neutral and has a negative gamma, a loss is experienced when there is a large movement in the underlying asset price. We can conclude that the bank is likely to have lost money.

14.23. For a non-dividend paying stock, put-call parity gives at a general time t:

$$p + S = c + Ke^{-r(T-t)}$$

(a) Differentiating with respect to S:

$$\frac{\partial p}{\partial S} + 1 = \frac{\partial c}{\partial S}$$

or

$$\frac{\partial p}{\partial S} = \frac{\partial c}{\partial S} - 1$$

This shows that the delta of a European put equals the delta of the corresponding European call less 1.0.

(b) Differentiating with respect to S again

$$\frac{\partial^2 p}{\partial S^2} = \frac{\partial^2 c}{\partial S^2}$$

Hence the gamma of a European put equals the gamma of a European call.
(c) Differentiating the put-call parity relationship with respect to σ

$$\frac{\partial p}{\partial \sigma} = \frac{\partial c}{\partial \sigma}$$

showing that the vega of a European put equals the vega of a European call.
(d) Differentiating the put-call parity relationship with respect to T

$$\frac{\partial p}{\partial t} = rKe^{-r(T-t)} + \frac{\partial c}{\partial t}$$

This is in agreement with the thetas of European calls and puts given in Section 14.5 since $N(d_2) = 1 - N(-d_2)$.

CHAPTER 15
Volatility Smiles

15.1. When both tails of the stock price distribution are less heavy than those of the lognormal distribution, Black–Scholes will tend to produce relatively high prices for options that are either significantly out of the money or significantly in the money. This leads to an implied volatility pattern similar to that in Figure 15.6. When the right tail is heavier and the left tail is less heavy, Black–Scholes will tend to produce relatively low prices for out-of-the-money calls and in-the-money puts. It will tend to produce relatively high prices for out-of-the-money puts and in the-money calls. This leads to the implied volatility being an increasing function of strike price.

15.2. When the asset price is positively correlated with volatility, the volatility tends to increase as the asset price increases, producing less heavy left tails and heavy right tails. Implied volatility is an increasing function of the strike price.

15.3. Jumps tend to make both tails of the stock price distribution heavier than those of the lognormal distribution. This creates a volatility smile similar to that in Figure 15.1 of the text. The volatility smile is likely to be more pronounced for a three-month option than a six-month option.

15.4. The put–call parity relationship

$$c - p = S_0 e^{-qT} - K e^{-rT}$$

should hold for all option pricing models. Because the terms on the right hand side of this equation are independent of the option pricing model used, $c - p$ is independent of the option pricing model used.

15.5. Because the implied probability distribution in Figure 15.4 has a less heavy right tail than the lognormal distribution, it should lead to lower prices for out-of-the-money calls. Because it has a heavier left tail, it should lead to higher prices for out-of-the-money puts. This argument shows that, if σ^* is the volatility corresponding to the lognormal distribution in Figure 15.4, the implied volatility for high strike price calls must be less than σ^*, and the implied volatility for low strike price puts must be greater than σ^*. It follows that Figure 15.3 is consistent with Figure 15.4.

15.6. With the notation in the text

$$c_{\text{bs}} + K e^{-rT} = p_{bs} + S_0 e^{-qT}$$

$$c_{\text{mkt}} + K e^{-rT} = p_{mkt} + S_0 e^{-qT}$$

It follows that

$$c_{\text{bs}} - c_{\text{mkt}} = p_{\text{bs}} - p_{\text{mkt}}$$

In this case $c_{mkt} = 3.00$; $c_{bs} = 3.50$; and $p_{bs} = 1.00$. It follows that p_{mkt} should be 0.50.

15.7. The probability distribution of the stock price in one month is not lognormal. Possibly it consists of two lognormal distributions superimposed upon each other and is bimodal. Black–Scholes is inappropriate because it assumes that the stock price at any future time is lognormal.

15.8. There are a number of problems in testing an option pricing model empirically. These include the problem of obtaining synchronous data on stock prices and option prices, the problem of estimating the dividends that will be paid on the stock during the option's life, the problem of distinguishing between situations where the market is inefficient and situations where the option pricing model is incorrect, and the problems of estimating stock price volatility.

15.9. In this case the probability distribution of the exchange rate has a less heavy left tail and a less heavy right tail than the lognormal distribution. We are in the opposite situation to that described for foreign currencies in Section 15.2. Both out-of-the-money and in-the-money calls and puts can be expected to have lower implied volatilities than at-the-money calls and puts. The pattern of implied volatilities is likely to be similar to Figure 15.6.

15.10. A deep-out-of-the-money option has a low value. Decreases in its volatility reduce its value. However, this reduction is small because the value can never go below zero. Increases in its volatility, on the other hand, can lead to significant percentage increases in the value of the option. The option does, therefore, have some of the same attributes as an option on volatility.

15.11. As explained in the chapter, put–call parity implies that European put and call options have the same implied volatility. If a call option has an implied volatility of 30% and a put option has an implied volatility of 33%, the call is priced too low relative to the put. The correct trading strategy is to buy the call, sell the put and short the stock. This does not depend on the lognormal assumption underlying Black–Scholes. Put–call parity is true for any set of assumptions.

15.12. Suppose that p is the probability of a favorable ruling. The expected price of Microsoft tomorrow is

$$75p + 50(1 - p) = 50 + 25p$$

This must be the price of Microsoft today. (We ignore the expected return to an investor over one day.) Hence

$$50 + 25p = 60$$

or $p = 0.4$.

If the ruling is favorable, the volatility, σ, will be 25%. Other option parameters are $S_0 = 75$, $r = 0.06$, and $T = 0.5$. For a value of K equal to 50, DerivaGem gives the value of a European call option price as 26.502.

Figure 15.1   Implied Volatilities in Problem 15.12

If the ruling is unfavorable, the volatility, σ will be 40% Other option parameters are $S_0 = 50$, $r = 0.06$, and $T = 0.5$. For a value of K equal to 50, DerivaGem gives the value of a European call option price as 6.310.

The value today of a European call option with a strike price today is the weighted average of 26.502 and 6.310 or:

$$0.4 \times 26.502 + 0.6 \times 6.310 = 14.387$$

DerivaGem can be used to calculate the implied volatility when the option has this price. The parameter values are $S_0 = 60$, $K = 50$, $T = 0.5$, $r = 0.06$ and $c = 14.387$. The implied volatility is 47.76%.

These calculations can be repeated for other strike prices. The results are shown in the table below. The pattern of implied volatilities is shown in Figure 15.1.

Strike Price	Call Option Price Favorable Outcome	Call Option Price Unfavorable Outcome	Weighted Price	Implied Volatility (%)
30	45.887	21.001	30.955	46.67
40	36.182	12.437	21.935	47.78
50	26.502	6.310	14.387	47.76
60	17.171	2.826	8.564	46.05
70	9.334	1.161	4.430	43.22
80	4.159	0.451	1.934	40.36

15.13. As pointed out in Chapters 3 and 13 an exchange rate behaves like a stock that provides a dividend yield equal to the foreign risk-free rate. Whereas the growth rate in a non-dividend-paying stock in a risk-neutral world is r, the growth rate in the exchange rate in a risk-neutral world is $r - r_f$. Exchange rates have low systematic risks and so we can reasonably assume that this is also the growth rate in the real world. In this case the foreign risk-free rate equals the domestic risk-free rate ($r = r_f$). The expected growth rate in the exchange rate is therefore zero. If S_T is the exchange rate at time T its probability distribution is given by equation (12.3) with $\mu = 0$:

$$\ln S_T \sim \phi(\ln S_0 - \sigma^2 T/2, \sigma\sqrt{T})$$

where S_0 is the exchange rate at time zero and σ is the volatility of the exchange rate. In this case $S_0 = 0.7000$ and $\sigma = 0.12$, and $T = 0.25$ so that

$$\ln S_T \sim \phi(\ln 0.8 - 0.12^2 \times 0.25/2, 0.12\sqrt{0.25})$$

or

$$\ln S_T \sim \phi(-0.2240, 0.06)$$

(a) $\ln 0.70 = -0.3567$. The probability that $S_T < 0.70$ is the same as the probability that $\ln S_T < -0.3567$. It is

$$N\left(\frac{-0.3567 + 0.2240}{0.06}\right) = N(-2.2117)$$

This is 1.35%.

(b) $\ln 0.75 = -0.2877$. The probability that $S_T < 0.75$ is the same as the probability that $\ln S_T < -0.2877$. It is

$$N\left(\frac{-0.2877 + 0.2240}{0.06}\right) = N(-1.0617)$$

This is 14.42%. The probability that the exchange rate is between 0.70 and 0.75 is therefore $14.42 - 1.35 = 13.07\%$.

(c) $\ln 0.80 = -0.2231$. The probability that $S_T < 0.80$ is the same as the probability that $\ln S_T < -0.2231$. It is

$$N\left(\frac{-0.2231 + 0.2240}{0.06}\right) = N(0.0150)$$

This is 50.60%. The probability that the exchange rate is between 0.75 and 0.80 is therefore $50.60 - 14.42 = 36.18\%$.

(d) $\ln 0.85 = -0.1625$. The probability that $S_T < 0.85$ is the same as the probability that $\ln S_T < -0.1625$. It is

$$N\left(\frac{-0.1625 + 0.2240}{0.06}\right) = N(1.0250)$$

This is 84.73%. The probability that the exchange rate is between 0.80 and 0.85 is therefore $84.73 - 50.60 = 34.13\%$.

(e) $\ln 0.90 = -0.1054$. The probability that $S_T < 0.90$ is the same as the probability that $\ln S_T < -0.1054$. It is

$$N\left(\frac{-0.1054 + 0.2240}{0.06}\right) = N(1.9767)$$

This is 97.60%. The probability that the exchange rate is between 0.85 and 0.90 is therefore $97.60 - 84.73 = 12.87\%$.

(f) The probability that the exchange rate is greater than 0.90 is $100 - 97.60 = 2.40\%$

The volatility smile encountered for foreign exchange options is shown in Figure 15.1 of the text and implies the probability distribution in Figure 15.2. Figure 15.2 suggests that we would expect the probabilities in (a), (c), (d), and (f) to be too low and the probabilities in (b) and (d) to be too high.

15.14. The difference between the two implied volatilities is consistent with Figure 15.3. For equities the volatility smile is downward sloping. A high strike price option has a lower implied volatility than a low strike price option. The reason is that traders consider that the probability of a large downward movement in the stock price is higher than that predicted by the lognormal probability distribution. The implied distribution assumed by traders is shown in Figure 15.4.

To use DerivaGem to calculate the price of the first option, proceed as follows. Select Equity as the Underlying Type in the first worksheet. Select Analytic European as the Option Type. Input the stock price as 40, volatility as 35%, risk-free rate as 5%, time to exercise as 0.5 year, and exercise price as 30. Leave the dividend table blank because we are assuming no dividends. Select the button corresponding to call. Do not select the implied volatility button. Hit the *Enter* key and click on calculate. DerivaGem will show the price of the option as 11.155. Change the volatility to 28% and the strike price to 50. Hit the *Enter* key and click on calculate. DerivaGem will show the price of the option as 0.725.

Put–call parity is

$$c + Ke^{-rT} = p + S_0$$

so that

$$p = c + Ke^{-rT} - S_0$$

For the first option, $c = 11.155$, $S_0 = 40$, $r = 0.054$, $K = 30$, and $T = 0.5$ so that

$$p = 11.155 + 30e^{-0.05 \times 0.5} - 40 = 0.414$$

For the second option, $c = 0.725$, $S_0 = 40$, $r = 0.06$, $K = 50$, and $T = 0.5$ so that

$$p = 0.725 + 50e^{-0.05 \times 0.5} - 40 = 9.490$$

To use DerivaGem to calculate the implied volatility of the first put option, input the stock price as 40, the risk-free rate as 5%, time to exercise as 0.5 year, and the exercise price as 30. Input the price as 0.414 in the second half of the Option Data table. Select the buttons for a put option and implied volatility. Hit the *Enter* key and click on calculate. DerivaGem will show the implied volatility as 34.99%.

Similarly, to use DerivaGem to calculate the implied volatility of the first put option, input the stock price as 40, the risk-free rate as 5%, time to exercise as 0.5 year, and the exercise price as 50. Input the price as 9.490 in the second half of the Option Data table. Select the buttons for a put option and implied volatility. Hit the *Enter* key and click on calculate. DerivaGem will show the implied volatility as 27.99%.

These results are what we would expect. DerivaGem gives the implied volatility of a put with strike price 30 to be almost exactly the same as the implied volatility of a call with a strike price of 30. Similarly, it gives the implied volatility of a put with strike price 30 to be almost exactly the same as the implied volatility of a call with a strike price of 30.

15.15. When plain vanilla call and put options are being priced, traders do use the Black–Scholes model as an interpolation tool. They calculate implied volatilities for the options whose prices they can observe in the market. By interpolating between strike prices and between times to maturity, they estimate implied volatilities for other options. These implied volatilities are then substituted into Black–Scholes to calculate prices for these options. In practice much of the work in producing a table such as 15.2 in the over-the-counter market is done by brokers. Brokers often act as intermediaries between participants in the over-the-counter market and usually have more information on the trades taking place than any individual financial institution. The brokers provide a table such as 15.2 to their clients as a service.

CHAPTER 16
Value at Risk

16.1. The standard deviation of the daily change in the investment in each asset is $1,000. The variance of the portfolio's daily change is

$$1,000^2 + 1,000^2 + 2 \times 0.3 \times 1,000 \times 1,000 = 2,600,000$$

The standard deviation of the portfolio's daily change is the square root of this or $1,612.45. The standard deviation of the 5-day change is

$$1,612.45 \times \sqrt{5} = \$3,605.55$$

From the tables of $N(x)$ we see that $N(-2.33) = 0.01$. This means that 1% of a normal distribution lies more than 2.33 standard deviations below the mean. The 5-day 99 percent value at risk is therefore $2.33 \times 3,605.55 = \$8,401$.

16.2. The three alternative procedures mentioned in the chapter for handling interest rates when the model building approach is used to calculate VaR involve (a) the use of the duration model, (b) the use of cash flow mapping, and (c) the use of principal components analysis. When historical simulation is used we need to assume that the change in the zero-coupon yield curve between Day m and Day $m+1$ is the same as that between Day i and Day $i+1$ for different values of i. In the case of a LIBOR, the zero curve is usually calculated from deposit rates, Eurodollar futures quotes, and swap rates. We can assume that the percentage change in each of these between Day m and Day $m+1$ is the same as that between Day i and Day $i+1$. In the case of a Treasury curve it is usually calculated from the yields on Treasury instruments. Again we can assume that the percentage change in each of these between Day m and Day $m+1$ is the same as that between Day i and Day $i+1$.

16.3. The approximate relationship between the daily change in the portfolio value, δP, and the daily change in the exchange rate, δS, is

$$\delta P = 56\delta S$$

The percentage daily change in the exchange rate, δx, equals $\delta S/1.5$. It follows that

$$\delta P = 56 \times 1.5\delta x$$

or

$$\delta P = 84\delta x$$

The standard deviation of δx equals the daily volatility of the exchange rate, or 0.7 percent. The standard deviation of δP is therefore $84 \times 0.007 = 0.588$. It follows that the 10-day 99 percent VaR for the portfolio is

$$0.588 \times 2.33 \times \sqrt{10} = 4.33$$

16.4. The relationship is

$$\delta P = 56 \times 1.5\delta x + \frac{1}{2} \times 1.5^2 \times 16.2 \times \delta x^2$$

or

$$\delta P = 84\delta x + 18.225\delta x^2$$

The first two moments of δP are

$$\frac{1}{2} \times 1.5^2 \times 16.2 \times 0.007^2 = 0.000893$$

and

$$1.5^2 \times 56^2 \times 0.007^2 + \frac{3}{4} \times 1.5^4 \times 16.2^2 \times 0.007^4 = 0.346$$

The mean and standard deviation of δP are therefore 0.000893 and $\sqrt{0.346 - 0.000893^2}$ = 0.588, respectively. The 10-day 99% VaR is therefore

$$\sqrt{10} \times 2.33 \times 0.588 - 10 \times 0.000893 = 4.32$$

16.5. The factors calculated from a principal components analysis are uncorrelated. The daily variance of the portfolio is

$$6^2 \times 20^2 + 4^2 \times 8^2 = 15,424$$

and the daily standard deviation is $\sqrt{15,424} = \$124.19$. Since $N(-1.282) = 0.9$, the 5-day 90% value at risk is

$$124.19 \times \sqrt{5} \times 1.282 = \$356.01$$

16.6. The linear model assumes that the percentage daily change in each market variable has a normal probability distribution. The historical simulation model assumes that the probability distribution observed for the percentage daily changes in the market variables in the past is the probability distribution that will apply over the next day.

16.7. When a final exchange of principal is added in, the floating side is equivalent a zero coupon bond with a maturity date equal to the date of the next payment. The fixed side is a coupon-bearing bond, which is equivalent to a portfolio of zero-coupon bonds. The swap can therefore be mapped into a portfolio of zero-coupon bonds with maturity dates corresponding to the payment dates. Each of the zero-coupon bonds can then be mapped into positions in the adjacent standard-maturity zero-coupon bonds.

16.8. Value at risk is the loss that is expected to be exceeded $(100 - X)\%$ of the time in N days for specified parameter values, X and N. Conditional Value at Risk is the expected loss conditional that the loss is greater than the Value at Risk.

16.9. The change in the value of an option is not linearly related to the change in the value of the underlying variables. When the change in the values of underlying variables is normal, the change in the value of the option is non-normal. The linear model assumes that it is normal and is, therefore, only an approximation.

16.10. The 0.3-year cash flow is mapped into a 3-month zero-coupon bond and a 6-month zero-coupon bond. The 0.25 and 0.50 year rates are 5.50 and 6.00 respectively. Linear interpolation gives the 0.30-year rate as 5.60%. The present value of $50,000 received at time 0.3 years is
$$\frac{50,000}{1.056^{0.30}} = 49,189.32$$

The volatility of 0.25-year and 0.50-year zero-coupon bonds are 0.06% and 0.10% per day respectively. The interpolated volatility of a 0.30-year zero-coupon bond is therefore 0.068% per day.

Assume that α of the value of the 0.30-year cash flow gets allocated to a 3-month zero-coupon bond and $1 - \alpha$ to a six-month zero coupon bond. To match variances we must have

$$0.00068^2 = 0.0006^2\alpha^2 + 0.001^2(1 - \alpha)^2 + 2 \times 0.9 \times 0.0006 \times 0.001\alpha(1 - \alpha)$$

or

$$0.28\alpha^2 - 0.92\alpha + 0.5376 = 0$$

Using the formula for the solution to a quadratic equation

$$\alpha = \frac{-0.92 + \sqrt{0.92^2 - 4 \times 0.28 \times 0.5376}}{2 \times 0.28} = 0.760259$$

this means that a value of $0.760259 \times 49,189.32 = \$37,397$ is allocated to the three-month bond and a value of $0.239741 \times 49,189.32 = \$11,793$ is allocated to the six-month bond. The 0.3-year cash flow is therefore equivalent to a position of $37,397 in a 3-month zero-coupon bond and a position of $11,793 in a 6-month zero-coupon bond. This is consistent with the results in Table 16.7 of Appendix 16A.

16.11. The 6.5-year cash flow is mapped into a 5-year zero-coupon bond and a 7-year zero-coupon bond. The 5-year and 7-year rates are 6% and 7% respectively. Linear interpolation gives the 6.5-year rate as 6.75%. The present value of $1,000 received at time 6.5 years is
$$\frac{1,000}{1.0675^{6.5}} = 654.05$$

The volatility of 5-year and 7-year zero-coupon bonds are 0.50% and 0.58% per day respectively. The interpolated volatility of a 6.5-year zero-coupon bond is therefore 0.056% per day.

Assume that α of the value of the 6.5-year cash flow gets allocated to a 5-year zero-coupon bond and $1 - \alpha$ to a 7-year zero coupon bond. To match variances we must have

$$.56^2 = .50^2\alpha^2 + .58^2(1 - \alpha)^2 + 2 \times 0.6 \times .50 \times .58\alpha(1 - \alpha)$$

or

$$.2384\alpha^2 - .3248\alpha + .0228 = 0$$

Using the formula for the solution to a quadratic equation

$$\alpha = \frac{.3248 - \sqrt{.3248^2 - 4 \times .2384 \times .0228}}{2 \times .2384} = 0.074243$$

this means that a value of $0.074243 \times 654.05 = \$48.56$ is allocated to the 5-year bond and a value of $0.925757 \times 654.05 = \$605.49$ is allocated to the 7-year bond. The 6.5-year cash flow is therefore equivalent to a position of \$48.56 in a 3-month zero-coupon bond and a position of \$605.49 in a 7-year zero-coupon bond.

The equivalent 5-year and 7-year cash flows are $48.56 \times 1.06^5 = 64.98$ and $605.49 \times 1.07^7 = 972.28$.

16.12. The contract is a long position in a sterling bond combined with a short position in a dollar bond. The value of the sterling bond is $1.53e^{-0.05 \times 0.5}$ or \$1.492 million. The value of the dollar bond is $1.5e^{-0.05 \times 0.5}$ or \$1.463 million. The variance of the change in the value of the contract in one day is

$$1.492^2 \times 0.0006^2 + 1.463^2 \times 0.0005^2 - 2 \times 0.8 \times 1.492 \times 0.0006 \times 1.463 \times 0.0005$$

$$= 0.000000288$$

The standard deviation is therefore \$0.000537 million. The 10-day 99% VaR is $0.000537 \times \sqrt{10} \times 2.33 = \$0.00396$ million.

16.13. If we assume only one factor, the model is

$$\delta P = -0.08 f_1$$

The standard deviation of f_1 is 17.49. The standard deviation of δP is therefore $0.08 \times 17.49 = 1.40$ and the 1-day 99 percent value at risk is $1.40 \times 2.33 = 3.26$. If we assume three factors, our exposure to the third factor is

$$10 \times (-0.37) + 4 \times (-0.38) - 8 \times (-0.30) - 7 \times (-0.12) + 2 \times (-0.04) = -2.06$$

The model is therefore

$$\delta P = -0.08 f_1 - 4.40 f_2 - 2.06 f_3$$

The variance of δP is

$$0.08^2 \times 17.49^2 + 4.40^2 \times 6.05^2 + 2.06^2 \times 3.1062 = 751.36$$

The standard deviation of δP is $\sqrt{751.36} = 27.41$ and the 1-day 99% value at risk is $27.41 \times 2.33 = \$63.87$.

The example illustrates that the relative importance of different factors depends on the portfolio being considered. Normally the second factor is less important than the first, but in this case it is much more important.

16.14. The delta of the options is the rate if change of the value of the options with respect to the price of the asset. When the asset price increases by a small amount the value of the options decrease by 30 times this amount. The gamma of the options is the rate of change of their delta with respect to the price of the asset. When the asset price increases by a small amount, the delta of the portfolio decreases by five times this amount.

Suppose that δS is the change in the asset price in one day and δx is the proportional change in the asset price. The quadratic model is

$$\delta P = -30\delta S - .5 \times 5 \times (\delta S)^2$$

or

$$\delta P = -30 \times 20\delta x - 0.5 \times 5 \times 20^2 \times (\delta x)^2$$

which simplifies to

$$\delta P = -600\delta x - 1,000(\delta x)^2$$

From the equations in Section 16.5 of the text the first three moments of the portfolio value are

$$\frac{1}{2} \times 20^2 \times (-5) \times 0.01^2 = -0.1$$

$$20^2 \times 30^2 \times 0.01^2 + \frac{3}{4} \times 20^4 \times 5^2 \times 0.01^4 = 36.03$$

and

$$\frac{9}{2} \times 20^4 \times 30^2 \times (-5) \times 0.01^4 + \frac{15}{8} \times 20^6 \times (-5)^3 \times 0.01^6 = -32.415$$

The mean change in the portfolio value in one day is -0.1 and the standard deviation of the change in one day is $\sqrt{36.03 - 0.1^2} = 6.002$. The skewness is

$$\frac{-32.415 - 3 \times 36.03 \times (-0.1) + 2 \times (-0.1)^3}{6.002^3} = -21.608 = -0.10$$

Using only the first two moments the 1-day 99% value at risk is therefore $0.1 + 2.33 \times 6.002 = \$14.08$

When three moments are considered, Appendix 16B shows that the 1 percentile of the distribution is

$$-0.1 - 6.002w_q$$

where

$$w_q = -2.33 + \frac{1}{6} \times (2.33^2 - 1) \times (-0.1) = 2.404$$

The one percentile point is therefore $-0.1 - 6.002 \times 2.404 = -14.529$ showing that the 1-day 99% VaR is 14.529.

16.15. Define σ as the volatility per year, $\delta\sigma$ as the change in σ in one day, and δw and the proportional change in σ in one day. We measure in σ as a multiple of 1% so that the current value of σ is $1 \times \sqrt{252} = 15.87$. The delta-gamma-vega model is

$$\delta P = -30\delta S - .5 \times 5 \times (\delta S)^2 - 2\delta\sigma$$

or

$$\delta P = -30 \times 20\delta x - 0.5 \times 5 \times 20^2(\delta x)^2 - 2 \times 15.87\delta w$$

which simplifies to

$$\delta P = -600\delta x - 1,000(\delta x)^2 - 31.74\delta w$$

The change in the portfolio value now depends on two market variables. Once the daily volatility of σ and the correlation between σ and S have been estimated we can use the results in Appendix 16B to estimate moments of δP. An alternative approach is would be to use Monte Carlo simulation in conjunction with the model.

CHAPTER 17
Estimating Volatilities and Correlations

17.1. Define u_i as $(S_i - S_{i-1})/S_{i-1}$, where S_i is value of a market variable on day i. In the EWMA model, the variance rate of the market variable (i.e., the square of its volatility) calculated for day n is a weighted average of the u_{n-i}^2's $(i = 1, 2, 3, \ldots)$. For some constant λ $(0 < \lambda < 1)$ the weight given to u_{n-i-1}^2 is λ times the weight given to u_{n-i}^2. The volatility estimated for day n, σ_n, is related to the volatility estimated for day $n-1$, σ_{n-1}, by

$$\sigma_n^2 = \lambda \sigma_{n-1}^2 + (1-\lambda) u_{n-1}^2$$

This formula shows that the EWMA model has one very attractive property. To calculate the volatility estimate for day n, it is sufficient to know the volatility estimate for day $n-1$ and u_{n-1}.

17.2. The EWMA model produces a forecast of the daily variance rate for day n which is a weighted average of (i) the forecast for day $n-1$, and (ii) the square of the proportional change on day $n-1$. The GARCH (1,1) model produces a forecast of the daily variance for day n which is a weighted average of (i) the forecast for day $n-1$, (ii) the square of the proportional change on day $n-1$. and (iii) a long run average variance rate. GARCH (1,1) adapts the EWMA model by giving some weight to a long run average variance rate. Whereas the EWMA has no mean reversion, GARCH (1,1) is consistent with a mean-reverting variance rate model.

17.3. In this case $\sigma_{n-1} = 0.015$ and $u_n = 0.5/30 = 0.01667$, so that equation (17.7) gives

$$\sigma_n^2 = 0.94 \times 0.015^2 + 0.06 \times 0.01667^2 = 0.0002281$$

The volatility estimate on day n is therefore $\sqrt{0.0002281} = 0.015103$ or 1.5103%.

17.4. Reducing λ from 0.95 to 0.85 means that more weight is put on recent observations of u_i^2 and less weight is given to older observations. Volatilities calculated with $\lambda = 0.85$ will react more quickly to new information and will "bounce around" much more than volatilities calculated with $\lambda = 0.95$.

17.5. The volatility per day is $30/\sqrt{252} = 1.89\%$. There is a 99% chance that a normally distributed variable will lie within 2.57 standard deviations. We are therefore 99% confident that the daily change will be less than $2.57 \times 1.89 = 4.86\%$.

17.6. The weight given to the long-run average variance rate is $1 - \alpha - \beta$ and the long-run average variance rate is $\omega/(1 - \alpha - \beta)$. Increasing ω increases the long-run average variance rate; Increasing α increases the weight given to the most recent data item, reduces the weight given to the long-run average variance rate, and increases the level of the long-run average variance rate. Increasing β increases the weight given to the previous variance estimate, reduces the weight given to the long-run average variance rate, and increases the level of the long-run average variance rate.

17.7. The proportional daily change is $-0.005/1.5000 = -0.003333$. The current daily variance estimate is $0.006^2 = 0.000036$. The new daily variance estimate is

$$0.9 \times 0.000036 + 0.1 \times 0.003333^2 = 0.000033511$$

The new volatility is the square root of this. It is 0.00579 or 0.579%.

17.8. With the usual notation $u_{n-1} = 20/1040 = 0.01923$ so that

$$\sigma_n^2 = 0.000002 + 0.06 \times 0.01923^2 + 0.92 \times 0.01^2 = 0.0001162$$

so that $\sigma_n = 0.01078$. The new volatility estimate is therefore 1.078% per day.

17.9. (a) The volatilities and correlation imply that the current estimate of the covariance is $0.25 \times 0.016 \times 0.025 = 0.0001$.
(b) If the prices of the assets at close of trading are \$20.5 and \$40.5, the proportional changes are $0.5/20 = 0.025$ and $0.5/40 = 0.0125$. The new covariance estimate is

$$0.95 \times 0.0001 + 0.05 \times 0.025 \times 0.0125 = 0.0001106$$

The new variance estimate for asset A is

$$0.95 \times 0.016^2 + 0.05 \times 0.025^2 = 0.00027445$$

so that the new volatility is 0.0166. The new variance estimate for asset B is

$$0.95 \times 0.025^2 + 0.05 \times 0.0125^2 = 0.000601562$$

so that the new volatility is 0.0245. The new correlation estimate is

$$\frac{0.0001106}{0.0166 \times 0.0245} = 0.272$$

17.10. The long-run average variance rate is $\omega/(1 - \alpha - \beta)$ or $0.000004/0.03 = 0.0001333$. The long-run average volatility is $\sqrt{0.0001333}$ or 1.155%. The equation describing the way the variance rate reverts to its long-run average is equation (17.13)

$$E[\sigma_{n+k}^2] = V_L + (\alpha + \beta)^k(\sigma_n^2 - V_L)$$

In this case

$$E[\sigma_{n+k}^2] = 0.0001333 + 0.97^k(\sigma_n^2 - 0.0001333)$$

If the current volatility is 20% per year, $\sigma_n = 0.2/\sqrt{252} = 0.0126$. The expected variance rate in 20 days is

$$0.0001333 + 0.97^{20}(0.0126^2 - 0.0001333) = 0.0001471$$

The expected volatility in 20 days is therefore $\sqrt{0.0001471} = 0.0121$ or 1.21% per day.

17.11. Using the notation in the text $\sigma_{u,n-1} = 0.01$ and $\sigma_{v,n-1} = 0.012$ and the most recent estimate of the covariance between the asset returns is $\text{cov}_{n-1} = 0.01 \times 0.012 \times 0.50 = 0.00006$. The variable $u_{n-1} = 1/30 = 0.03333$ and the variable $v_{n-1} = 1/50 = 0.02$. The new estimate of the covariance, cov_n, is

$$0.000001 + 0.04 \times 0.03333 \times 0.02 + 0.94 \times 0.00006 = 0.0000841$$

The new estimate of the variance of the first asset, $\sigma^2_{u,n}$ is

$$0.000003 + 0.04 \times 0.03333^2 + 0.94 \times 0.01^2 = 0.0001414$$

so that $\sigma_{u,n} = \sqrt{0.0001414} = 0.01189$ or 1.189%. The new estimate of the variance of the second asset, $\sigma^2_{v,n}$ is

$$0.000003 + 0.04 \times 0.02^2 + 0.94 \times 0.012^2 = 0.0001544$$

so that $\sigma_{v,n} = \sqrt{0.0001544} = 0.01242$ or 1.242%. The new estimate of the correlation between the assets is therefore $0.0000841/(0.01189 \times 0.01242) = 0.569$.

17.12. The FT-SE expressed in dollars is XY where X is the FT-SE expressed in sterling and Y is the exchange rate (value of one pound in dollars). Define x_i as the proportional change in X on day i and y_i as the proportional change in Y on day i. The proportional change in XY is approximately $x_i + y_i$. The standard deviation of x_i is 0.018 and the standard deviation of y_i is 0.009. The correlation between the two is 0.4. The variance of $x_i + y_i$ is therefore

$$0.018^2 + 0.009^2 + 2 \times 0.018 \times 0.009 \times 0.4 = 0.0005346$$

so that the volatility of $x_i + y_i$ is 0.0231 or 2.31%. This is the volatility of the FT-SE expressed in dollars. Note that it is greater than the volatility of the FT-SE expressed in sterling. This is the impact of the positive correlation. When the FT-SE increases the value of sterling measured in dollars also tends to increase. This creates an even bigger increase in the value of FT-SE measured in dollars. Similarly for a decrease in the FT-SE.

17.13. Continuing with the notation in Problem 17.12, define z_i as the proportional change in the value of the S&P 500 on day i. The covariance between x_i and z_i is $0.7 \times 0.018 \times 0.016 = 0.0002016$. The covariance between y_i and z_i is $0.3 \times 0.009 \times 0.016 = 0.0000432$.

114

The covariance between $x_i + y_i$ and z_i equals the covariance between x_i and z_i plus the covariance between y_i and z_i. It is

$$0.0002016 + 0.0000432 = 0.0002448$$

The correlation between $x_i + y_i$ and z_i is

$$\frac{0.0002448}{0.016 \times 0.0231} = 0.662$$

Note that the volatility of the S&P 500 drops out in this calculation.

17.14.

$$\sigma_n^2 = \omega + \alpha u_{n-1}^2 + \beta \sigma_{n-1}^2$$

so that

$$\sigma_n^2 - \sigma_{n-1}^2 = \omega + (\beta - 1)\sigma_{n-1}^2 + \alpha u_{n-1}^2$$

The variable u_{n-1}^2 has a mean of σ_{n-1}^2 and a variance of

$$E(u_{n-1})^4 - [E(u_{n-1}^2)]^2 = 2\sigma_{n-1}^4$$

The standard deviation of u_{n-1}^2 is $\sqrt{2}\sigma_{n-1}^2$. Assuming the u_i are generated by a Wiener process, dz, we can therefore write

$$u_{n-1}^2 = \sigma_{n-1}^2 + \sqrt{2}\sigma_{n-1}^2 \epsilon$$

where ϵ is a random sample from a standard normal distribution. Substituting this into the equation for $\sigma_n^2 - \sigma_{n-1}^2$ we get

$$\sigma_n^2 - \sigma_{n-1}^2 = \omega + (\alpha + \beta - 1)\sigma_{n-1}^2 + \alpha\sqrt{2}\sigma_{n-1}^2 \epsilon$$

We can write $\delta V = \sigma_n^2 - \sigma_{n-1}^2$ and $V = \sigma_{n-1}^2$. Also $a = 1 - \alpha - \beta$, $aV_L = \omega$, and $\xi = \alpha\sqrt{2}$ so that

$$\delta V = a(V_L - V) + \xi \epsilon V$$

Because time is measured in days, $\delta t = 1$ and

$$\delta V = a(V_L - V)\delta t + \xi V \epsilon \sqrt{\delta t}$$

The result follows.

When time is measured in years $\delta t = 1/252$ so that

$$\delta V = a(V_L - V)252\delta t + \xi V \epsilon \sqrt{252}\sqrt{\delta t}$$

and the process for V is

$$dV = 252a(V_L - V)\,dt + \xi V \sqrt{252}\,dz$$

CHAPTER 18
Numerical Procedures

18.1. Delta, gamma, and theta can be determined from a single binomial tree. Vega is determined by making a small change to the volatility and recomputing the option price using a new tree. Rho is calculated by making a small change to the interest rate and recomputing the option price using a new tree.

18.2. In this case, $S_0 = 60$, $K = 60$, $r = 0.1$, $\sigma = 0.45$, $T = 0.25$, and $\delta t = 0.0833$. Also

$$u = e^{\sigma\sqrt{\delta t}} = e^{0.45\sqrt{0.0833}} = 1.1387$$

$$d = \frac{1}{u} = 0.8782$$

$$a = e^{r\delta t} = e^{0.1 \times 0.0833} = 1.0084$$

$$p = \frac{a - u}{u - d} = 0.4998$$

$$1 - p = 0.5002$$

The output from DerivaGem for this example is shown in the Figure 18.1. The calculated price of the option is $5.16.

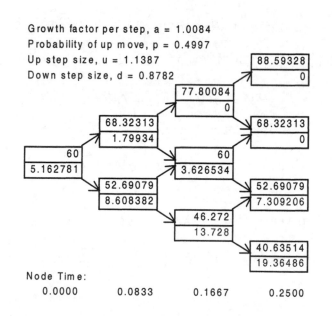

Growth factor per step, a = 1.0084
Probability of up move, p = 0.4997
Up step size, u = 1.1387
Down step size, d = 0.8782

Figure 18.1 Tree for Problem 18.2

18.3. The control variate technique is implemented by
  (a) valuing an American option using a binomial tree in the usual way ($= f_A$).
  (b) valuing the European option with the same parameters as the American option using the same tree ($= f_E$).
  (c) valuing the European option using Black–Scholes ($= f_{BS}$).
The price of the American option is estimated as $f_A + f_{BS} - f_E$.

18.4. In this case $F_0 = 198$, $K = 200$, $r = 0.08$, $\sigma = 0.3$, $T = 0.75$, and $\delta t = 0.25$. Also

$$u = e^{0.3\sqrt{0.25}} = 1.1618$$

$$d = \frac{1}{u} = 0.8607$$

$$a = 1$$

$$p = \frac{a - d}{u - d} = 0.4626$$

$$1 - p = 0.5373$$

The output from DerivaGem for this example is shown in the Figure 18.2. The calculated price of the option is 20.34 cents.

Growth factor per step, a = 1.0000
Probability of up move, p = 0.4626
Up step size, u = 1.1618
Down step size, d = 0.8607

Figure 18.2 Tree for Problem 18.4

18.5. A binomial tree cannot be used in the way described in this chapter. This is an example of what is known as a history-dependent option. The payoff depends on the path followed by the stock price as well as its final value. The option cannot be valued by starting at the end of the tree and working backward since the payoff at the final branches is not known unambiguously. Chapter 20 describes an extension of the binomial tree approach that can be used to handle options where the payoff depends on the average value of the stock price.

18.6. Suppose a dividend equal to D is paid during a certain time interval. If S is the stock price at the beginning of the time interval, it will be either $Su - D$ or $Sd - D$ at the end of the time interval. At the end of the next time interval, it will be one of $(Su - D)u$, $(Su - D)d$, $(Sd - D)u$ and $(Sd - D)d$. Since $(Su - D)d$ does not equal $(Sd - D)u$ the tree does not recombine. If S is equal to the stock price less the present value of future dividends, this problem is avoided.

18.7. With the usual notation
$$p = \frac{a - d}{u - d}$$
$$1 - p = \frac{u - a}{u - d}$$

If $a < d$ or $a > u$, one of the two probabilities is negative. This happens when
$$e^{(r-q)\delta t} < e^{-\sigma\sqrt{\delta t}}$$

or
$$e^{(r-q)\delta t} > e^{\sigma\sqrt{\delta t}}$$

This in turn happens when $(q - r)\sqrt{\delta t} > \sigma$ or $(r - q)\sqrt{\delta t} > \sigma$ Hence negative probabilities occur when
$$\sigma < |(r - q)\sqrt{\delta t}|$$

This is the condition in footnote 8.

18.8. When the dividend yield is constant
$$u = e^{\sigma\sqrt{\delta t}}$$
$$d = \frac{1}{u}$$
$$p = \frac{a - d}{u - d}$$
$$a = e^{(r-q)\delta t}$$

Making the dividend yield, q, a function of time makes a, and therefore p, a function of time. However, it does not affect u or d. It follows that if q is a function of time we can use the same tree by making the probabilities a function of time. The interest rate r can also be a function of time as described in Section 18.4.

18.9. In Monte Carlo simulation sample values for the derivative security in a risk-neutral world are obtained by simulating paths for the underlying variables. On each simulation run, values for the underlying variables are first determined at time δt, then at time $2\delta t$, then at time $3\delta t$, etc. At time $i\delta t$ $(i = 0, 1, 2 \ldots)$ it is not possible to determine whether early exercise is optimal since the range of paths which might occur after time $i\delta t$ have not been investigated. In short, Monte Carlo simulation works by moving forward from time t to time T. Other numerical procedures which accommodate early exercise work by moving backwards from time T to time t.

18.10. In this case, $S_0 = 50$, $K = 49$, $r = 0.05$, $\sigma = 0.30$, $T = 0.75$, and $\delta t = 0.25$. Also

$$u = e^{\sigma\sqrt{\delta t}} = e^{0.30\sqrt{0.25}} = 1.0126$$

$$d = \frac{1}{u} = 0.8607$$

$$a = e^{r\delta t} = e^{0.1 \times 0.0833} = 1.0084$$

$$p = \frac{a - u}{u - d} = 0.5043$$

$$1 - p = 0.4957$$

The output from DerivaGem for this example is shown in the Figure 18.3. The calculated price of the option is $4.29. Using 100 steps the price obtained is $3.91

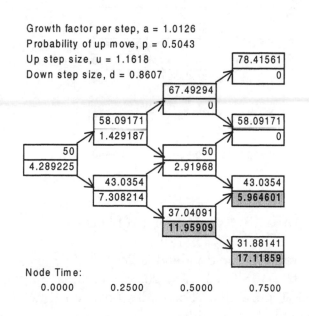

Figure 18.3   Tree for Problem 18.10

18.11. In this case $F_0 = 400$, $K = 420$, $r = 0.06$, $\sigma = 0.35$, $T = 0.75$, and $\delta t = 0.25$. Also

$$u = e^{0.35\sqrt{0.25}} = 1.1912$$

$$d = \frac{1}{u} = 0.8395$$

$$a = 1$$

$$p = \frac{a-d}{u-d} = 0.4564$$

$$1 - p = 0.5436$$

The output from DerivaGem for this example is shown in the Figure 18.4. The calculated price of the option is 42.07 cents. Using 100 time steps the price obtained is 38.64. The options delta is calculated from the tree is

$$(79.971 - 11.419)/(476.498 - 335.783) = 0.487$$

. When 100 steps are used the estimate of the option's delta is 0.483.

Growth factor per step, a = 1.0000
Probability of up move, p = 0.4564
Up step size, u = 1.1912
Down step size, d = 0.8395

| | 676.1835 |
| | 256.1835 |

567.627
147.627

476.4985
79.971

476.4985
56.49849

400
42.06767

400
25.39985

335.7828
11.41894

335.7828
0

281.8752
0

236.6221
0

Node Time:
0.0000   0.2500   0.5000   0.7500

Figure 18.4   Tree for Problem 18.11

18.12. In this case the present value of the dividend is $2e^{-0.03 \times 0.125} = 1.9925$. We first build a tree for $S_0 = 20 - 1.9925 = 18.0075$, $K = 20$, $r = 0.03$, $\sigma = 0.25$, and $T = 0.25$ with $\delta t = 0.08333$. This gives Figure 18.5. For nodes between times 0 and 1.5 months we then add the present value of the dividend to the stock price. The result is the tree in Figure 18.6. The price of the option calculated from the tree is 0.674. When 100 steps are used the price obtained is 0.690.

120

Time step, dt = 0.0833 years, 30.42 days
Growth factor per step, a = 1.0025
Probability of up move, p = 0.4993
Up step size, u = 1.0748
Down step size, d = 0.9304

22.36047

20.8036

19.35512

18.0075

16.75371

15.58721

19.35512

18.0075

16.75371
0

14.50193
0

Node Time:

| 0.0000 | 0.0833 | 0.1667 | 0.2500 |

Figure 18.5 First tree for Problem 18.12

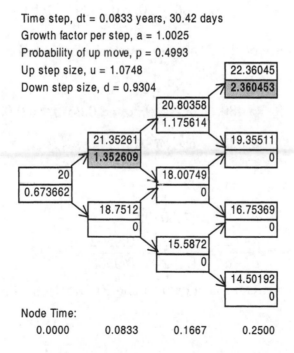

Time step, dt = 0.0833 years, 30.42 days
Growth factor per step, a = 1.0025
Probability of up move, p = 0.4993
Up step size, u = 1.0748
Down step size, d = 0.9304

22.36045
2.360453

20.80358
1.175614

21.35261
1.352609

20
0.673662

18.00749
0

18.7512
0

15.5872
0

19.35511
0

16.75369
0

14.50192
0

Node Time:

| 0.0000 | 0.0833 | 0.1667 | 0.2500 |

Figure 18.6 Final Tree for Problem 18.12

18.13. In this case $S_0 = 20$, $K = 18$, $r = 0.15$, $\sigma = 0.40$, $T = 1$, and $\delta t = 0.25$. The

121

parameters for the tree are

$$u = e^{\sigma\sqrt{\delta t}} = e^{0.4\sqrt{0.25}} = 1.2214$$

$$d = 1/u = 0.8187$$

$$a = e^{r\delta t} = 1.0382$$

$$p = \frac{a-d}{u-d} = \frac{1.0382 - 0.8187}{1.2214 - 0.8187} = 0.545$$

The tree produced by DerivaGem for the American option is shown in Figure 18.7. The estimated value of the American option is $1.29.

As shown in Figure 18.8, the same tree can be used to value a European put option with the same parameters. The estimated value of the European option is $1.14. The option parameters are $S = 20$, $K = 18$, $r = 0.15$, $\sigma = 0.40$ and $T = 1$

$$d_1 = \frac{\ln(20/18) + 0.15 + 0.40^2/2}{0.40} = 0.8384$$

$$d_2 = d_1 - 0.40 = 0.4384$$

$$N(-d_1) = 0.2009; \quad N(-d_2) = 0.3306$$

The true European put price is therefore

$$18e^{-0.15} \times 0.3306 - 20 \times 0.2009 = 1.10$$

The control variate estimate of the American put price is therefore $1.29 + 1.10 - 1.14 = $1.25.

18.14. In this case $S_0 = 484$, $K = 480$, $r = 0.10$, $\sigma = 0.25$ $q = 0.03$, $T = 0.1667$, and $\delta t = 0.04167$

$$u = e^{\sigma\sqrt{\delta t}} = e^{0.25\sqrt{0.04167}} = 1.0524$$

$$d = \frac{1}{u} = 0.9502$$

$$a = e^{(r-q)\delta t} = 1.00292$$

$$p = \frac{a-d}{u-d} = \frac{1.0029 - 0.9502}{1.0524 - 0.9502} = 0.516$$

The tree produced by DerivaGem is shown in the Figure 18.9. The estimated price of the option is $14.93.

18.15. First the delta of the American option is estimated in the usual way from the tree. Denote this by Δ_A^*. Then the delta of a European option which has the same parameters as the American option is calculated in the same way using the same tree. Denote

Figure 18.7   Tree to evaluate American option for Problem 18.13

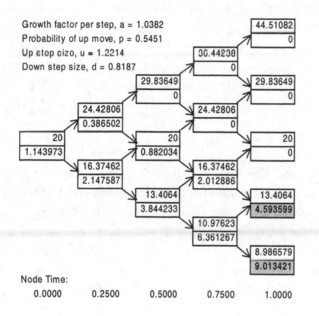

Figure 18.8   Tree to evaluate European option in Problem 18.13

this by Δ_B^*. Finally the true European delta, Δ_B, is calculated using the formulas in Chapter 14. The control variate estimate of delta is then:

$$\Delta_A^* - \Delta_B^* + \Delta_B$$

Figure 18.9   Tree to evaluate option in Problem 18.14

18.16. In this case a simulation requires two sets of samples from standardized normal distributions. The first is to generate the volatility movements. The second is to generate the stock price movements once the volatility movements are known. The control variate technique involves carrying out a second simulation on the assumption that the volatility is constant. The same random number stream is used to generate stock price movements as in the first simulation. An improved estimate of the option price is

$$f_A^* - f_B^* + f_B$$

where f_A^* is the option value from the first simulation (when the volatility is stochastic), f_B^* is the option value from the second simulation (when the volatility is constant) and f_B is the true Black-Scholes value when the volatility is constant.

To use the antithetic variable technique, two sets of samples from standardized normal distributions must be used for each of volatility and stock price. Denote the volatility samples by $\{V_1\}$ and $\{V_2\}$ and the stock price samples by $\{S_1\}$ and $\{S_2\}$.

$\{V_1\}$ is antithetic to $\{V_2\}$ and $\{S_1\}$ is antithetic to $\{S_2\}$. Thus if

$$\{V_1\} = +0.83, +0.41, -0.21\ldots$$

then

$$\{V_2\} = -0.83, -0.41, +0.21\ldots$$

Similarly for $\{S_1\}$ and $\{S_2\}$.

An efficient way of proceeding is to carry out six simulations in parallel:

    Simulation 1: Use $\{S_1\}$ with volatility constant

    Simulation 2: Use $\{S_2\}$ with volatility constant

Simulation 3: Use $\{S_1\}$ and $\{V_1\}$
Simulation 4: Use $\{S_1\}$ and $\{V_2\}$
Simulation 5: Use $\{S_2\}$ and $\{V_1\}$
Simulation 6: Use $\{S_2\}$ and $\{V_2\}$

If f_i is the option price from simulation i, simulations 3 and 4 provide an estimate $0.5(f_3 + f_4)$ for the option price. When the control variate technique is used we combine this estimate with the result of simulation 1 to obtain $0.5(f_3 + f_4) - f_1 + f_B$ as an estimate of the price where f_B is, as above, the Black-Scholes option price. Similarly simulations 2, 5 and 6 provide an estimate $0.5(f_5 + f_6) - f_2 + f_B$. Overall the best estimate is:

$$0.5[0.5(f_3 + f_4) - f_1 + f_B + 0.5(f_5 + f_6) - f_2 + f_B]$$

18.17. For an American call option on a currency

$$\frac{\partial f}{\partial t} + (r - r_f)S\frac{\partial f}{\partial S} + \frac{1}{2}\sigma^2 S^2 \frac{\partial^2 f}{\partial S^2} = rf$$

With the notation in the text this becomes

$$\frac{f_{i+1,j} - f_{ij}}{\delta t} + (r - r_f)j\delta S\frac{f_{i,j+1} - f_{i,j-1}}{2\delta S} + \frac{1}{2}\sigma^2 j^2 \delta S^2 \frac{f_{i,j+1} - 2f_{i,j} + f_{i,j-1}}{\delta S^2} = rf_{ij}$$

for $j = 1, 2 \ldots M - 1$ and $i = 0, 1 \ldots N - 1$. Rearranging terms we obtain

$$a_j f_{i,j-1} + b_j f_{ij} + c_j f_{i,j+1} = f_{i+1,j}$$

where

$$a_j = \frac{1}{2}(r - r_f)j\delta t - \frac{1}{2}\sigma^2 j^2 \delta t$$

$$b_j = 1 + \sigma^2 j^2 \delta t + r\delta t$$

$$c_j = -\frac{1}{2}(r - r_f)j\delta t - \frac{1}{2}\sigma^2 j^2 \delta t$$

Equations (18.26), (18.27) and (18.28) become

$$f_{Nj} = \max[j\delta S - K, 0] \quad j = 0, 1 \ldots M$$
$$f_{i0} = 0 \quad i = 0, 1 \ldots N$$
$$f_{iM} = M\delta S - K \quad i = 0, 1 \ldots N$$

18.18. We consider stock prices of $0, $4, $8, $12, $16, $20, $24, $28, $32, $36 and $40. Using equation (18.32) with $r = 0.10$, $\delta t = 0.0833$, $\delta S = 4$, $\sigma = 0.30$, $K = 21$, $T = 0.3333$ we obtain the table shown below. The option price is $1.56.

Grid for Finite Difference Approach in Problem 18.18.

Stock Price	Time To Maturity (Months)				
($)	4	3	2	1	0
40	0.00	0.00	0.00	0.00	0.00
36	0.00	0.00	0.00	0.00	0.00
32	0.01	0.00	0.00	0.00	0.00
28	0.07	0.04	0.02	0.00	0.00
24	0.38	0.30	0.21	0.11	0.00
20	1.56	1.44	1.31	1.17	1.00
16	5.00	5.00	5.00	5.00	5.00
12	9.00	9.00	9.00	9.00	9.00
8	13.00	13.00	13.00	13.00	13.00
4	17.00	17.00	17.00	17.00	17.00
0	21.00	21.00	21.00	21.00	21.00

18.19. In this case $\delta t = 0.25$ and $\sigma = 0.4$ so that

$$u = e^{0.4\sqrt{0.25}} = 1.2214$$

$$d = \frac{1}{u} = 0.8187$$

The futures prices provide estimates of the growth rate in copper in a risk-neutral world. During the first three months this growth rate (with continuous compounding) is

$$4 \ln \frac{0.59}{0.60} = -6.72\% \text{ per annum}$$

The parameter p for the first three months is therefore

$$\frac{e^{-0.0672 \times 0.25} - 0.8187}{1.2214 - 0.8187} = 0.4088$$

The growth rate in copper is equal to -13.79%, -21.63% and -30.78% in the following three quarters. Therefore, the parameter p for the second three months is

$$\frac{e^{-0.1379 \times 0.25} - 0.8187}{1.2214 - 0.8187} = 0.3660$$

For the third quarter it is

$$\frac{e^{-0.2163 \times 0.25} - 0.8187}{1.2214 - 0.8187} = 0.3195$$

For the final quarter, it is

$$\frac{e^{-0.3078 \times 0.25} - 0.8187}{1.2214 - 0.8187} = 0.2663$$

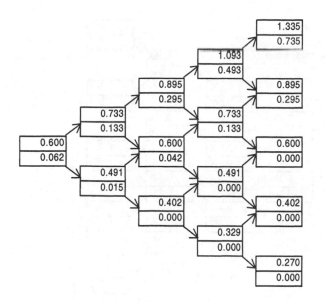

Figure 18.10   Tree to value option in Problem 18.19: At each node, upper number is price of copper and lower number is option price

The tree for the movements in copper prices in a risk-neutral world is shown in Figure 18.10. The value of the option is $0.062.

18.20. In this problem we use exactly the same tree for copper prices as in Problem 18.19. However, the values of the derivative are different. On the final nodes the values of the derivative equal the square of the price of copper. On other nodes they are calculated in the usual way. The current value of the security is $0.275 (see Figure 18.11).

18.21. Define S_t as the current asset price, S_{max} as the highest asset price considered and S_{min} as the lowest asset price considered. (In the example in the text $S_{min} = 0$). Let

$$Q_1 = \frac{S_{max} - S_t}{\delta S} \quad \text{and} \quad Q_2 = \frac{S_t - S_{min}}{\delta S}$$

and let N be the number of time intervals considered. From the structure of the calculations in the explicit version of the finite difference method, we can see that the values assumed for the derivative security at $S = S_{min}$ and $S = S_{max}$ affect the derivative security's value at time t if

$$N \geq \max(Q_1, Q_2)$$

18.22. A similar approach to that suggested for the binomial tree approach in Section 18.3 can be used. The grid can be used to model the stock price less the present value of

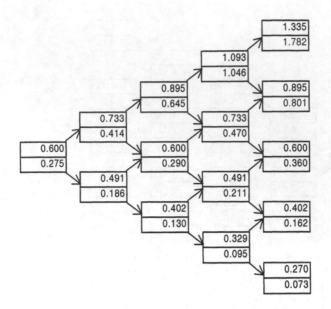

Figure 18.11 Tree to value derivative in Problem 18.20. At each
node, upper number is price of copper and lower
number is derivative security price.

future dividends during the life of the derivative security. This is the variable which is
denoted by S^* in Section 18.3. The volatility that must be estimated is the volatility of
S^* rather than the volatility of S. These two volatilities may be significantly different
when a long-lived derivative security is being valued.

18.23. The basic approach is similar to that described in Section 18.8. The only difference is
the boundary conditions. For a sufficiently small value of the stock price, $S_{\min}$, it can
be assumed that conversion will never take place and the convertible can be valued
as a straight bond. The highest stock price which needs to be considered, $S_{\max}$, is
$18. When this is reached the value of the convertible bond is $36. At maturity the
convertible is worth the greater of $2S_T$ and $25 where S_T is the stock price.
The convertible can be valued by working backwards through the grid using either
the explicit or the implicit finite difference method in conjunction with the boundary
conditions. In formulas (18.25) and (18.32) the present value of the income on the
convertible between time $t + i\,\delta t$ and $t + (i + 1)\,\delta t$ discounted to time $t + i\,\delta t$ must
be added to the right-hand side. Chapter 27 considers the pricing of convertibles in
more detail.

18.24. Suppose x_1, x_2, and x_3 are random samples from three independent normal distributions. Random samples with the required correlation structure are ϵ_1, ϵ_2, ϵ_3 where

$$\epsilon_1 = x_1$$

$$\epsilon_2 = \rho_{12}x_1 + x_2\sqrt{1 - \rho_{12}^2}$$

and

$$\epsilon_3 = \alpha_1 x_1 + \alpha_2 x_2 + \alpha_3 x_3$$

where

$$\alpha_1 = \rho_{13}$$

$$\alpha_1 \rho_{12} + \alpha_2 \sqrt{1 - \rho_{12}^2} = \rho_{23}$$

and

$$\alpha_1^2 + \alpha_2^2 + \alpha_3^2 = 1$$

This means that

$$\alpha_1 = \rho_{13}$$

$$\alpha_2 = \frac{\rho_{23} - \rho_{13}\rho_{12}}{\sqrt{1 - \rho_{12}^2}}$$

$$\alpha_3 = \sqrt{1 - \alpha_1^2 - \alpha_2^2}$$

CHAPTER 19
Exotic Options

19.1. A forward start option is an option that is paid for now but will start at some time in the future. The strike price is usually equal to the price of the asset at the time the option starts. A chooser option is an option where, at some time in the future, the holder chooses whether the option is a call or a put.

19.2. A lookback call provides a payoff of $S_T - S_{\min}$. A lookback put provides a payoff of $S_{\max} - S_T$. A combination of a lookback call and a lookback put therefore provides a payoff of $S_{\max} - S_{\min}$.

19.3. No, it is never optimal to choose early. The resulting cash flows are the same regardless of when the choice is made. There is no point in the holder making a commitment earlier than necessary. This argument applies when the holder chooses between two American options providing the options cannot be exercised before the 2-year point. If the early exercise period starts as soon as the choice is made, the argument does not hold. For example, if the stock price fell to almost nothing in the first six months, the holder would choose a put option at this time and exercise it immediately.

19.4. The payoffs are as follows:

$c_1 : \max(\overline{S} - K, 0)$
$c_2 : \max(S_T - \overline{S}, 0)$
$c_3 : \max(S_T - K, 0)$
$p_1 : \max(K - \overline{S}, 0)$
$p_2 : \max(\overline{S} - S_T, 0)$
$p_3 : \max(K - S_T, 0)$

The payoff from $c_1 - p_1$ is always $\overline{S} - K$; The payoff from $c_2 - p_2$ is always $S_T - \overline{S}$; The payoff from $c_3 - p_3$ is always $S_T - K$; It follows that

$$c_1 - p_1 + c_2 - p_2 = c_3 - p_3$$

or

$$c_1 + c_2 - c_3 = p_1 + p_2 - p_3$$

19.5. Substituting for c, put-call parity gives

$$\max(c, p) = \max\left[p,\ p + S_1 e^{-q(T_2 - T_1)} - Ke^{-r(T_2 - T_1)}\right]$$

$$= p + \max\left[0,\ S_1 e^{-q(T_2 - T_1)} - Ke^{-r(T_2 - T_1)}\right]$$

This shows that the chooser option can be decomposed into
1. A put option with strike price K and maturity T_2; and
2. $e^{-q(T_2-T_1)}$ call options with strike price $Ke^{-(r-q)(T_2-T_1)}$ and maturity T_1.

19.6. Consider the formula for c_{do} when $H \geq K$

$$c_{do} = S_0 N(x_1)e^{-qT} - Ke^{-rT}N(x_1 - \sigma\sqrt{T}) - S_0 e^{-qT}(H/S_0)^{2\lambda}N(y_1)$$

$$+Ke^{-rT}(H/S_0)^{2\lambda-2}N(y_1 - \sigma\sqrt{T})$$

Substituting $H = K$ and noting that

$$\lambda = \frac{r - q + \sigma^2/2}{\sigma^2}$$

we obtain $x_1 = d_1$ so that

$$c_{do} = c - S_0 e^{-qT}(H/S_0)^{2\lambda}N(y_1) + Ke^{-rT}(H/S_0)^{2\lambda-2}N(y_1 - \sigma\sqrt{T})$$

The formula for c_{di} when $H \leq K$ is

$$c_{di} = S_0 e^{-qT}(H/S_0)^{2\lambda}N(y) - Ke^{-rT}(H/S_0)^{2\lambda-2}N(y - \sigma\sqrt{T})$$

Since $c_{do} = c - c_{di}$

$$c_{do} = c - S_0 e^{-qT}(H/S_0)^{2\lambda}N(y) + Ke^{-rT}(H/S_0)^{2\lambda-2}N(y - \sigma\sqrt{T})$$

From the formulas in the text $y_1 = y$ when $H = K$. The two expression for c_{do} are therefore equivalent when $H = K$

19.7. The option is in the money only when the asset price is less than the strike price. However, in these circumstances the barrier has been hit and the option has ceased to exist.

19.8. The argument is similar to that given in Chapter 8 for a regular option on a non-dividend-paying stock. Consider a portfolio consisting of the option and cash equal to the present value of the terminal strike price. The initial cash position is

$$Ke^{gT-rT}$$

By time τ ($0 \leq \tau \leq T$), the cash grows to

$$Ke^{-r(T-\tau)+gT} = Ke^{g\tau}e^{-(r-g)(T-\tau)}$$

Since $r > g$, this is less than $Ke^{g\tau}$ and therefore is less than the amount required to exercise the option. It follows that, if the option is exercised early, the terminal value of the portfolio is less than S_T. At time T the cash balance is Ke^{gT}. This is exactly what is required to exercise the option. If the early exercise decision is delayed until time T, the terminal value of the portfolio is therefore

$$\max[S_T, Ke^{gT}]$$

This is at least as great as S_T. It follows that early exercise cannot be optimal.

19.9. When the strike price of an option on a non-dividend-paying stock is defined as 10% greater that the stock price, the value of the option is proportional to the stock price. The same argument as that given in the text for forward start options shows that if t_1 is the time when the option starts and t_2 is the time when it finishes, the option has the same value as an option starting today with a life of $t_2 - t_1$ and a strike price of 1.1 times the current stock price.

19.10. Assume that we start calculating averages from time zero. The relationship between $A(t + \delta t)$ and $A(t)$ is

$$A(t + \delta t) \times (t + \delta t) = A(t) \times t + S(t) \times \delta t$$

where $S(t)$ is the stock price at time t and terms of higher order than δt are ignored. If we continue to ignore terms of higher order than δt, it follows that

$$A(t + \delta t) = A(t)\left[1 - \frac{\delta t}{t}\right] + S(t)\frac{\delta t}{t}$$

Taking limits as δt tends to zero

$$dA(t) = \frac{S(t) - A(t)}{t}dt$$

The process for $A(t)$ has a stochastic drift and no dz term. The process makes sense intuitively. Once some time has passed, the change in S in the next small portion of time has only a second order effect on the average. If S equals A the average has no drift; if $S > A$ the average is drifting up; if $S < A$ the average is drifting down.

19.11. In an Asian option the payoff becomes more certain as time passes and the delta always approaches zero as the maturity date is approached. This makes delta hedging easy. Barrier options cause problems for delta hedgers when the asset price is close to the barrier because delta is discontinuous.

19.12. The value of the option is given by the formula in the text

$$V_0 e^{-q_2 T} N(d_1) - U_0 e^{-q_1 T} N(d_2)$$

where

$$d_1 = \frac{\ln(V_0/U_0) + (q_1 - q_2 + \sigma^2/2)T}{\sigma\sqrt{T}}$$

$$d_2 = d_1 - \sigma\sqrt{T}$$

and

$$\sigma = \sqrt{\sigma_1^2 + \sigma_2^2 - 2\rho\sigma_1\sigma_2}$$

In this case, $V_0 = 380$, $U_0 = 400$, $q_1 = 0$, $q_2 = 0$, $T = 1$, and

$$\sigma = \sqrt{0.2^2 + 0.2^2 - 2 \times 0.7 \times 0.2 \times 0.2} = 0.1549$$

Because $d_1 = -0.2537$ and $d_2 = -0.4086$, the option price is

$$380N(-0.2537) - 400N(-0.4086) = 15.38$$

or $15.38.

19.13. No. If the future's price is above the spot price during the life of the option, it is possible that the spot price will hit the barrier when the futures price does not.

19.14. (a) The put–call relationship is

$$cc + K_1 e^{-rT_1} = pc + c$$

where cc is the price of the call on the call, pc is the price of the put on the call, c is the price today of the call into which the options can be exercised at time T_1, and K_1 is the exercise price for cc and pc. The proof is similar to that in Chapter 8 for the usual put–call parity relationship. Both sides of the equation represent the values of portfolios that will be worth $\max(c, K_1)$ at time T_1. From the formulas in the text, the relationships

$$M(a, b; \rho) = N(a) - M(a, -b; -\rho) = N(b) - M(-a, b, ; -\rho)$$

in Appendix 12C, and the relationship

$$N(x) = 1 - N(-x)$$

we obtain

$$cc - pc = Se^{-qT_2}N(b_1) - K_2 e^{-rT_2}N(b_2) - K_1 e^{-rT_1}$$

Since

$$c = Se^{-qT_2}N(b_1) - K_2 e^{-rT_2}N(b_2)$$

put–call parity is consistent with the formulas
(b) The put–call relationship is

$$cp + K_1 e^{-rT_1} = pp + p$$

where cp is the price of the call on the put, pp is the price of the put on the put, p is the price today of the put into which the options can be exercised at time T_1, and K_1

is the exercise price for cc and pc. The proof is similar to that in Chapter 8 for the usual put–call parity relationship. Both sides of the equation represent the values of portfolios that will be worth $\max(p, K_1)$ at time T_1. From the formulas in the text, the relationships

$$M(a, b; \rho) = N(a) - M(a, -b; -\rho) = N(b) - M(-a, b, ; -\rho)$$

in Appendix 12C, and the relationship

$$N(x) = 1 - N(-x)$$

it follows that

$$cp - pp = -Se^{-qT_2}N(-b_1) + K_2e^{-rT_2}N(-b_2) - K_1e^{-rT_1}$$

Because

$$p = -Se^{-qT_2}N(-b_1) - K_2e^{-rT_2}N(-b_2)$$

put–call parity is consistent with the formulas.

19.15. As we increase the frequency we observe a more extreme minimum which increases the value of a lookback call.

19.16. As we increase the frequency with which the asset price is observed, the asset price becomes more likely to hit the barrier and the value of a down-and-out call goes down. For a similar reason the value of a down-and-in call goes up. The adjustment mentioned in the text, suggested by Broadie, Glasserman, and Kou, moves the barrier further out as the asset price is observed less frequently. This increases the price of a down-and-out option and reduces the price of a down-and-in option.

19.17. If the barrier is reached the down-and-out option is worth nothing while the down-and-in option has the same value as a regular option. If the barrier is not reached the down-and-in option is worth nothing while the down-and-out option has the same value as a regular option. This is why a down-and-out call option plus a down-and-in call option is worth the same as a regular option. A similar argument cannot be used for American options.

19.18. This is a cash-or-nothing call. The value is $100N(d_2)e^{-0.08 \times 0.5}$ where

$$d_2 = \frac{\ln(960/1000) + (0.08 - 0.03 - 0.2^2/2) \times 0.5}{0.2 \times \sqrt{0.5}} = -0.1826$$

Since $N(d_2) = 0.4276$ the value of the derivative is \$41.08.

19.19. This is a regular call with a strike price of \$20 that ceases to exist if the futures price hits \$18. With the notation in the text $H = 18$, $K = 20$, $S = 19$, $r = 0.05$, $\sigma = 0.4$, $q = 0.05$, $T = 0.25$. From this $\lambda = 0.5$ and

$$y = \frac{\ln[18^2/(19 \times 20)]}{0.4\sqrt{0.25}} + 0.5 \times 0.4\sqrt{0.25} = -0.69714$$

The value of a down-and-out call plus a down-and-in call equals the value of a regular call. Substituting into the formula given when $H < K$ we get $c_{di} = 0.4638$. The regular Black Scholes formula gives $c = 1.0902$. Hence $c_{do} = 0.6264$. (These answers can be checked with DerivaGem).

19.20. DerivaGem shows that the value is 53.38. Note that the Minimum to date and Maximum to date should be set equal to the current value of the index for a new deal. (See material on DerivaGem at the end of the book.)

19.21. We can use the analytic approximation given in the text.

$$M_1 = \frac{(e^{0.05 \times 0.5} - 1) \times 30}{0.05 \times 0.5} = 30.378$$

Also $M_2 = 936.9$ so that $\sigma = 17.41\%$. The option can be valued as a futures option with $F_0 = 30.378$, $K = 30$, $r = 5\%$, $\sigma = 17.41\%$, and $t = 0.5$. The price is 1.637.

19.22. (a) The price of a regular European call option is 7.116.
(b) The price of the down-and-out call option is 4.696.
(c) The price of the down-and-in call option is 2.419.
The price of a regular European call is the sum of the prices of down-and-out and down-and-in options.

CHAPTER 20
More on Models and Numerical Procedures

20.1. It follows immediately from the equations in Section 20.1 that

$$p - c = Ke^{-rT} - S_0 e^{-qT}$$

in all cases.

20.2. The probability of N jumps in time δt is

$$\frac{e^{-\lambda \delta t}(\lambda \delta t)^N}{N!}$$

When δt is small we can ignore terms of order $(\delta t)^2$ and higher so that the probability of no jumps is $1 - \lambda \delta t$ and the probability of one jump is $\lambda \delta t$. During each time step of length δt we first sample a random number between 0 and 1 to determine whether a jump takes place. Suppose for example that $\lambda = 0.8$ and $\delta t = 0.1$ so that the probability of no jumps is 0.92 and the probability of one jump is 0.08. If the random number is between 0 and 0.92 there is no jump; if it is between 0.92 and 1, there is one jump. If there is a jump we sample from the appropriate distribution to determine the size of the jump. The change in the asset price in time δt is then given by

$$\frac{\delta S}{S} = (\mu - \lambda k)\delta t + \sigma \epsilon \sqrt{\delta t} + Q$$

where $Q = 0$ if there is no jump and Q is the size of the jump if a jump takes place. We can adjust this procedure to sample $\ln S$ rather than S and to allow for more than one jump in time δt.

20.3. With the notation in the text the value of a call option, c is

$$\sum_{n=0}^{\infty} \frac{e^{-\lambda'T}(\lambda'T)^n}{n!} c_n$$

where c_n is the Black–Scholes price of a call option where the variance rate is

$$\sigma^2 + \frac{ns^2}{T}$$

and the risk-free rate is

$$r - \lambda k + \frac{n\gamma}{T}$$

where $\gamma = \ln(1 + k)$. Similarly the value of a put option p is

$$\sum_{n=0}^{\infty} \frac{e^{-\lambda' T}(\lambda' T)^n}{n!} p_n$$

where p_n is the Black–Scholes price of a put option with this variance rate and risk-free rate. It follows that

$$p - c = \sum_{n=0}^{\infty} \frac{e^{-\lambda' T}(\lambda' T)^n}{n!}(p_n - c_n)$$

From put–call parity

$$p_n - c_n = K e^{(-r+\lambda k)T} e^{-n\gamma} - S_0 e^{-qT}$$

Because

$$e^{-n\gamma} = (1 + k)^{-n}$$

it follows that

$$p - c = \sum_{n=0}^{\infty} \frac{e^{-\lambda' T + \lambda k T}(\lambda' T/(1+k))^n}{n!} K e^{-rT} - \sum_{n=0}^{\infty} \frac{e^{-\lambda' T}(\lambda' T)^n}{n!} S_0 e^{-qT}$$

Using $\lambda' = \lambda(1 + k)$ this becomes

$$\frac{1}{e^{\lambda T}} \sum_{n=0}^{\infty} \frac{(\lambda T)^n}{n!} K e^{-rT} - \frac{1}{e^{\lambda' T}} \sum_{n=0}^{\infty} \frac{(\lambda' T)^n}{n!} S_0 e^{-qT}$$

From the expansion of the exponential function we get

$$e^{\lambda T} = \sum_{n=0}^{\infty} \frac{(\lambda T)^n}{n!}$$

$$e^{\lambda' T} = \sum_{n=0}^{\infty} \frac{(\lambda' T)^n}{n!}$$

Hence

$$p - c = K e^{-rT} - S_0 e^{-qT}$$

showing that put–call parity holds.

20.4. The average variance rate is

$$\frac{6 \times 0.2^2 + 6 \times 0.22^2 + 12 \times 0.24^2}{24} = 0.0509$$

The volatility used should be $\sqrt{0.0509} = 0.2256$ or 22.56%.

20.5. In a risk-neutral world the process for the asset price exclusive of jumps is

$$\frac{dS}{S} = (r - q - \lambda k)\, dt + \sigma\, dz$$

In this case $k = -1$ so that the process is

$$\frac{dS}{S} = (r - q + \lambda)\, dt + \sigma\, dz$$

The asset behaves like a stock paying a dividend yield of $q - \lambda$. This shows that, conditional on no jumps, call price

$$S_0 e^{-(q-\lambda)T} N(d_1) - K e^{-rT}$$

where

$$d_1 = \frac{\ln(S_0/K) + (r - q + \lambda + \sigma^2/2)T}{\sigma\sqrt{T}}$$

$$d_2 = d_1 - \sigma\sqrt{T}$$

There is a probability of $e^{-\lambda T}$ that there will be no jumps and a probability of $1 - e^{-\lambda T}$ that there will be one or more jumps so that the final asset price is zero. It follows that there is a probability of $e^{-\lambda T}$ that the value of the call is given by the above equation and $1 - e^{-\lambda T}$ that it will be zero. Because jumps have no systematic risk it follows that the value of the call option is

$$e^{-\lambda T}[S_0 e^{-(q-\lambda)T} N(d_1) - K e^{-rT}]$$

or

$$S_0 e^{-qT} N(d_1) - K e^{-(r+\lambda)T}$$

This is the required result. The value of a call option is an increasing function of the risk-free interest rate (see Chapter 8). It follows that the possibility of jumps increases the value of the call option in this case.

20.6. (a) Suppose that S_1 is the stock price at time t_1 and S_T is the stock price at time T. From equation (12.3), it follows that in a risk- neutral world:

$$\ln S_1 - \ln S_0 \sim \phi\left[\left(r_1 - \frac{\sigma_1^2}{2}\right)t_1, \sigma_1\sqrt{t_1}\right]$$

$$\ln S_T - \ln S_1 \sim \phi\left[\left(r_2 - \frac{\sigma_2^2}{2}\right)t_2, \sigma_2\sqrt{t_2}\right]$$

Since the sum of two independent normal distributions is normal with mean equal to the sum of the means and variance equal to the sum of the variances

$$\ln S_T - \ln S_0 = (\ln S_T - \ln S_1) + (\ln S_1 - \ln S_0)$$

$$\sim \phi\left(r_1 t_1 + r_2 t_2 - \frac{\sigma_1^2 t_1}{2} - \frac{\sigma_2^2 t_2}{2}, \sqrt{\sigma_1^2 t_1 + \sigma_2^2 t_2}\right)$$

(b) Because

$$r_1t_1 + r_2t_2 = \bar{r}T$$

and

$$\sigma_1^2t_1 + \sigma_2^2t_2 = \overline{V}T$$

it follows that:

$$\ln S_T - \ln S_0 \sim \phi\left[\left(\bar{r} - \frac{\overline{V}}{2}\right)T, \sqrt{\overline{V}T}\right]$$

(c) If σ_i and r_i are the volatility and risk-free interest rate during the ith subinterval ($i = 1, 2, 3$), an argument similar to that in (a) shows that:

$$\ln S_T - \ln S_0 \sim \phi\left(r_1t_1 + r_2t_2 + r_3t_3 - \frac{\sigma_1^2t_1}{2} - \frac{\sigma_2^2t_2}{2} - \frac{\sigma_3^2t_3}{2}, \sqrt{\sigma_1^2t_1 + \sigma_2^2t_2 + \sigma_3^2t_3}\right)$$

where t_1, t_2 and t_3 are the lengths of the three subintervals. It follows that the result in (b) is still true.

(d) The result in (b) remains true as the time between time zero and time T is divided into more subintervals, each having its own risk-free interest rate and volatility. In the limit, it follows that, if r and σ are known functions of time, the stock price distribution at time T is the same as that for a stock with a constant interest rate and variance rate with the constant interest rate equal to the average interest rate and the constant variance rate equal to the average variance rate.

20.7. The equations are:

$$S(t + \delta t) = S(t)\exp[(r - q - V(t)/2)\delta t + \epsilon_1\sqrt{V(t)\delta t}]$$

$$V(t + \delta t) - V(t) = a[V_L - V(t)]\delta t + \xi\epsilon_2 V(t)^\alpha\sqrt{\delta t}$$

20.8. The IVF model is designed to match the volatility surface today. There is no guarantee that the volatility surface given by the model at future times will be the same as today—or that it will be even reasonable.

20.9. The IVF model ensures that the risk-neutral probability distribution of the asset price at any future time conditional on its value today is correct (or at least consistent with the market prices of options). When a derivative's payoff depends on the value of the asset at only one time the IVF model therefore calculates the expected payoff from the asset correctly. The value of the derivative is the present value of the expected payoff. When interest rates are constant the IVF model calculates this present value correctly.

20.10. In this case $S_0 = 1.6$, $r = 0.05$, $r_f = 0.08$, $\sigma = 0.15$, $T = 1.5$, $\delta t = 0.5$. This means that

$$u = e^{0.15\sqrt{0.5}} = 1.1119$$

$$d = \frac{1}{u} = 0.8994$$

$$a = e^{(0.05-0.08)\times 0.5} = 0.9851$$

$$p = \frac{a-d}{u-d} = 0.4033$$

$$1 - p = 0.5967$$

The option pays off

$$S_T - S_{\min}$$

The tree is shown in Figure 20.1. At each node, the upper number is the exchange rate, the middle number(s) are the minimum exchange rate(s) so far, and the lower number(s) are the value(s) of the option. The tree shows that the value of the option today is 0.131.

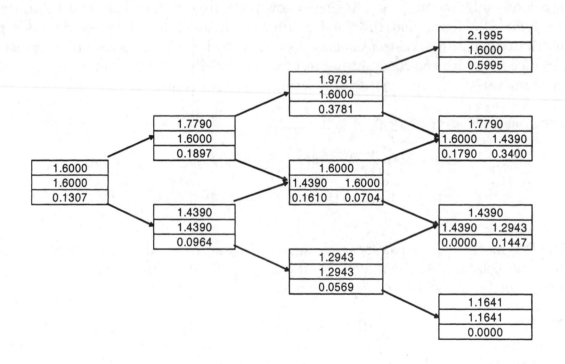

Figure 20.1   Binomial tree for Problem 20.10.

20.11. In this case we construct a tree shown in Figure 20.2 for $Y(t) = G(t)/S(t)$ where $G(t)$ is the minimum value of the exchange rate to date and $S(t)$ is the current exchange rate. We use the tree to value the option in units of the foreign currency. That is we

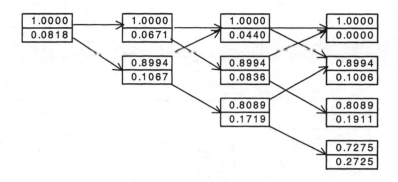

Figure 20.2   Tree for Problem 20.11.

value an instrument that pays off $1 - Y(t)$. The tree shows that the value of the option is 0.0818 units of the foreign currency or $0.0818 \times 1.6 = 0.131$ units of the domestic currency. This is consistent with the answer to Problem 20.10.

20.12. In this case $S_0 = 40$, $K = 40$, $r = 0.1$, $\sigma = 0.35$, $T = 0.25$, $\delta t = 0.08333$. This means that

$$u = e^{0.35\sqrt{0.08333}} = 1.1063$$

$$d = \frac{1}{u} = 0.9039$$

$$a = e^{0.1 \times 0.08333} = 1.008368$$

$$p = \frac{a - d}{u - d} = 0.5161$$

$$1 - p = 0.4839$$

The option pays off

$$40 - \overline{S}$$

where $\overline{S}$ denotes the geometric average. The tree is shown in Figure 20.3. At each node, the upper number is the exchange rate, the middle number(s) are the geometric average(s), and the lower number(s) are the value(s) of the option. The geometric averages are calculated using the first, the last and all intermediate stock prices on the path. The tree shows that the value of the option today is $1.40.

20.13. As mentioned in Section 20.5, for the procedure to work it must be possible to calculate the value of the path function at time $\tau + \delta t$ from the value of the path function at time τ and the value of the underlying asset at time $\tau + \delta t$. When S_{ave} is calculated from time zero until the end of the life of the option (as in the example considered

141

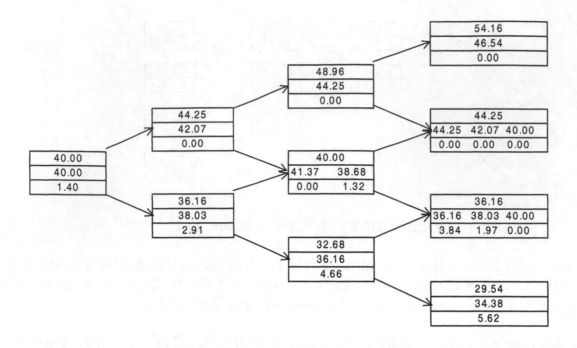

Figure 20.3 Binomial tree for Problem 20.12.

in Section 20.5) this condition is satisfied. When it is calculated over the last three months it is not satisfied. This is because, in order to update the average with a new observation on S, it is necessary to know the observation on S from three months ago that is now no longer part of the average calculation.

20.14. We consider the situation where the average at node X is 53.83. If there is an up movement to node Y the new average becomes:

$$\frac{53.83 \times 5 + 54.68}{6} = 53.97$$

Interpolating, the value of the option at node Y when the average is 53.97 is

$$\frac{(53.97 - 51.12) \times 8.635 + (54.26 - 53.97) \times 8.101}{54.26 - 51.12} = 8.586$$

Similarly if there is a down movement the new average will be

$$\frac{53.83 \times 5 + 45.72}{6} = 52.48$$

142

In this case the option price is 4.416. The option price at node X when the average is 53.83 is therefore:

$$8.586 \times 0.5056 + 4.416 \times 0.4944)e^{-0.1 \times 0.05} = 6.492$$

20.15. Under the least squares approach we exercise at time $t = 1$ in paths 4, 6, 7, and 8. We exercise at time $t = 2$ for none of the paths. We exercise at time $t = 3$ for path 3. Under the exercise boundary parameterization approach we exercise at time $t = 1$ for paths 6 and 8. We exercise at time $t = 2$ for path 7. We exercise at time $t = 3$ for paths 3 and 4. For the paths sampled the exercise boundary parameterization approach gives a higher value for the option. However, it may be biased upward. As mentioned in the text, one the early exercise boundary has been determined in the exercise boundary parameterization approach a new Monte Carlo simulation should be carried out.

20.16. If the average variance rate is 0.06, the value of the option is given by Black-Scholes with a volatility of $\sqrt{0.06} = 24.495\%$; it is 12.460. If the average variance rate is 0.09, the value of the option is given by Black-Scholes with a volatility of $\sqrt{0.09} = 30.000\%$; it is 14.655. If the average variance rate is 0.12, the value of the option is given by Black-Scholes with a volatility of $\sqrt{0.12} = 34.641\%$; it is 16.506. The value of the option is the Black-Scholes price integrated over the probability distribution of the average variance rate. It is

$$0.2 \times 12.460 + 0.5 \times 14.655 + 0.3 \times 16.506 = 14.77$$

CHAPTER 21
Martingales and Measures

21.1. The market price of risk for a variable that is not the price of a traded security is the market price of risk of a traded security whose price is instantaneously perfectly positively correlated with the variable.

21.2. If its market price of risk is zero, gold must, after storage costs have been paid, provide an expected return equal to the risk-free rate of interest. In this case, the expected return after storage costs must be 6% per annum. It follows that the expected growth rate in the price of gold must be 7% per annum.

21.3. Suppose that S is the security price and μ is the expected return from the security. Then:

$$\frac{dS}{S} = \mu dt + \sigma_1 dz_1 + \sigma_2 dz_2$$

where dz_1 and dz_2 are Wiener processes, $\sigma_1 dz_1$ is the component of the risk in the return attributable to the price of copper and $\sigma_2 dz_2$ is the component of the risk in the return attributable to the yen-$ exchange rate.

If the price of copper is held fixed, $dz_1 = 0$ and:

$$\frac{dS}{S} = \mu dt + \sigma_2 dz_2$$

Hence σ_2 is 8% per annum or 0.08. If the yen-$ exchange rate is held fixed, $dz_2 = 0$ and:

$$\frac{dS}{S} = \mu dt + \sigma_1 dz_1$$

Hence σ_1 is 12% per annum or 0.12.
From equation (21.13)

$$\mu - r = \lambda_1 \sigma_1 + \lambda_2 \sigma_2$$

where λ_1 and λ_2 are the market prices of risk for copper and the yen-$ exchange rate. In this case, $r = 0.07$, $\lambda_1 = 0.5$ and $\lambda_2 = 0.1$. Therefore

$$\mu - 0.07 = 0.5 \times 0.12 + 0.1 \times 0.08$$

so that

$$\mu = 0.138$$

i.e., the expected return is 13.8% per annum.

If the two variables affecting S are uncorrelated, we can use the result that the sum of normally distributed variables is normal with variance of the sum equal to the sum of the variances. This leads to:

$$\sigma_1 dz_1 + \sigma_2 dz_2 = \sqrt{\sigma_1^2 + \sigma_2^2} dz_3$$

where dz_3 is a Wiener process. Hence the process for S becomes:

$$\frac{dS}{S} = \mu dt + \sqrt{\sigma_1^2 + \sigma_2^2} dz_3$$

If follows that the volatility of S is $\sqrt{\sigma_1^2 + \sigma_2^2}$ or 14.4% per annum.

21.4. It can be argued that the market price of risk for the second variable is zero. This is because the risk is unsystematic, i.e., it is totally unrelated to other risks in the economy. To put this another way, there is no reason why investors should demand a higher return for bearing the risk since the risk can be totally diversified away.

21.5. Suppose that the price, f, of the derivative depends on the prices, S_1 and S_2, of two traded securities. Suppose further that:

$$dS_1 = \mu_1 S_1 dt + \sigma_1 S_1 dz_1$$

$$dS_2 = \mu_2 S_2 dt + \sigma_2 S_2 dz_2$$

where dz_1 and dz_2 are Wiener processes with correlation ρ. From Ito's lemma [see equation (21A.3)]

$$df = \left(\mu_1 S_1 \frac{\partial f}{\partial S_1} + \mu_2 S_2 \frac{\partial f}{\partial S_2} + \frac{\partial f}{\partial t} + \frac{1}{2}\sigma_1^2 S_1^2 \frac{\partial^2 f}{\partial S_1^2} + \frac{1}{2}\sigma_2^2 S_2^2 \frac{\partial^2 f}{\partial S_2^2} \right.$$
$$\left. + \rho\sigma_1\sigma_2 S_1 S_2 \frac{\partial^2 f}{\partial S_1 \partial S_2} \right) dt + \sigma_1 S_1 \frac{\partial f}{\partial S_1} dz_1 + \sigma_2 S_2 \frac{\partial f}{\partial S_2} dz_2$$

To eliminate the dz_1 and dz_2 we choose a portfolio, Π, consisting of

$$
\begin{array}{ll}
-1: & \text{derivative} \\
+\frac{\partial f}{\partial S_1}: & \text{first traded security} \\
+\frac{\partial f}{\partial S_2}: & \text{second traded security}
\end{array}
$$

$$\Pi = -f + \frac{\partial f}{\partial S_1} S_1 + \frac{\partial f}{\partial S_2} S_2$$

$$d\Pi = -df + \frac{\partial f}{\partial S_1} dS_1 + \frac{\partial f}{\partial S_2} dS_2$$

$$= -\left(\frac{\partial f}{\partial t} + \frac{1}{2}\sigma_1^2 S_1^2 \frac{\partial^2 f}{\partial S_1^2} + \frac{1}{2}\sigma_2^2 S_2^2 \frac{\partial^2 f}{\partial S_2^2} + \rho\sigma_1\sigma_2 S_1 S_2 \frac{\partial^2 f}{\partial S_1 \partial S_2} \right) dt$$

Since the portfolio is instantaneously risk-free it must instantaneously earn the risk-free rate of interest. Hence

$$d\Pi = r\Pi dt$$

Combining the above equations

$$-\left[\frac{\partial f}{\partial t} + \frac{1}{2}\sigma_1^2 S_1^2 \frac{\partial^2 f}{\partial S_1^2} + \frac{1}{2}\sigma_2^2 S_2^2 \frac{\partial^2 f}{\partial S_2^2} + \rho\sigma_1\sigma_2 S_1 S_2 \frac{\partial^2 f}{\partial S_1 \partial S_2}\right] dt = r\left[-f + \frac{\partial f}{\partial S_1}S_1 + \frac{\partial f}{\partial S_2}S_2\right] dt$$

so that:

$$\frac{\partial f}{\partial t} + rS_1\frac{\partial f}{\partial S_1} + rS_2\frac{\partial f}{\partial S_2} + \frac{1}{2}\sigma_1^2 S_1^2 \frac{\partial^2 f}{\partial S_1^2} + \frac{1}{2}\sigma_2^2 S_2^2 \frac{\partial^2 f}{\partial S_2^2} + \rho\sigma_1\sigma_2 S_1 S_2 \frac{\partial^2 f}{\partial S_1 \partial S_2} = rf$$

21.6. The process for x can be written

$$\frac{dx}{x} = \frac{a(x_0 - x)}{x}dt + \frac{c}{\sqrt{x}}dz$$

Hence the expected growth rate in x is:

$$\frac{a(x_0 - x)}{x}$$

and the volatility of x is

$$\frac{c}{\sqrt{x}}$$

In a risk neutral world the expected growth rate should be changed to

$$\frac{a(x_0 - x)}{x} - \lambda\frac{c}{\sqrt{x}}$$

so that the process is

$$\frac{dx}{x} = \left[\frac{a(x_0 - x)}{x} - \lambda\frac{c}{\sqrt{x}}\right]dt + \frac{c}{\sqrt{x}}dz$$

i.e.

$$dx = \left[a(x_0 - x) - \lambda c\sqrt{x}\right]dt + c\sqrt{x}dz$$

Hence the drift rate should be reduced by $\lambda c\sqrt{x}$.

21.7. As suggested in the hint we form a new security f^* which is the same as f except that all income produced by f is reinvested in f. Assuming we start doing this at time zero, the relationship between f and f^* is

$$f^* = fe^{qt}$$

146

If μ^* and σ^* are the expected return and volatility of f^*, Ito's lemma shows that

$$\mu^* = \mu + q$$

$$\sigma^* = \sigma$$

From equation (21.9)

$$\mu^* - r = \lambda \sigma^*$$

It follows that

$$\mu + q - r = \lambda \sigma$$

21.8. As suggested in the hint, we form two new securities f^* and g^* which are the same as f and g at time zero, but are such that income from f is reinvested in f and income from g is reinvested in g. By construction f^* and g^* are non-income producing and their values at time t are related to f and g by

$$f^* = f e^{q_f t} \qquad g^* = g e^{q_g t}$$

From Ito's lemma, the securities g and g^* have the same volatility. We can apply the analysis given in Section 21.3 to f^* and g^* so that from equation (21.15)

$$f_0^* = g_0^* E_g \left(\frac{f_T^*}{g_T^*} \right)$$

or

$$f_0 = g_0 E_g \left(\frac{f_T e^{q_f T}}{g_T e^{q_g T}} \right)$$

or

$$f_0 = g_0 e^{(q_f - q_g)T} E_g \left(\frac{f_T}{g_T} \right)$$

21.9. This statement implies that the interest rate has a negative market price of risk. Since bond prices and interest rates are negatively correlated, the statement implies that the market price of risk for a bond price is positive. The statement is reasonable. When interest rates increase, there is a tendency for the stock market to decrease. This implies that interest rates have negative systematic risk, or equivalently that bond prices have positive systematic risk.

21.10 (a) In the traditional risk-neutral world the process followed by S is

$$dS = (r - q)S \, dt + \sigma_S S \, dz$$

where r is the instantaneous risk-free rate. The market price of dz-risk is zero.

(b) In the traditional risk-neutral world for currency B the process is

$$dS = (r - q + \rho_{QS}\sigma_S\sigma_Q)S\,dt + \sigma_S S\,dz$$

where Q is the exchange rate (units of A per unit of B), σ_Q is the volatility of Q and ρ_{QS} is the coefficient of correlation between Q and S. The market price of dz-risk is $\rho_{QS}\sigma_Q$

(c) In a world that is forward risk neutral with respect to a zero-coupon bond in currency A maturing at time T

$$dS = (r - q + \sigma_S\sigma_P)S\,dt + \sigma_S S\,dz$$

where σ_P is the bond price volatility. The market price of dz-risk is σ_P

(d) In a world that is forward risk neutral with respect to a zero-coupon bond in currency B maturing at time T

$$dS = (r - q + \sigma_S\sigma_P + \rho_{FS}\sigma_S\sigma_F)S\,dt + \sigma_S S\,dz$$

where F is the forward exchange rate, σ_F is the volatility of F (units of A per unit of B, and ρ_{FS} is the correlation between F and S. The market price of dz-risk is $\sigma_P + \rho_{FS}\sigma_F$.

21.11. Define

$P(t,T)$: Price in yen at time t of a bond paying 1 yen at time T

$E_T(\cdot)$: Expectation in world that is forward risk neutral with respect to $P(t,T)$

F: Dollar forward price of gold for a contract maturing at time T

F_0: Value of F at time zero

σ_F: Volatility of F

G: Forward exchange rate (dollars per yen)

σ_G: Volatility of G

We assume that S_T is lognormal. We can work in a world that is forward risk neutral with respect to $P(t,T)$ to get the value of the call as

$$P(0,T)[E_T(S_T)N(d_1) - N(d_2)]$$

where

$$d_1 = \frac{\ln[E_T(S_T)/K] + \sigma_F^2 T/2}{\sigma_F\sqrt{T}}$$

$$d_2 = \frac{\ln[E_T(S_T)/K] - \sigma_F^2 T/2}{\sigma_F\sqrt{T}}$$

The expected gold price in a world that is forward risk-neutral with respect to a zero-coupon dollar bond maturing at time T is F_0. It follows from equation (21.36) that

$$E_T(S_T) = F_0 e^{\rho\sigma_F\sigma_G T}$$

Hence the option price, measured in yen, is

$$P(0,T)[F_0 e^{\rho \sigma_F \sigma_G T} N(d_1) - K N(d_2)]$$

where

$$d_1 = \frac{\ln[F_0 e^{\rho \sigma_F \sigma_G T}/K] + \sigma_F^2 T/2}{\sigma_F \sqrt{T}}$$

$$d_2 = \frac{\ln[F_0 e^{\rho \sigma_F \sigma_G T}/K] - \sigma_F^2 T/2}{\sigma_F \sqrt{T}}$$

21.12. Equation (21A.4) in Appendix 21A gives:

$$d \ln f = \left[r + \sum_{i=1}^{n} (\lambda_i \sigma_{f,i} - \sigma_{f,i}^2/2) \right] dt + \sum_{i=1}^{n} \sigma_{f,i} dz_i$$

$$d \ln g = \left[r + \sum_{i=1}^{n} (\lambda_i \sigma_{g,i} - \sigma_{g,i}^2/2) \right] dt + \sum_{i=1}^{n} \sigma_{g,i} dz_i$$

so that

$$d \ln \frac{f}{g} = d(\ln f - \ln g) = \left[\sum_{i=1}^{n} (\lambda_i \sigma_{f,i} - \lambda_i \sigma_{g,i} - \sigma_{f,i}^2/2 + \sigma_{g,i}^2/2) \right] dt + \sum_{i=1}^{n} (\sigma_{f,i} - \sigma_{g,i}) dz_i$$

Applying Ito's lemma again

$$d\frac{f}{g} = \frac{f}{g} \left[\sum_{i=1}^{n} (\lambda_i \sigma_{f,i} - \lambda_i \sigma_{g,i} - \sigma_{f,i}^2/2 + \sigma_{g,i}^2/2) + (\sigma_{f,i} - \sigma_{g,i})^2 \right] dt + \frac{f}{g} \sum_{i=1}^{n} (\sigma_{f,i} - \sigma_{g,i}) dz_i$$

When $\lambda_i = \sigma_{g,i}$ the coefficient of dt is zero and f/g is a martingale.

21.13. Consider the case where v depends on m traded securities f_i, f_2, ..., f_m and the ith component of the volatility of f_j is $\sigma_{i,j}$. With the notation in Section 21.7 when the numeraire changes from g to h the expected growth rate of f_j changes by

$$\sum_{i=1}^{n} (\sigma_{h,i} - \sigma_{g,i}) \sigma_{i,j}$$

Equation (21A.5) in Appendix 21A shows that the drift rate v changes by

$$\sum_{j=1}^{m} \frac{\partial v}{\partial f_j} \sum_{i=1}^{n} (\sigma_{h,i} - \sigma_{g,i}) \sigma_{i,j} f_j$$

The ith component of the volatility of v, $\sigma_{v,i}$ is from equation (21A.5) given by

$$v\sigma_{v,i} = \sum_{j=1}^{m} \frac{\partial v}{\partial f_j}\sigma_{i,j}f_j$$

so that the drift rate of v changes by

$$\sum_{i=1}^{n}(\sigma_{h,i} - \sigma_{g,i})v\sigma_{v,i}$$

This is the same as saying that the growth rate of v changes by

$$\sum_{i=1}^{n}(\sigma_{h,i} - \sigma_{g,i})\sigma_{v,i}$$

and proves equation (21.33).

21.14. Equation (21A.4) in Appendix 21A gives:

$$d\ln h = \ldots + \sum_{i=1}^{n}\sigma_{h,i}dz_i$$

$$d\ln g = \ldots + \sum_{i=1}^{n}\sigma_{g,i}dz_i$$

so that

$$d\ln\frac{h}{g} = \ldots + \sum_{i=1}^{n}(\sigma_{h,i} - \sigma_{g,i})dz_i$$

Applying Ito's lemma again

$$d\frac{h}{g} = \ldots + \frac{h}{g}\sum_{i=1}^{n}(\sigma_{h,i} - \sigma_{g,i})dz_i$$

This proves the result.

21.15. Define g^* as the money market account in currency Y denominated in currency Y. Then

$$dh = r_X h\,dt$$
$$dg^* = r_Y g^*\,dt$$

where r_X and r_Y are the risk-free rates in currencies X and Y. We suppose that the exchange rate S follows the process

$$dS = \ldots + \sigma_S S\,dz_s$$

Because $g = g^*/S$, $h/g = Sh/g^*$. From equation (21A.3)

$$d\left(\frac{Sh}{g^*}\right) = \ldots + \frac{h}{g^*}\sigma_S S\,dz_s$$

It follows that

$$d\frac{h}{g} = \ldots + \sigma_S\frac{h}{g}dz_s$$

This proves the required result.

CHAPTER 22
Interest Rate Derivatives:
The Standard Market Models

22.1. An amount
$$\$20,000,000 \times 0.02 \times 0.25 = \$100,000$$
would be paid out 3 months later.

22.2. A swaption is an option to enter into an interest rate swap at a certain time in the future with a certain fixed rate being used. An interest rate swap can be regarded as the exchange of a fixed-rate bond for a floating-rate bond. A swaption is therefore the option to exchange a fixed-rate bond for a floating-rate bond. The floating-rate bond will be worth its face value at the beginning of the life of the swap. The swaption is therefore an option on a fixed-rate bond with the strike price equal to the face value of the bond.

22.3 In this case, $F_0 = (125 - 10)e^{0.1 \times 1} = 127.09$, $K = 110$, $r = 0.1$, $\sigma = 0.08$, and $T = 1.0$.

$$d_1 = \frac{\ln(127.09/110) + (0.08^2/2)}{0.08} = 1.8456$$
$$d_2 = d_1 - 0.08 = 1.7656$$

The value of the put option is

$$110e^{-0.1}N(-1.7656) - 115N(-1.8456) = 0.12$$

or \$0.12.

22.4. The value of the derivative is $100R_0 P(0,5)$ where $P(0,5)$ is the value of a five-year zero-coupon bond today and R_0 is the forward rate for a one-year period starting in four years, expressed with annual compounding. If the payoff is made in four years the value is $100(R_0 + c)P(0,4)$ where c is the convexity adjustment given by equation (22.16):

$$c = 5R_0^2 \sigma_R^2/(1 + R_0)$$

If the payoff is made in six years the value is $100(R_0 - c)P(0,6)$.

22.5. (a) A convexity adjustment is necessary for the swap rate
(b) No convexity or timing adjustments are necessary.

22.6. When spot volatilities are used to value a cap, a different volatility is used to value each caplet. When flat volatilities are used, the same volatility is used to value each caplet within a given cap. Spot volatilities are a function of the maturity of the caplet. Flat volatilities are a function of the maturity of the cap.

22.7. In this case $L = 1000$, $\delta_k = 0.25$, $F_k = 0.12$, $R_K = 0.13$, $r = 0.115$, $\sigma_k = 0.12$, $t_k = 1.25$, $P(0, t_{k+1}) = 0.8416$.

$$L\delta_k = 250$$

$$d_1 = \frac{\ln(0.12/0.13) + 0.12^2 \times 1.25/2}{0.12\sqrt{1.25}} = -0.5295$$

$$d_2 = -0.5295 - 0.12\sqrt{1.25} = -0.6637$$

The value of the option is

$$250 \times 0.8416 \times [0.12N(-0.5295) - 0.13N(-0.6637)]$$

$$= 0.59$$

or $0.59.

22.8. The implied volatility measures the standard deviation of the logarithm of the bond price at the maturity of the option divided by the square root of the time to maturity. In the case of a five year option on a ten year bond, the bond has five years left at option maturity. In the case of a nine year option on a ten year bond it has one year left. The standard deviation of a one year bond price observed in nine years can be normally be expected to be considerably less than that of a five year bond price observed in five years. (See Figure 22.1.) We would therefore expect the price to be too high.

22.9. The present value of the principal in the four year bond is $100e^{-4 \times 0.1} = 67.032$. The present value of the coupons is, therefore, $102 - 67.032 = 34.968$. This means that the forward price of the five-year bond is

$$(105 - 34.968)e^{4 \times 0.1} = 104.475$$

The parameters in Black's model are therefore $F_0 = 104.475$, $K = 100$, $r = 0.1$, $T = 4$, and $\sigma = 0.02$.

$$d_1 = \frac{\ln 1.04475 + 0.5 \times 0.02^2 \times 4}{0.02\sqrt{4}} = 1.1144$$

$$d_2 = d_1 - 0.02\sqrt{4} = 1.0744$$

The price of the European call is

$$e^{-0.1 \times 4}[104.475N(1.1144) - 100N(1.0744)] = 3.19$$

or $3.19.

22.10. The option should be valued using Black's model in equations (22.1) and (22.2) with the bond price volatility being

$$4.2 \times 0.07 \times 0.22 = 0.0647$$

or 6.47%.

22.11. A 5-year zero-cost collar where the strike price of the cap equals the strike price of the floor is the same as an interest rate swap agreement to receive floating and pay a fixed rate equal to the strike price. The common strike price is the swap rate. Note that the swap is actually a forward swap that excludes the first exchange. (See footnote 2 of Chapter 22.)

22.12. There are two way of expressing the put–call parity relationship for bond options. The first is in terms of bond prices:

$$c + I + Ke^{-RT} = p + B$$

where c is the price of a European call option, p is the price of the corresponding European put option, I is the present value of the bond coupon payments during the life of the option, K is the strike price, T is the time to maturity, B is the bond price, and R is the risk-free interest rate for a maturity equal to the life of the options. To prove this we can consider two portfolios. The first consists of a European put option plus the bond; the second consists of the European call option, and an amount of cash equal to the present value of the coupons plus the present value of the strike price. Both can be seen to be worth the same at the maturity of the options.
The second way of expressing the put–call parity relationship is

$$c + Ke^{-RT} = p + F_0 e^{-RT}$$

where F_0 is the forward bond price. This can also be proved by considering two portfolios. The first consists of a European put option plus a forward contract on the bond plus the present value of the forward price; the second consists of a European call option plus the present value of the strike price. Both can be seen to be worth the same at the maturity of the options.

22.13. The put–call parity relationship for European swap options is

$$c + V = p$$

where c is the value of a call option to pay a fixed rate of s_K and receive floating, p is the value of a put option to receive a fixed rate of s_K and pay floating, and V is the value of the forward swap underlying the swap option where s_K is received and floating is paid. This can be proved by considering two portfolios. The first consists of the put option; the second consists of the call option and the swap. Suppose that the actual swap rate at the maturity of the options is greater than s_K. The call will be exercised and the put will not be exercised. Both portfolios are then worth zero. Suppose next that the actual swap rate at the maturity of the options is less than s_K. The put option is exercised and the call option is not exercised. Both portfolios are equivalent to a swap where s_K is received and floating is paid. In all states of the world the two portfolios are worth the same at time T. They must therefore be worth the same today. This proves the result.

22.14. Suppose that the cap and floor have the same strike price and the same time to maturity. The following put–call parity relationship must hold:

$$\text{cap} + \text{swap} = \text{floor}$$

where the swap is an agreement to receive the cap rate and pay floating over the whole life of the cap/floor. If the implied Black volatilities for the cap equals that for the floor, the Black formulas show that this relationship holds. In other circumstances it does not hold and there is an arbitrage opportunity. The broker quotes in Table 22.1 do not present an arbitrage opportunity because the cap offer is always higher than the floor bid and the floor offer is always higher than the cap bid.

22.15. Yes. If a discount bond price at some future time is lognormal, there is some chance that the price will be above par. This in turn implies that the yield to maturity on the bond is negative.

22.16. There are two differences. The discounting is done over a 1.0-year period instead of over a 1.25-year period. Also a convexity adjustment to the forward rate is necessary. From equation (22.16) the convexity adjustment is:

$$\frac{0.07^2 \times 0.2^2 \times 0.25 \times 1}{1 + 0.25 \times 0.07} = 0.00005$$

or about half a basis point.
In the formula for the caplet we set $F_k = 0.07005$ instead of 0.07. This means that $d_1 = -0.5642$ and $d_2 = -0.7642$. With continuous compounding the 15-month rate is 6.5% and the forward rate between 12 and 15 months is 6.94%. The 12 month rate is therefore 6.39% The caplet price becomes

$$0.25 \times 10,000e^{-0.0639 \times 1.0}[0.07005N(-0.5642) - 0.08N(-0.7642)] = 5.31$$

or \$5.31.

22.17 The convexity adjustment discussed in Section 20.11 leads to the instrument being worth an amount slightly different from zero. Define $G(y)$ as the value as seen in five years of a two-year bond with a coupon of 10% as a function of its yield.

$$G(y) = \frac{0.1}{1 + y} + \frac{1.1}{(1 + y)^2}$$

$$G'(y) = -\frac{0.1}{(1+y)^2} - \frac{2.2}{(1+y)^3}$$

$$G''(y) = \frac{0.2}{(1+y)^3} + \frac{6.6}{(1+y)^4}$$

It follows that $G'(0.1) = -1.7355$ and $G''(0.1) = 4.6582$ and the convexity adjustment that must be made for the two-year swap- rate is

$$0.5 \times 0.1^2 \times 0.2^2 \times 5 \times \frac{4.6582}{1.7355} = 0.00268$$

We can therefore value the instrument on the assumption that the swap rate will be 10.268% in five years. The value of the instrument is

$$\frac{0.268}{1.1^5} = 0.167$$

or $0.167.

22.18. In this case we have to make a timing adjustment as well as a convexity adjustment to the forward swap rate. For (a) equation (22.18) shows that the timing adjustment involves multiplying the swap rate by

$$\exp\left[-\frac{0.8 \times 0.20 \times 0.20 \times 0.1 \times 5}{1 + 0.1}\right] = 0.9856$$

so that it becomes $10.268 \times 0.9856 = 10.120$. The value of the instrument is

$$\frac{0.120}{1.1^5} = 0.075$$

or $0.075.
For (b) equation (22.18) shows that the timing adjustment involves multiplying the swap rate by

$$\exp\left[-\frac{0.95 \times 0.2 \times 0.2 \times 0.1 \times 2 \times 5}{1 + 0.1}\right] = 0.9627$$

so that it becomes $10.268 \times 0.9627 = 9.885$. The value of the instrument is now

$$-\frac{0.115}{1.1^5} = 0.086$$

or $-0.086.

22.19. In equation (22.14), $L = 10,000,000$, $s_K = 0.05$, $s_0 = 0.05$, $d_1 = 0.2\sqrt{4}/2 = 0.2$, $d_2 = -.2$, and

$$A = \frac{1}{1.05^5} + \frac{1}{1.05^6} + \frac{1}{1.05^7} = 2.2404$$

The value of the swap option (in millions of dollars) is

$$10 \times 2.2404[0.05N(0.2) - 0.05N(-0.2)] = 0.178$$

This is the same as the answer given by DerivaGem. (For the purposes of using the DerivaGem software note that the interest rate is 4.879% with continuous compounding for all maturities.)

22.20. The price of the bond at time t is $e^{-R(T-t)}$ where T is the time when the bond matures. Using Ito's lemma the volatility of the bond price is

$$\sigma \frac{\partial}{\partial R} e^{-R(T-t)} = -\sigma(T-t)e^{-R(T-t)}$$

This tends to zero as t approaches T.

22.21. (a) The process for y is

$$dy = \alpha y \, dt + \sigma_y y \, dz$$

The forward bond price is $G(y)$. From Ito's lemma, its process is

$$d[G(y)] = [G'(y)\alpha y + \frac{1}{2}G''(y)\sigma_y^2 y^2] \, dt + G'(y)\sigma_y y \, dz$$

(b) Since the expected growth rate of $G(y)$ is zero

$$G'(y)\alpha y + \frac{1}{2}G''(y)\sigma_y^2 y^2 = 0$$

or

$$\alpha = -\frac{1}{2}\frac{G''(y)}{G'(y)}\sigma_y^2 y$$

(c) Assuming as an approximation that y always equals its initial value of y_0, this shows that the growth rate of y is

$$-\frac{1}{2}\frac{G''(y_0)}{G'(y_0)}\sigma_y^2 y_0$$

The variable y starts at y_0 and ends as y_T. The convexity adjustment to y_0 when we are calculating the expected value of y_T in a world that is forward risk neutral with respect to a zero-coupon bond maturing at time T is approximately $y_0 T$ times this or

$$-\frac{1}{2}\frac{G''(y_0)}{G'(y_0)}\sigma_y^2 y_0^2 T$$

This is consistent with equation (22.15).

22.22. The cash price of the bond is

$$4e^{-0.05 \times 0.50} + 4e^{-0.05 \times 1.00} + \ldots + 4e^{-0.05 \times 10} + 100e^{-0.05 \times 10} = 122.82$$

As there is no accrued interest this is also the quoted price of the bond. The interest paid during the life of the option has a present value of

$$4e^{-0.05 \times 0.5} + 4e^{-0.05 \times 1} + 4e^{-0.05 \times 1.5} + 4e^{-0.05 \times 2} = 15.04$$

The forward price of the bond is therefore

$$(122.82 - 15.04)e^{0.05 \times 2.25} = 120.61$$

The duration of the bond at option maturity is

$$\frac{0.25 \times 4e^{-0.05 \times 0.25} + \ldots + 7.75 \times 4e^{-0.05 \times 7.75} + 7.75 \times 100e^{-0.05 \times 7.75}}{4e^{-0.05 \times 0.25} + 4e^{-0.05 \times 0.75} + \ldots + 4e^{-0.05 \times 7.75} + 100e^{-0.05 \times 7.75}}$$

or 5.99. The bond price volatility is therefore $5.99 \times 0.05 \times 0.2 = 0.0599$. We can therefore value the bond option using Black's model with $F_0 = 120.61$, $P(0, 2.25) = e^{-0.05 \times 2.25} = 0.8936$, $\sigma = 5.99\%$, and $T = 2.25$. When the strike price is the cash price $K = 115$ and the value of the option is 1.78. When the strike price is the quoted price $K = 117$ and the value of the option is 2.41.

22.23. We choose the Caps and Swap Options worksheet of DerivaGem and choose Cap/Floor as the Underlying Type. We enter the 1-, 2-, 3-, 4-, 5-year zero rates as 6%, 6.4%, 6.7%, 6.9%, and 7.0% in the Term Structure table. We enter Semiannual for the Settlement Frequency, 100 for the Principal, 0 for the Start (Years), 5 for the End (Years), 8% for the Cap/Floor Rate, and $3 for the Price. We select Black-European as the Pricing Model and choose the Cap button. We check the Imply Volatility box and Calculate. The implied volatility is 24.79%. We then uncheck Implied Volatility, select Floor, check Imply Breakeven Rate. The floor rate that is calculated is 6.71%. This is the floor rate for which the floor is worth $3. A collar when the floor rate is 6.71% and the cap rate is 8% has zero cost.

22.24. We prove this result by considering two portfolios. The first consists of the swap option to receive s_K; the second consists of the swap option to pay s_K and the forward swap. Suppose that the actual swap rate at the maturity of the options is greater than s_K. The swap option to pay s_K will be exercised and the swap option to receive s_K will not be exercised. Both portfolios are then worth zero since the swap option to pay s_K is neutralized by the forward swap. Suppose next that the actual swap rate at the maturity of the options is less than s_K. The swap option to receive s_K is exercised and the swap option to pay s_K is not exercised. Both portfolios are then equivalent to a swap where s_K is received and floating is paid. In all states of the world the two portfolios are worth the same at time T_1. They must therefore be worth the same today. This proves the result. When s_K equals the current forward swap rate $f = 0$

and $V_1 = V_2$. A swap option to pay fixed is therefore worth the same as a similar swap option to receive fixed when the fixed rate in the swap option is the forward swap rate.

22.25. We choose the Caps and Swap Options worksheet of DerivaGem and choose Swap Option as the Underlying Type. We enter 100 as the Principal, 1 as the Start (Years), 6 as the End (Years), 6% as the Swap Rate, and Semiannual as the Settlement Frequency. We choose Black-European as the pricing model, enter 21% as the Volatility and check the Pay Fixed button. We do not check the Imply Breakeven Rate and Imply Volatility boxes. The value of the swap option is 5.63.

22.26. (a) To calculate flat volatilities from spot volatilities we choose a strike rate and use the spot volatilities to calculate caplet prices. We then sum the caplet prices to obtain cap prices and imply flat volatilities from Black's model. The answer is slightly dependent on the strike price chosen. This procedure ignores any volatility smile in cap pricing. (b) To calculate spot volatilities from flat volatilities the first step is usually to interpolate between the flat volatilities so that we have a flat volatility for each caplet payment date. We choose a strike price and use the flat volatilities to calculate cap prices. By subtracting successive cap prices we obtain caplet prices from which we can imply spot volatilities. The answer is slightly dependent on the strike price chosen. This procedure also ignores any volatility smile in caplet pricing.

CHAPTER 23

Interest Rate Derivatives: Models of the Short Rate

23.1. Equilibrium models usually start with assumptions about economic variables and derive the behavior of interest rates. The initial term structure is an output from the model. In a no-arbitrage model the initial term structure is an input. The behavior of interest rates in a no-arbitrage model is designed to be consistent with the initial term structure.

23.2. If the price of a traded security followed a mean-reverting or path-dependent process there would be a market inefficiency. The short-term interest rate is not the price of a traded security. In other words we cannot trade something whose price is always the short-term interest rate. There is therefore no market inefficiency when the short-term interest rate follows a mean-reverting or path-dependent process. We can trade bonds and other instruments whose prices do depend on the short rate. The prices of these instruments do not follow mean-reverting or path-dependent processes.

23.3. In Vasicek's model the standard deviation stays at 1%. In the Rendleman and Bartter model the standard deviation is proportional to the level of the short rate. When the short rate increases from 4% to 8% the standard deviation increases from 1% to 2%. In the Cox, Ingersoll, and Ross model the standard deviation of the short rate is proportional to the square root of the short rate. When the short rate increases from 4% to 8% the standard deviation of the short rate increases from 1% to 1.414%.

23.4. In a one-factor model there is one source of uncertainty driving all rates. This usually means that in any short period of time all rates move in the same direction (but not necessarily by the same amount). In a two-factor model, there are two sources of uncertainty driving all rates. The first source of uncertainty usually gives rise to a roughly parallel shift in rates. The second gives rise to a twist where long and short rates moves in opposite directions.

23.5. No. The approach in Section 23.4 relies on the argument that, at any given time, all bond prices are moving in the same direction. This is not true when there is more than one factor.

23.6. In Vasicek's model, $a = 0.1$, $b = 0.1$, and $\sigma = 0.02$ so that

$$B(t, t + 10) = \frac{1}{0.1}(1 - e^{-0.1 \times 10}) = 6.32121$$

$$A(t, t+10) = \exp\left[\frac{(6.32121 - 10)(0.1^2 \times 0.1 - 0.0002)}{0.01} - \frac{0.0004 \times 6.32121^2}{0.4}\right]$$

$$= 0.71587$$

The bond price is therefore $0.71587e^{-6.32121 \times 0.1} = 0.38046$

In the Cox, Ingersoll, and Ross model, $a = 0.1$, $b = 0.1$ and $\sigma = 0.02/\sqrt{0.1} = 0.0632$. Also

$$\gamma = \sqrt{a^2 + 2\sigma^2} = 0.13416$$

Define

$$\beta = (\gamma + a)(e^{10\gamma} - 1) + 2\gamma = 0.92992$$

$$B(t, t+10) = \frac{2(e^{10\gamma} - 1)}{\beta} = 6.07650$$

$$A(t, t+10) = \left(\frac{2\gamma e^{5(a+\gamma)}}{\beta}\right)^{2ab/\sigma^2} = 0.69746$$

The bond price is therefore $0.69746e^{-6.07650 \times 0.1} = 0.37986$

23.7. Using the notation in the text, $s = 3$, $T = 1$, $L = 100$, $K = 87$, and

$$\sigma_P = \frac{0.015}{0.1}(1 - e^{-2 \times 0.1})\sqrt{\frac{1 - e^{-2 \times 0.1 \times 1}}{2 \times 0.1}} = 0.025886$$

Also using the formulas in the text $P(0, 1) = 0.94988$, $P(0, 3) = 0.85092$, and $h = 1.14277$ so that the call price is

$$100 \times 0.85092 \times N(1.14277) - 87 \times 0.94988 \times N(1.11688) = 2.59$$

or $2.59.

23.8. The put price is

$$87 \times 0.94988 \times N(-1.11688) - 100 \times 0.85092 \times N(-1.14277) = 0.14$$

Since the underlying bond pays no coupon, put–call parity states that the put price plus the bond price should equal the call price plus the present value of the strike price. The bond price is 85.09 and the present value of the strike price is $87 \times 0.94988 = 82.64$. Put–call parity is therefore satisfied:

$$82.64 + 2.59 = 85.09 + 0.14$$

23.9. The first stage is to calculate the value of r at time 2.1 years which is such that the value of the bond at that time is 99. Denoting this value of r by r^*, we must solve

$$2.5A(2.1, 2.5)e^{-B(2.1, 2.5)r^*} + 102.5A(2.1, 3.0)e^{-B(2.1, 3.0)r^*} = 99$$

160

The solution to this is $r^* = 0.063$. Since

$$2.5A(2.1, 2.5)e^{-B(2.1,2.5)\times 0.063} = 2.43624$$

and

$$102.5A(2.1, 3.0)e^{-B(2.1,3.0)\times 0.063} = 96.56373$$

the call option on the coupon-bearing bond can be decomposed into a call option with a strike price of 2.43624 on a bond that pays off 2.5 at time 2.5 years and a call option with a strike price of 96.56373 on a bond that pays off 102.5 at time 3.0 years. The formulas in the text show that the value of the first option is 0.0015 and the value of the second option is 0.1229. The total value of the option is therefore 0.1244.

23.10. Put-call parity shows that:

$$c + I + PV(K) = p + B_0$$

or

$$p = c + PV(K) - (B_0 - I)$$

where c is the call price, K is the strike price, I is the present value of the coupons, and B_0 is the bond price. In this case $c = 0.1244$, $PV(K) = 99 \times P(0, 2.1) = 85.9093$, $B_0 - I = 2.5 \times P(0, 2.5) + 102.5 \times P(0, 3) = 85.3124$ so that the put price is

$$0.1244 + 85.9093 - 85.3124 = 0.7213$$

23.11. Using the notation in the text $P(0, T) = e^{-0.1 \times 1} = 0.9048$ and $P(0, s) = e^{-0.1 \times 5} = 0.6065$. Also

$$\sigma_P = \frac{0.01}{0.08}(1 - e^{-4 \times 0.08})\sqrt{\frac{1 - e^{-2 \times 0.08 \times 1}}{2 \times 0.08}} = 0.0329$$

and $h - -0.4192$ so that the call price is

$$100 \times 0.6065N(h) - 68 \times 0.9048N(h - \sigma_P) = 0.439$$

23.12. The relevant parameters for the Hull–White model are $a = 0.05$ and $\sigma = 0.015$. Setting $\delta t = 0.4$

$$\hat{B}(2.1, 3) = \frac{B(2.1, 3)}{B(2.1, 2.5)} \times 0.4 = 0.88888$$

Also from equation (23.23), $\hat{A}(2.1, 3) = 0.99925$ The first stage is to calculate the value of R at time 2.1 years which is such that the value of the bond at that time is 99. Denoting this value of R by R^*, we must solve

$$2.5e^{-R^* \times 0.4} + 102.5\hat{A}(2.1, 3)e^{-\hat{B}(2.1,3)R^*} = 99$$

The solution to this for R^* turns out to be 6.626%. The option on the coupon bond is decomposed into an option with a strike price of 96.565 on a zero-coupon bond with a principal of 102.5 and an option with a strike price of 2.435 on a zero-coupon bond with a principal of 2.5. The first option is worth 0.0105 and the second option is worth 0.9341. The total value of the option is therefore 0.9446.

23.13. From Section 23.16 the instantaneous futures rate for the Ho–Lee model is

$$G(0,t) = F(0,t) + \frac{\sigma^2 t^2}{2}$$

so that

$$G_t(0,t) = F_t(0,t) + \sigma^2 t$$

This is the expression for $\theta(t)$ in equation (23.13) showing that $G_t(0,t)$ is indeed the drift of the short rate.

23.14. From Section 23.16 the instantaneous futures rate for the Hull-White model is

$$G(0,t) = F(0,t) + \frac{\sigma^2}{2a^2}(1 - e^{-at})^2$$

so that

$$G_t(0,t) = F_t(0,t) + \frac{\sigma^2}{a}(1 - e^{-at})e^{-at}$$

$$G_t(0,t) + a[G(0,t) - r] = F_t(0,t) + aF(0,t) - ar + \frac{\sigma^2}{a}(1 - e^{-at})e^{-at} + \frac{\sigma^2}{2a}(1 - e^{-at})^2$$

$$= F_t(0,t) + aF(0,t) - ar + \frac{\sigma^2}{2a}(1 - e^{-2at})$$

From equation (23.18) this is the same as the drift of r, $\theta(t) - ar$.

23.15. The time step, δt, is 1 so that $\delta r = 0.015\sqrt{3} = 0.02598$. Also $j_{\max} = 4$ showing that the branching method should change four steps from the center of the tree. With only three steps we never reach the point where the branching changes. The tree is shown in Figure 23.1.

23.16. A two-year zero-coupon bond pays off $100 at the ends of the final branches. At node B it is worth $100e^{-0.12 \times 1} = 88.69$. At node C it is worth $100e^{-0.10 \times 1} = 90.48$. At node D it is worth $100e^{-0.08 \times 1} = 92.31$. It follows that at node A the bond is worth

$$(88.69 \times 0.25 + 90.48 \times 0.5 + 92.31 \times 0.25)e^{-0.1 \times 1} = 81.88$$

or $81.88

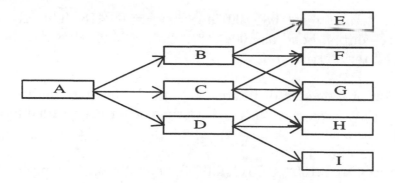

Node	A	B	C	D	E	F	G	H	I
r	10.00%	12.61%	10.01%	7.41%	15.24%	12.64%	10.04%	7.44%	4.84%
p_u	0.1667	0.1429	0.1667	0.1929	0.1217	0.1429	0.1667	0.1929	0.2217
p_m	0.6666	0.6642	0.6666	0.6642	0.6567	0.6642	0.6666	0.6642	0.6567
p_d	0.1667	0.1929	0.1667	0.1429	0.2217	0.1929	0.1667	0.1429	0.1217

Figure 23.1   Tree for Problem 23.15.

23.17. A two-year zero-coupon bond pays off \$100 at time two years. At node B it is worth $100e^{-0.0693\times1} = 93.30$. At node C it is worth $100e^{-0.0520\times1} = 94.93$. At node D it is worth $100e^{-0.0347\times1} = 96.59$. It follows that at node A the bond is worth

$$(93.30 \times 0.167 + 94.93 \times 0.666 + 96.59 \times 0.167)e^{-0.0382\times1} = 91.37$$

or \$91.37. Because $91.37 = 100e^{-0.04512\times2}$, the price of the two-year bond agrees with the initial term structure.

23.18. An 18-month zero-coupon bond pays off \$100 at the final nodes of the tree. At node E it is worth $100e^{-0.088\times0.5} = 95.70$. At node F it is worth $100e^{-0.0648\times0.5} = 96.81$. At node G it is worth $100e^{-0.0477\times0.5} = 97.64$. At node H it is worth $100e^{-0.0351\times0.5} = 98.26$. At node I it is worth $100e^{0.0259\times0.5} = 98.71$. At node B it is worth

$$(0.118 \times 95.70 + 0.654 \times 96.81 + 0.228 \times 97.64)e^{-0.0564\times0.5} = 94.17$$

Similarly at nodes C and D it is worth 95.60 and 96.68. The value at node A is therefore

$$(0.167 \times 94.17 + 0.666 \times 95.60 + 0.167 \times 96.68)e^{-0.0343\times0.5} = 93.92$$

The 18-month zero rate is $0.08 - 0.05e^{-0.18 \times 1.5} = 0.0418$. This gives the price of the 18-month zero-coupon bond as $100e^{-0.0418 \times 1.5} = 93.92$ showing that the tree agrees with the initial term structure.

23.19. The calibration of a one-factor interest rate model involves determining its volatility parameters so that it matches the market prices of actively traded interest rate options as closely as possible.

23.20. The option prices are 0.1302, 0.0814, 0.0580, and 0.0274. The implied Black volatilities are 14.28%, 13.64%, 13.24%, and 12.81%

23.21. When t_2 approaches t_1, $B(t_1, t_2)$ approaches zero and $B(t_1, t_2)/(t_2 - t_1)$ approaches 1.0. The convexity adjustment in equation (23.32) becomes

$$\frac{\sigma^2 B(0,t)^2}{2} = \frac{\sigma^2}{2a^2}(1 - e^{-at})^2$$

where t is the common value of t_1 and t_2. The instantaneous futures rate is therefore

$$F(0,t) + \frac{\sigma^2}{2a^2}(1 - e^{-at})^2$$

From equation (23.27) this is the same as $\alpha(t)$. This is what we would expect since $\alpha(t)$ is the expected short term interest rate in the traditional risk-neutral world and the futures price of a variable equals its expected future spot price in this world.

23.22. From equation (23.14)

$$P(t, t + \delta t) = A(t, t + \delta t)e^{-r(t)\delta t}$$

Also

$$P(t, t + \delta t) = e^{-R(t)\delta t}$$

so that

$$e^{-R(t)\delta t} = A(t, t + \delta t)e^{-r(t)\delta t}$$

or

$$e^{-r(t)(T-t)} = \frac{e^{-R(t)(T-t)}}{A(t, t + \delta t)^{(T-t)/\delta t}}$$

Hence equation (23.15) is true with

$$\hat{A}(t, T) = \frac{A(t, T)}{A(t, t + \delta t)^{(T-t)/\delta t}}$$

or

$$\ln \hat{A}(t, T) = \ln A(t, T) - \frac{T - t}{\delta t} \ln A(t, t + \delta t)$$

164

Substituting for $\ln A(t, T)$ and $\ln A(t, t + \delta t)$ we obtain equation (23.16).

23.23. From equation (23.19)

$$P(t, t + \delta t) = A(t, t + \delta t)e^{-r(t)B(t, t+\delta t)}$$

Also

$$P(t, t + \delta t) = e^{-R(t)\delta t}$$

so that

$$e^{-R(t)\delta t} = A(t, t + \delta t)e^{-r(t)B(t, t+\delta t)}$$

or

$$e^{-r(t)B(t,T)} = \frac{e^{-R(t)B(t,T)\delta t / B(t, t+\delta t)}}{A(t, t + \delta t)^{B(t,T)/B(t, t+\delta t)}}$$

Hence equation (23.22) is true with

$$\hat{B}(t, T) = \frac{B(t, T)\delta t}{B(t, t + \delta t}$$

and

$$\hat{A}(t, T) = \frac{A(t, T)}{A(t, t + \delta t)^{B(t,T)/B(t, t+\delta t)}}$$

or

$$\ln \hat{A}(t, T) = \ln A(t, T) - \frac{B(t, T)}{B(t, t + \delta t)} \ln A(t, t + \delta t)$$

Substituting for $\ln A(t, T)$ and $\ln A(t, t + \delta t)$ we obtain equation (23.23).

CHAPTER 24
Interest Rate Derivatives:
More Advanced Models

24.1. (a) The expected growth rate of $P(t, T)$ in a risk-neutral world is r. Using Ito's lemma to determine the volatility components we get

$$dP(t, T) = rP(t, T)\, dt + \frac{\partial P(t, T)}{\partial r}\sigma_1\, dz_1 + \frac{\partial P(t, T)}{\partial u}\sigma_2\, dz_2$$

From equation (24.2) this becomes

$$dP(t, T) = rP(t, T)\, dt - B(t, T)P(t, T)\sigma_1\, dz_1 - C(t, T)P(t, T)\sigma_2\, dz_2$$

(b) Define $R(t, T)$ as the bond yield. Since

$$R(t, T) = -\frac{1}{T - t}\ln[P(t, T)]$$

we can use Ito's lemma (or Taylor Series expansion) to obtain

$$dR(t, T) = -\frac{1}{T - t}\left[r - B(t, T)^2\sigma_1^2/2 - C(t, T)^2\sigma_2^2/2 - \rho B(t, T)C(t, T)\sigma_1\sigma_2\right] dt$$

$$+ \frac{1}{T - t}B(t, T)\sigma_1\, dz_1 + \frac{1}{T - t}C(t, T)\sigma_2\, dz_2$$

(c) Define $B(t, t + T_1)$ as B_1, $B(t, t + T_2)$ as B_2, $C(t, t + T_1)$ as C_1, and $C(t, t + T_2)$ as C_2. The correlation between the T_2 and T_1 rates are

$$\frac{B_1 B_2\sigma_1^2 + C_1 C_2\sigma_2^2 + \rho B_1 C_2\sigma_1\sigma_2 + \rho B_2 C_1\sigma_1\sigma_2}{\sqrt{(B_1^2\sigma_1^2 + C_1^2\sigma_2^2 + 2\rho B_1 C_1\sigma_1\sigma_2)(B_2^2\sigma_1^2 + C_2^2\sigma_2^2 + 2\rho B_2 C_2\sigma_1\sigma_2)}}$$

For the data in Figure 24.1 of the text

$$B(t, t + 0.25) = 1 - e^{-0.25} = 0.2212$$

$$B(t, t + 10) = 1 - e^{-10} = 0.99955$$

$$C(t, t + 0.25) = \frac{1}{0.9}e^{-0.25} - \frac{1}{0.1 \times 0.9}e^{-0.1 \times 0.25} + 10 = 0.02856$$

$$C(t, t + 10) = \frac{1}{0.9}e^{-10} - \frac{1}{0.1 \times 0.9}e^{-0.1 \times 10} + 10 = 5.9125$$

The correlation between the three-month rate and the ten-year rate can be calculated from the above formula as 0.765.

24.2. The forward bond price between T and $T + \tau$ as seen at time t is

$$\frac{P(t, T + \tau)}{P(t, T)}$$

The forward interest rate between T and $T + \tau$ is therefore

$$\frac{1}{\tau} \ln \left(\frac{P(t, T + \tau)}{P(t, T)} \right)$$

or

$$\frac{1}{\tau} [\ln P(t, T + \tau) - \ln P(t, T)]$$

Taking limits the instantaneous forward rate for maturity T, $F(t,T)$ is given by

$$F(t, T) = -\frac{\partial \ln P(t, T)}{\partial T}$$

From equation (24.2) this is

$$-\frac{\partial}{\partial T} [\ln A(t, T) - B(t, T)r - C(t, T)u]$$

in the situation we are considering. This means that the process followed by the forward rate is:

$$dF(t, T) = \ldots + \frac{\partial B(t, T)}{\partial T} \sigma_1 dz_1 + \frac{\partial C(t, T)}{\partial T} \sigma_2 dz_2$$

24.3. In a Markov model the expected change and volatility of the short rate at time t depend only on the value of the short rate at time t. In a non-Markov model they depend on the history of the short rate prior to time t.

24.4. Equation (24.3) becomes

$$dP(t, T) = r(t)P(t, T)\, dt + \sum_k v_k(t, T, \Omega_t)P(t, T)\, dz_k$$

so that

$$d\ln[P(t, T_1)] = \left[r(t) - \sum_k \frac{v_k(t, T_1, \Omega_t)^2}{2} \right] dt + \sum_k v_k(t, T_1, \Omega_t)\, dz_k(t)$$

and

$$d \ln[P(t, T_2)] = \left[r(t) - \sum_k \frac{v_k(t, T_2, \Omega_t)^2}{2} \right] dt + v_k(t, T_2, \Omega_t) \, dz_k(t)$$

From equation (24.4)

$$df(t, T_1, T_2) = \frac{\sum_k [v_k(t, T_2, \Omega_t)^2 - v_k(t, T_1, \Omega_t)^2]}{2(T_2 - T_1)} dt + \sum_k \frac{v_k(t, T_1, \Omega_t) - v_k(t, T_2, \Omega_t)}{T_2 - T_1} dz_k(t)$$

Putting $T_1 = T$ and $T_2 = T + \delta t$ and taking limits as δt tends to zero this becomes

$$dF(t, T) = \sum_k \left[v_k(t, T, \Omega_t) \frac{\partial v_k(t, T, \Omega_t)}{\partial T} \right] dt - \sum_k \left[\frac{\partial v_k(t, T, \Omega_t)}{\partial T} \right] dz_k(t)$$

Using $v_k(t, t, \Omega_t) = 0$

$$v_k(t, T, \Omega_t) = \int_t^T \frac{\partial v_k(t, \tau, \Omega_t)}{\partial \tau} d\tau$$

The result in equation (24.10) follows by substituting

$$s_k(t, T, \Omega_t) = \frac{\partial v_k(t, T, \Omega_t)}{\partial T}$$

24.5. Using the notation in Section 24.2, when s is constant, $v_T(t, T) = s$, $v_{TT}(t, T) = 0$. Integrating $v_T(t, T)$

$$v(t, T) = sT + \alpha(t)$$

for some function α. Using the fact that $v(T, T) = 0$, we must have

$$v(t, T) = s(T - t)$$

Substituting into equation (24.9) we get

$$dr = F_t(0, t) \, dt + \left[\int_0^t s^2 d\tau \right] dt + s \, dz(t)$$

or

$$dr = [F_t(0, t) + s^2 t] \, dt + s \, dz$$

This is the Ho-Lee model as given by equations (23.12) and (23.13).

24.6. Using the notation in Section 24.2, when $v_T(t, T) = s(t, T) = \sigma e^{-a(T-t)}$ so that $v_{TT}(t, T) = -a\sigma e^{-a(T-t)}$. Integrating $v_T(t, T)$

$$v(t, T) = -\frac{1}{a} \sigma e^{-a(T-t)} + \alpha(t)$$

168

for some function α. Using the fact that $v(T,T) = 0$, we must have

$$v(t,T) = \frac{\sigma}{a}[1 - e^{-a(T-t)}] = \sigma B(t,T)$$

In this case

$$v_{tt}(\tau, t) = -a v_t(\tau, t)$$

so that combining equation (24.9) with equation (24.8), we get

$$dr = F_t(0,t)\, dt + \left\{ \int_0^t [v(\tau,t)v_{tt}(\tau,t) + v_t(\tau,t)^2]d\tau \right\} dt + a[F(0,t) - r(t)]\, dt$$

$$+ a\left[\int_0^t v(\tau,t)v_t(\tau,t)d\tau \right] dt + \sigma\, dz(t)$$

Substituting for $v(t,T)$, this reduces to

$$dr = F_t(0,t)\, dt + a[F(0,t) - r(t)]\, dt + \sigma^2 \left[\int_0^t e^{-2a(t-\tau)}\, d\tau \right] dt + \sigma\, dz(t)$$

so that

$$dr = F_t(0,t)\, dt + a[F(0,t) - r(t)]\, dt + \frac{\sigma^2}{2a}[1 - e^{-2at}]\, dt + \sigma\, dz(t)$$

This is the result in equations (23.17) and (23.18).

24.7. When $v(t,T) = x(t)[y(T) - y(t)]$, the component of the drift in the second term in equation (24.9) is a function only of t. Also

$$v_{tt}(\tau, t) = x(\tau)y_{tt}(t)$$

and

$$v_t(\tau, t) = x(\tau)y_t(t)$$

so that, using equation (24.8), the third term becomes

$$\frac{y_{tt}(t)}{y_t(t)} \left[r(t) - F(0,t) - \int_0^t v(\tau,t)v_t(\tau,t)d\tau \right] dt$$

This is a function only of r and t. The coefficient of $dz(t)$ is a function only of t. It follows that the process for r is Markov.

24.8. A ratchet cap tends to provide relatively low payoffs if a high (low) interest rate at one reset date is followed by a high (low) interest rate at the next reset date. High payoffs occur when a low interest rate is followed by a high interest rate. As the number of factors increase, the correlation between successive forward rates declines and there is a greater chance that a low interest rate will be followed by a high interest rate.

24.9. Equation (24.14) can be written

$$dF_k(t) = \zeta_k(t)F_k(t) \sum_{i=m(t)}^{k} \frac{\delta_i F_i(t)\zeta_i(t)}{1 + \delta_i F_i(t)} + \zeta_k(t)F_k(t)\,dz$$

As δ_i tends to zero, $\zeta_i(t)F_i(t)$ becomes the standard deviation of the instantaneous t_i-maturity forward rate at time t. Using the notation of equation (24.7) this is $s(t, t_i)$. As δ_i tends to zero

$$\sum_{i=m(t)}^{k} \frac{\delta_i F_i(t)\zeta_i(t)}{1 + \delta_i F_i(t)}$$

tends to

$$\int_{\tau=t}^{t_k} s(t, \tau)\,d\tau$$

Equation (24.14) therefore becomes

$$dF_k(t) = s(t, t_k) \int_{\tau=t}^{t_k} s(t, \tau)\,d\tau + s(t, t_k)\,dz$$

This is the HJM result in equation (24.7)

24.10. In a ratchet cap, the cap rate equals the previous reset rate, R, plus a spread. In the notation of the text it is $R_j + s$. In a sticky cap the cap rate equal the previous capped rate plus a spread. In the notation of the text it is $\min(R_j, K_j) + s$. The cap rate in a ratchet cap is always at least a great as that in a sticky cap. Since the value of a cap is a decreasing function of the cap rate, it follows that a sticky cap is more expensive.

24.11. When prepayments increase, the principal is received sooner. This increases the value of a PO. When prepayments increase, less interest is received. This decreases the value of an IO.

24.12. A bond yield is the discount rate that causes the bond's price to equal the market price. The same discount rate is used for all maturities. An OAS is the parallel shift to the Treasury zero curve that causes the price of an instrument such as a mortgage-backed security to equal its market price.

24.13. When there are p factors equation (24.11) becomes

$$dF_k = \sum_{q=1}^{p} \zeta_{k,q} F_k(t) dz_q$$

Using equation (21.33), equation (24.12) becomes

$$dF_k(t) = \sum_{q=1}^{p} \zeta_{k,q}[v_{m(t),q} - v_{k+1,q}]F_k(t)dt + \sum_{q=1}^{p} \zeta_{k,q}(F_k(t)dz_q$$

Equation coefficients of dz_q in

$$\ln P(t, t_i) - \ln P(t, t_{i+1}) = \ln[1 + \delta_i F_i(t)]$$

equation (24.13) becomes

$$v_{i,q}(t) - v_{i+1,q}(t) = \frac{\delta_i F_i(t)\zeta_{i,q}}{1 + \delta_i F_i(t)}$$

Equation (24.19) follows.

24.14. From the equations on page 582

$$s(t) = \frac{P(t, T_0) - P(t, T_N)}{\sum_{i=0}^{N-1} \tau_i P(t, T_{i+1})}$$

and

$$\frac{P(t, T_i)}{P(t, T_0)} = \prod_{j=0}^{i-1} \frac{1}{1 + \tau_j G_j(t)}$$

so that

$$s(t) = \frac{1 - \prod_{j=0}^{N-1} \frac{1}{1+\tau_j G_j(t)}}{\sum_{i=0}^{N-1} \tau_i \prod_{j=0}^{i} \frac{1}{1+\tau_j G_j(t)}}$$

(We employ the convention that empty sums equal zero and empty products equal one.) Equivalently

$$s(t) = \frac{\prod_{j=0}^{N-1}[1 + \tau_j G_j(t)] - 1}{\sum_{i=0}^{N-1} \tau_i \prod_{j=i+1}^{N-1}[1 + \tau_j G_j(t)]}$$

or

$$\ln s(t) = \ln\left\{\prod_{j=0}^{N-1}[1 + \tau_j G_j(t)] - 1\right\} - \ln\left\{\sum_{i=0}^{N-1} \tau_i \prod_{j=i+1}^{N-1}[1 + \tau_j G_j(t)]\right\}$$

so that

$$\frac{1}{s(t)}\frac{\partial s(t)}{\partial G_k(t)} = \frac{\tau_k \gamma_k(t)}{1 + \tau_k G_k(t)}$$

where

$$\gamma_k(t) = \frac{\prod_{j=0}^{N-1}[1 + \tau_j G_j(t)]}{\prod_{j=0}^{N-1}[1 + \tau_j G_j(t)] - 1} - \frac{\sum_{i=0}^{k-1} \tau_i \prod_{j=i+1}^{N-1}[1 + \tau_j G_j(t)]}{\sum_{i=0}^{N-1} \tau_i \prod_{j=i+1}^{N-1}[1 + \tau_j G_j(t)]}$$

171

From Ito's lemma the qth component of the volatility of $s(t)$ is

$$\sum_{k=0}^{N-1} \frac{1}{s(t)} \frac{\partial s(t)}{\partial G_k(t)} \beta_{k,q}(t) G_k(t)$$

or

$$\sum_{k=0}^{N-1} \frac{\tau_k \beta_{k,q}(t) G_k(t) \gamma_k(t)}{1 + \tau_k G_k(t)}$$

The variance rate of $s(t)$ is therefore

$$V(t) = \sum_{q=1}^{p} \left[\sum_{k=0}^{N-1} \frac{\tau_k \beta_{k,q}(t) G_k(t) \gamma_k(t)}{1 + \tau_k G_k(t)} \right]^2$$

24.15.

$$1 + \tau_j G_j(t) = \prod_{m=1}^{M} [1 + \tau_{j,m} G_{j,m}(t)]$$

so that

$$\ln[1 + \tau_j G_j(t)] = \sum_{m=1}^{M} \ln[1 + \tau_{j,m} G_{j,m}(t)]$$

Equating coefficients of dz_q

$$\frac{\beta_{k,q}(t) G_j(t)}{1 + \tau_j G_j(t)} = \sum_{m=1}^{M} \frac{\tau_{j,m} \beta_{k,m,q}(t) G_{j,m}(t)}{1 + \tau_{j,m} G_{j,m}(t)}$$

If we assume that $G_{j,m}(t) = G_{j,m}(0)$ for the purposes of calculating the swap volatility we see from equation (24.21) that the volatility becomes

$$\sqrt{\frac{1}{T_0} \int_{t=0}^{T_0} \sum_{q=1}^{p} \left[\sum_{k=n}^{N-1} \sum_{m=1}^{M} \frac{\tau_{k,m} \beta_{k,m,q}(t) G_{k,m}(0) \gamma_k(0)}{1 + \tau_{k,m} G_{k,m}(0)} \right]^2 dt}$$

This is equation (24.22).

CHAPTER 25
Swaps Revisited

25.1. The target payment dates are July 11, 2001; January 11, 2002; July 11, 2002; January 11, 2003; July 11, 2003; January 11, 2004; July 11, 2004; January 11, 2005; July 11, 2005; January 11, 2006. These occur on Wed, Fri, Thurs, Sat, Fri, Sun, Sun, Tues, Mon, and Wed respectively with no holidays. The actual payment dates are therefore July 11, 2001; January 11, 2002; July 11, 2002; January 13, 2003; July 11, 2003; January 12, 2004; July 12, 2004; January 11, 2005; July 11, 2005; January 11, 2006. The fixed rate daycount convention is Actual/365. There are 181 days between January 11, 2001 and July 11, 2001. This means that the fixed payments on July 11, 2001 is

$$\frac{181}{365} \times 0.06 \times 100,000,000 = \$2,975,342$$

Similarly subsequent fixed cash flows are: \$3,024,658, \$2,975,342, \$3,024,658, \$2,975,342, \$3,024,658, \$2,991,781, \$3,024,658, \$2,975,342, \$3,024,658.

25.2. Yes. The swap is the same as one on twice the principal where half the fixed rate is exchanged for the LIBOR rate.

25.3. The final fixed payment is in millions of dollars:

$$[(4 \times 1.0415 + 4) \times 1.0415 + 4] \times 1.0415 + 4 = 17.0238$$

The final floating payment assuming forward rates are realized is

$$[(4.05 \times 1.041 + 4.05) \times 1.041 + 4.05] \times 1.041 + 4.05 = 17.2238$$

The value of the swap is therefore $-0.2000/(1.04^4) = -0.1710$ or $-\$171,000$.

25.4. The value is zero. The receive side is the same as the pay side with the cash flows compounded forward at LIBOR. Compounding cash flows forward at LIBOR does not change their value.

25.5. In theory, a new floating-for-floating swap should involve exchanging LIBOR in one currency for LIBOR in another currency (with no spreads added). In practice, macroeconomic effects give rise to spreads. Financial institutions often adjust the discount rates they use to allow for this. Suppose that USD LIBOR is always exchanged Swiss franc LIBOR plus 15 basis points. Financial institutions would discount USD cash flows at USD LIBOR and Swiss franc cash flows at LIBOR plus 15 basis points. This would ensure that the floating-for-floating swap is valued consistently with the market.

25.6. In this case $y_i = 0.05$, $\sigma_{y,i} = 0.13$, $\tau_i = 0.5$, $F_i = 0.05$, $\sigma_{F,i} = 0.18$, and $\rho_i = 0.7$ for all i. It is still true that $G_i'(y_i) = -437.603$ and $G_i''(y_i) = 2261.23$. Equation (25.3) gives the total convexity/timing adjustment as $0.0000892t_i$ or 0.892 basis points per year until the swap rate is observed. The swap rate in three years should be assumed to be 5.0268%. The value of the swap is $97,282.

25.7. In a plain vanilla swap we can enter into a series of FRAs to exchange the floating cash flows for their values if the "assume forward rates are realized rule" is used. In the case of a compounding swap Section 25.2 shows that we are able to enter into a series of FRAs that exchange the final floating rate cash flow for its value when the "assume forward rates are realized rule" is used. There is no way of entering into FRAs so that the floating-rate cash flows in a LIBOR-in-arrears swap are exchanged for their values when the "assume forward rates are realized rule" is used.

25.8. Suppose that the fixed rate accrues only when the floating reference rate is below R_X and above R_Y where $R_Y < R_X$. In this case the swap is a regular swap plus two series of binary options, one for each day of the life of the swap. Using the notation in the text, the risk-neutral probability that LIBOR will be above R_X on day i is $N(d_2)$ where

$$d_2 = \frac{\ln(F_i/R_X) - \sigma_i^2 t_i^2/2}{\sigma_i \sqrt{t_i}}$$

The probability that it will be below R_Y where $R_Y < R_X$ is $N(-d_2')$ where

$$d_2' = \frac{\ln(F_i/R_Y) - \sigma_i^2 t_i^2/2}{\sigma_i \sqrt{t_i}}$$

From the viewpoint of the party paying fixed, the swap is a regular swap plus binary options. The binary options corresponding to day i have a total value of

$$\frac{QL}{n_2} P(0, s_i)[N(d_2) + N(-d_2')]$$

(This ignores the small timing adjustment mentioned in Section 25.6.)

CHAPTER 26
Credit Risk

26.1. From equation (26.1) the probability of default in the first three years is $1 - e^{-0.005 \times 3}$. The probability of default in the first six years is $1 - e^{-0.008 \times 6}$. The probability of default between years 3 and 6 is therefore $e^{-0.005 \times 3} - e^{-0.008 \times 6} = 0.0320$ or 3.2%.

26.2. The gradients indicate that on average we expect the creditworthiness of a BBB to decline faster than that of a AAA. When a company borrows a floating rate of interest and swaps it to fixed rate of interest, it is, as explained in Chapter 6, subject to rollover risk. The rollover risk is much higher for the BBB than for the AAA. This explains why a BBB often appears to have a comparative advantage (relative to a AAA) in floating-rate markets.

26.3. The risk-neutral default probability is the probability that would exist in a world where all participants are risk-neutral. It can be backed out from bond prices. The real-world probability is the true probability. It can be calculated from historical data. The risk-neutral probability of default is higher. Risk-neutral probabilities of default should be used for valuation. Real-world probabilities of default should be used for scenario analysis.

26.4. The hazard rate, $h(t)$ at time t is defined so that $h(t)\delta t$ is the probability of default between times t and $t + \delta t$ conditional on no default prior to time t. The default probability density $q(t)$ is defined so that $q(t)\delta t$ is the probability of default between times t and $t + \delta t$ as seen at time zero.

26.5. The value of the bond is the expected payoff in a risk-neutral world discounted at the risk-free rate. This is $99e^{-0.06 \times 1} = 93.2347$. Alternatively it is the expected payoff in the real world discounted at the appropriate risk-adjusted rate. If R is the appropriate risk-adjusted rate this is $99.75e^{-R}$. For the two prices to be the same we must have $R = 0.06755$. The excess expected return over the risk-free rate on the bond is 0.755%. This is 15.1% of the excess return of the market over the risk-free rate. Our estimate of the beta of the bond is therefore 0.151.

26.6. In this case $B_1 = 100.381$, $G_1 = 101.927$, $B_2 = 100.553$, $G_2 = 103.762$, $F_1(1) = 103.5$, and $F_2(2) = 103.5$. Also using equation (3.6), $F_2(1) = (103.762 - 3.5/1.025) \times 1.025^2 = 105.4274$. If the claim amount equals the no-default value:

$$\alpha_{11} = \frac{1}{1.025^2}(103.5 - 0.3 \times 103.5) = 68.9590$$

$$\alpha_{12} = \frac{1}{1.025^2}(105.4274 - 0.3 \times 105.4274) = 70.2431$$

$$\alpha_{22} = \frac{1}{1.025^4}(103.5 - 0.3 \times 103.5) = 65.6361$$

Hence

$$p_1 = \frac{101.927 - 100.381}{68.9590} = 0.0224$$

$$p_2 = \frac{103.762 - 100.553 - 0.0224 \times 70.2431}{65.6361} = 0.0249$$

If the claim amount equals the face value plus accrued interest, α_{11} and α_{22} are the same, but

$$\alpha_{12} = \frac{1}{1.025^2}(105.4274 - 0.3 \times 103.5) = 70.7935$$

This means that $p_1 = 0.0224$ as before while

$$p_2 = \frac{103.762 - 100.553 - 0.0224 \times 70.7935}{65.6361} = 0.0247$$

26.7. Suppose company A goes bankrupt when it has a number of outstanding contracts with company B. Netting means that the contracts with a positive value to A are netted against those with a negative value in order to determine how much, if anything, company A owes company B. Company A is not allowed to "cherry pick" by keeping the positive-value contracts and defaulting on the negative-value contracts.

The new transaction will increase the bank's exposure to the counterparty if the contract tends to have a positive value whenever the existing contract has a positive value and a negative value whenever the existing contract has a negative value. However, if the new transaction tends to offset the existing transaction, it is likely to have the incremental effect of reducing credit risk.

26.8. Equation (26.12) gives the relationship between $\beta_{AB}(T)$ and ρ_{AB}. This involves $Q_A(T)$ and $Q_B(T)$. These change as we move from the real world to the risk-neutral world. It follows that the relationship between $\beta_{AB}(T)$ and ρ_{AB} in the real world is not the same as in the risk-neutral world. If $\beta_{AB}(T)$ is the same in the two worlds, ρ_{AB} is not.

26.9. (a) In Credit Risk Plus a credit loss is recognized only when a default occurs. In CreditMetrics it is recognized when there is a credit downgrade as well as when there is a default.

(b) In Credit Risk Plus default correlation arises because the average default rate is uncertain. In CreditMetrics the Gaussian copula model is applied to credit ratings migration and this determines the joint probabilities of two companies defaulting. The correlations in the Gaussian copula model are usually assumed to be the same as the corresponding equity correlations.

26.10. In equation (26.12), $Q_A(2) = 0.2$, $Q_B(2) = 0.15$, and $\rho_{AB} = 0.3$. Also

$$u_A(2) = N^{-1}(0.2) = -0.84162$$

$$u_B(2) = N^{-1}(0.15) = -1.03643$$

$$M(-0.84162, -1.03643, 0.3) = 0.0522$$

$$\beta_{AB}(2) = \frac{0.0522 - 0.2 \times 0.15}{\sqrt{(0.2 - 0.2^2)(0.15 - 0.15^2)}} = 0.156$$

26.11. Suppose that the principal is \$100. The asset swap is structured so that the \$10 is paid initially. After that \$2.50 is paid every six months. In return LIBOR plus a spread is received on the principal of \$100. The present value of the fixed payments is

$$10 + 2.5e^{-0.06 \times 0.5} + 2.5e^{-0.06 \times 1} + \ldots + 2.5e^{-0.06 \times 5} + 100e^{-0.06 \times 5} = 105.3579$$

The spread over LIBOR must therefore have a present value of 5.3579. The present value of \$1 received every six months for five years is 8.5105. The spread received every six months must therefore be $5.3579/8.5105 = \$0.6296$. The asset swap spread is therefore $2 \times 0.6296 = 1.2592\%$ per annum.

26.12. When the claim amount is the no-default value, the loss for a corporate bond arising from a default at time t is

$$v(t)(1 - \hat{R})G$$

where G is the no-default value of the bond at time t. Suppose that the zero-coupon bonds comprising the corporate bond have no-default values at time t of $Z_1, Z_2, \ldots, Z_n$, respectively. The loss from the ith zero-coupon bond arising from a default at time t is

$$v(t)(1 - \hat{R})Z_i$$

The total loss from all the zero-coupon bonds is

$$v(t)(1 - \hat{R}) \sum_i^n Z_i = v(t)(1 - \hat{R})G$$

This shows that the loss arising from a default at time t is the same for the corporate bond as for the portfolio of its constituent zero-coupon bonds. It follows that the value of the corporate bond is the same as the value of its constituent zero-coupon bonds.

When the claim amount is the face value plus accrued interest, the loss for a corporate bond arising from a default at time t is

$$v(t)G - v(t)\hat{R}[L + a(t)]$$

where L is the face value and $a(t)$ is the accrued interest at time t. In general this is not the same as the loss from the sum of the losses on the constituent zero-coupon bonds.

26.13. From matrix multiplication the cumulative percentage probabilities of default are

Initial Rating	1 year	2 year	3 year	4 year	5 year
A	0.70	1.40	2.11	2.82	3.54
B	1.70	3.38	5.03	6.66	8.27
C	3.30	6.49	9.58	12.56	15.45
D	100.00	100.00	100.00	100.00	100.00

These are close to the numbers in Table 26.9.

CHAPTER 27
Credit Derivatives

27.1. The CDS buyer would pay $0.5 \times 0.0060 \times 300,000,000 = \$900,000$ at times 0.5, 1.0, 1.5, 2.0, 2.5, 3.0, 3.5, 4.0 years. An accrual payment of \$300,000 would be required at the time of the default. The payout to the CDS buyer at the time of the default is $0.6 \times 300,000,000 = \$180,000,000$.

27.2. In this case $A(t_i) = 0$ and $e(t_i) = 0$ for all i. Also, $v(t_1) = 0.9324$, $v(t_2) = 0.8694$, and $v(t_3) = 0.8106$, while $u(t_1) = 0.9490$, $u(t_2) = 1.8338$, and $u(t_3) = 2.6589$. From Table 26.5, $p_1 = 0.0224$, $p_2 = 0.0247$, $p_3 = 0.0269$, and $\pi = 0.9260$

$$s = \frac{0.7(0.0224 \times 0.9324 + 0.0247 \times 0.8694 + 0.0269 \times 0.8106)}{0.0224 \times 0.9490 + 0.0247 \times 1.8338 + 0.0269 \times 2.6589 + 0.9260 \times 2.6589} = 0.01733$$

The credit default swap spread is 173.3 basis points.

27.3. In this case $s^* = 0.056 - 0.04 = 0.016$, $\hat{R} = 0.4$, $a = 0.02$, $a^* = 0.014$ so that

$$s = \frac{0.016(1 - 0.4 - 0.02 \times 0.4)}{0.6 \times 1.014} = 0.01557$$

showing that the credit default swap spread is 155.7 basis points.

27.4. In the case of a binary swap the payoff in the event of a default is \$1 per \$1 of principal, not $1 - \hat{R} - A(t)\hat{R}$ per \$1 of principal. The formula is

$$s = \frac{\sum_{i=1}^{n} p_i v(t_i)}{\sum_{i=1}^{n} [u(t_i) + e(t_i)]p_i + \pi u(T)}$$

27.5. The spread for a binary CDS should be approximately $1/(1 - \hat{R})$ time the spread for a regular CDS. When $\hat{R}$ is 0.5, the spread for a binary CDS is about twice that for a regular CDS. When $\hat{R}$ is 0.1, the spread for a binary CDS is about $1/0.9 = 1.111$ times that for a regular CDS. The spread for a regular CDS is approximately the same in both cases. It follows that the spread for a binary CDS when the recovery rate is 50% is about $2/1.111 = 1.8$ times that when the recovery rate is 10%.

27.6. In a first-to-default basket credit default swap a group of reference entities is specified and there is a payoff when the first one defaults. The cost of the insurance provided by a basket CDS decreases as the correlation between the reference entities in the basket increases. To understand why this is so, consider two extremes. When the correlation is zero, the probability of a payoff is much higher than when there is only one reference entity. When the correlation is perfect, there is to all intents and purposes only one reference entity.

27.7. The total return swap receiver receives the return on a bond in exchange for LIBOR plus a spread. It is in the same position as it would be if it had borrowed funds at LIBOR plus a spread from the total return swap payer and bought the bond. However the total return swap payer has less credit risk. It's potential credit loss when the total return swap receiver defaults is the decrease in the value of the bond. If it had lent money to the receiver to buy the bond its potential credit loss would be the face value of the bond. It can therefore offer better financing terms using a total return swap than when lending money in the usual way to enable the receiver to buy the bond.

27.8. In an asset swap the bond's promised payments are swapped for LIBOR plus a spread. In a total return swap the bond's actual payments are swapped for LIBOR plus a spread.

27.9. When default risk is taken into account, the correct price is $e^{-0.01 \times 3} = 0.9704$ times the Black–Scholes price. The Black–Scholes model therefore overstates the value of the option by $(1 - 0.9704)/0.9704$ or 3.05%.

27.10. Assume that defaults happen only at the end of the life of the forward contract. In a default-free world the forward contract is the combination of a long European call and a short European put where the strike price of the options equals the delivery price and the maturity of the options equals the maturity of the forward contract. If the no-default value of the contract is positive at maturity, the call has a positive value and the put is worth zero. The impact of defaults on the forward contract is the same as that on the call. If the no-default value of the contract is negative at maturity, the call has a zero value and the put has a positive value. In this case defaults have no effect. Again the impact of defaults on the forward contract is the same as that on the call. It follows that the contract has a value equal to a long position in a call that is subject to default risk and short position in a default-free put.

27.11. Suppose that the forward contract provides a payoff at time T. With our usual notation, the value of a long forward contract is $S_T - Ke^{-rT}$. The credit exposure on a long forward contract is therefore $\max(S_T - Ke^{-rT}, 0)$; that is, it is a call on the asset price with strike price Ke^{-rT}. Similarly the credit exposure on a short forward contract is $\max(Ke^{-rT} - S_T, 0)$; that is, it is a put on the asset price with strike price Ke^{-rT}. The total credit exposure is, therefore, a straddle with strike price Ke^{-rT}.

27.12. The credit risk on a matched pair of interest rate swaps is $|B_{\text{fixed}} - B_{\text{floating}}|$. As maturity is approached all bond prices tend to par and this tends to zero. The credit risk on a matched pair of currency swaps is $|SB_{\text{foreign}} - B_{\text{fixed}}|$ where S is the exchange rate. The expected value of this tends to increase as the swap maturity is approached because of the uncertainty in S.

27.13. As time passes there is a tendency for the currency which has the lower interest rate to strengthen. This means that a swap where we are receiving this currency will tend to move in the money (i.e., have a positive value). Similarly a swap where we are paying the currency will tend to move out of the money (i.e., have a negative value). From this it follows that our expected exposure on the swap where we are receiving the low-interest currency is much greater than our expected exposure on the swap where we are receiving the high-interest currency. We should therefore look for counterparties with a low credit risk on the side of the swap where we are receiving the low-interest currency. On the other side of the swap we are far less concerned about the creditworthiness of the counterparty.

27.14. No, put–call parity does not hold when there is default risk. Suppose c^* and p^* are the no-default prices of a European call and put with strike price K and maturity T on a non-dividend-paying stock whose price is S, and that c and p are the corresponding values when there is default risk. The text shows that when we make the independence assumption (that is, we assume that the variables determining the no-default value of the option are independent of the variables determining default probabilities and recovery rates), $c = c^* e^{-[y(T)-y^*(T)]T}$ and $p = p^* e^{-[y(T)-y^*(T)]T}$. The relationship

$$c^* + Ke^{-y^*(T)T} = p^* + S$$

which holds in a no-default world therefore becomes

$$c + Ke^{-y(T)T} = p + Se^{-[y(T)-y^*(T)]T}$$

when there is default risk. This is not the same a regular put–call parity. What is more, the relationship depends on the independence assumption and cannot be deduced from the same sort of simple no-arbitrage arguments that we used in Chapter 8 for the put–call parity relationship in a no-default world.

27.15. An approach that is analogous to the approach used for European options is to increase the discount rate on the binomial or trinomial tree that is used to value the option from the risk-free rate to the risky rate. However this may understate the value of the option. This is because the option holder's decision on early exercise may be influenced by new information, received during the life of the option, on the fortunes of the option writer. An example may help to illustrate the point here. Suppose that company X sells a one-year American call option on a non-dividend-paying stock to company Y and that during the following six months company X experiences a series of large, well-publicized loan losses. Normally, the option would not be exercised early. But if the option is somewhat in the money at the end of the six months, company Y might choose to exercise the option at this time rather than wait and risk company X being liquidated before the option matures.

27.16. The statements in (a) and (b) are true. The statement in (c) is not. Suppose that v_X and v_Y are the exposures to X and Y. The expected value of $v_X + v_Y$ is the expected value of v_X plus the expected value of v_Y. The same is not true of 95% confidence limits.

27.17. The cost of defaults is uv where u is percentage loss from defaults during the life of the contract and v is the value of an option that pays off $\max(150S_T - 100, 0)$ in one year and S_T is the value in dollars of one AUD. The value of u is

$$u = 1 - e^{-(0.06-0.05)\times 1} = 0.009950$$

The variable v is 150 times a call option to buy one AUD for 0.6667. The formula for the call option in terms of forward prices is

$$[FN(d_1) - KN(d_2)]e^{-rT}$$

where

$$d_1 = \frac{\log(F/K) + \sigma^2 T/2}{\sigma\sqrt{T}}$$

$$d_2 = d_1 - \sigma\sqrt{T}$$

In this case $F = 0.6667$, $K = 0.6667$, $\sigma = 0.12$, $T = 1$, and $r = 0.05$ so that $d_1 = 0.06, d_2 = -0.06$ and the value of the call option is 0.0303. It follows that $v = 150 \times 0.0303 = 4.545$ so that the cost of defaults is

$$4.545 \times 0.009950 = 0.04522$$

27.18. In this case the costs of defaults is $u_1 v_1 + u_2 v_2$ where

$$u_1 = 1 - e^{-(0.055-0.05)\times 0.5} = 0.002497$$

$$u_2 = e^{-(0.055-0.05)\times 0.5} - e^{-(0.06-0.05)\times 1} = 0.007453$$

v_1 is the value of an option that pays off $\max(150S_T - 100, 0)$ in six months and v_2 is the value of a option that pays off $\max(150S_T - 100, 0)$ in one year. The calculations in Problem 27.17 show that v_2 is 4.545. Similarly $v_1 = 3.300$ so that the cost of defaults is

$$0.002497 \times 3.300 + 0.007453 \times 4.545 = 0.04211$$

27.19. In this case $\sigma = 0.25$, $\delta t = 0.5$, $r = 0.06$ and the tree parameters are $u = 1.1934$, $d = 0.8380$, $a = 1.0305$, $p = 0.5416$, and $1 - p = 0.4584$. The tree is shown in Figure 27.1. The top number at each node is the stock price; the second number is the value of the equity component of the convertible; the third number is the value of the debt component; the fourth number is the total value of the convertible. At node G and H the bond should be converted and is worth five times the stock price. At nodes I and J it should not be converted and is worth \$100. At node D the equity component is 142.41 and the debt component zero. (Neither calling nor converting change the value at this node.) At node E the value of the equity component is

$$0.5416 \times 119.34 \times e^{-0.06 \times 0.5} = 62.72$$

and the value of the debt component is

$$0.4584 \times 100 \times e^{-0.1 \times 0.5} = 43.60$$

The total value of the convertible is 106.32. The bond should be neither converted nor called at this node. At node F the convertible is worth $100e^{-0.1 \times 0.5} = 95.12$. Again it should be neither called nor converted. At node B, the value of the equity component is
$$(0.5416 \times 142.41 + 0.4584 \times 62.72)e^{-0.06 \times 0.5} = 105.88$$

The value of the debt component is

$$0.4584 \times 43.60 \times e^{-0.1 \times 0.5} = 19.01$$

The total value of the convertible is therefore 124.89. In this case the bond should be called. The holder can either take the 110 call price or convert into $5 \times 23.87 = 119.34$ of equity. The latter is the better alternative. The result of these calculations is therefore that the bond is worth 119.34, all of it equity, at node B. At node C the equity component is
$$0.5416 \times 62.72 \times e^{-0.06 \times 0.5} = 32.97$$

The debt component is

$$(0.5416 \times 43.60 + 0.4584 \times 95.12)e^{-0.1 \times 0.5} = 63.94$$

The total value at this node is 96.91 and the bond should be neither converted nor called. The value of the equity component at the initial node, A, is

$$(0.5416 \times 119.34 + 0.4584 \times 32.97)e^{-0.06 \times 0.5} = 77.39$$

The value of the debt component is

$$0.4584 \times 63.94 \times e^{-0.1 \times 0.5} = 27.88$$

The initial value of the convertible is therefore 105.27. The value of the bond without the conversion option is $100e^{-0.1 \times 1.5} = 86.07$. The value of the conversion option (net of the issuer's call option) is therefore $105.27 - 86.07 = 19.20$.

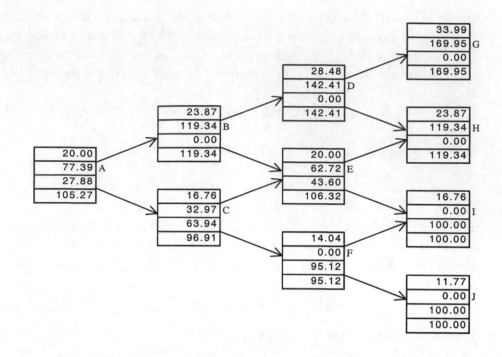

Figure 27.1   Tree for Problem 27.19

184

CHAPTER 28
Real Options

28.1. In the net present value approach, cash flows are estimated in the real world and discounted at a risk-adjusted discount rate. In the risk-neutral valuation approach, cash flows are estimated in the risk-neutral world and discounted at the risk-free interest rate. The risk-neutral valuation approach is arguably more appropriate for valuing real options because it is very difficult to determine the appropriate risk-adjusted discount rate when options are valued.

28.2. In a risk-neutral world the expected price of copper in six months is 75 cents. This corresponds to an expected growth rate of $2\ln(75/80) = -12.9\%$ per annum. The decrease in the growth rate when we move from the real world to the risk-neutral world is the volatility of copper times its market price of risk. This is $0.2 \times 0.5 = 0.1$ or 10% per annum. It follows that the expected growth rate of the price of copper in the real world is -2.9%.

28.3. In this case

$$\frac{dS}{S} = \mu(t)\, dt + \sigma\, dz$$

or

$$d\ln S = [\mu(t) - \sigma^2/2]\, dt + \sigma\, dz$$

so that $\ln S_T$ is normal with mean

$$\ln S_0 + \int_{t=0}^{T} \mu(t)dt - \sigma^2 T/2$$

and standard deviation $\sigma\sqrt{T}$. Section 28.5 shows that

$$\mu(t) = \frac{\partial}{\partial t}[\ln F(t)]$$

so that

$$\int_{t=0}^{T} \mu(t)dt = \ln F(T) - \ln F(0)$$

Since $F(0) = S_0$ the result follows.

28.4. Equation (28.5) gives

$$\mu - r = \sum_{i=1}^{n} \lambda_i \sigma_i$$

From equation (21A.3)

$$\mu f = \frac{\partial f}{\partial t} + \sum_i \frac{\partial f}{\partial \theta_i} m_i \theta_i + \frac{1}{2} \sum_{i,k} \rho_{ik} s_i s_k \theta_i \theta_k \frac{\partial^2 f}{\partial \theta_i \, \partial \theta_k}$$

$$\sigma_i f = \frac{\partial f}{\partial \theta_i} s_i \theta_i$$

Substituting into equation (28.5) we obtain

$$\frac{\partial f}{\partial t} + \sum_i \frac{\partial f}{\partial \theta_i} m_i \theta_i + \frac{1}{2} \sum_{i,k} \rho_{ik} s_i s_k \theta_i \theta_k \frac{\partial^2 f}{\partial \theta_i \, \partial \theta_k} - rf = \sum_{i=1}^n \lambda_i \frac{\partial f}{\partial \theta_i} s_i \theta_i$$

Simplifying this reduces to equation (28.6).

28.5. We explained the concept of a convenience yield for a commodity in Chapter 3. It is a measure of the benefits realized from ownership of the physical commodity that are not realized by the holders of a futures contract. If y is the convenience yield and u is the storage cost, equation (3.21) shows that the commodity behaves like an investment asset that provides a return equal to $y - u$. In a risk-neutral world its growth is, therefore,

$$r - (y - u) = r - y + u$$

The convenience yield of a commodity can be related to its market price of risk. From Section 28.2, the expected growth of the commodity price in a risk-neutral world is $m - \lambda s$, where m is its expected growth in the real world, s its volatility, and λ is its market price of risk. It follows that

$$m - \lambda s = r - y + u$$

or

$$y = r + u - m + \lambda s$$

28.6. In equation (28.7) $\rho = 0.2$, $\mu_m - r = 0.06$, and $\sigma_m = 0.18$. It follows that the market price of risk lambda is

$$\frac{0.2 \times 0.06}{0.18} = 0.067$$

28.7. The option can be valued using Black's model. In this case $F_0 = 24$, $K = 25$, $r = 0.05$, $\sigma = 0.2$, and $T = 3$. The value of a option to purchase one barrel of oil at \$25 is

$$e^{-rT}[F_0 N(d_1) - K N(d_2)]$$

where

$$d_1 = \frac{\ln(F_0/K) + \sigma^2 T/2}{\sigma\sqrt{T}}$$

$$d_2 = \frac{\ln(F_0/K) - \sigma^2 T/2}{\sigma \sqrt{T}}$$

This is 2.489. The value of the option to purchase one million barrels is therefore $2,489,000.

28.8. The expected growth rate of the car price in a risk-neutral world is $-0.25 - (-0.1 \times 0.15) = -0.235$ The expected value of the car in a risk-neutral world in four years, $\hat{E}(S_T)$, is therefore $30,000e^{-0.235 \times 4} = \$11,719$. Using the result in equation (12A.1) the value of the option is

$$e^{-rT}[\hat{E}(S_T)N(d_1) - KN(d_2)]$$

where

$$d_1 = \frac{\ln(\hat{E}(S_T)/K) + \sigma^2 T/2}{\sigma \sqrt{T}}$$

$$d_2 = \frac{\ln(\hat{E}(S_T)/K) - \sigma^2 T/2}{\sigma \sqrt{T}}$$

$r = 0.06$, $\sigma = 0.15$, $T = 4$, and $K = 10,000$. It is $1,832.

CHAPTER 29
Insurance, Weather, and Energy Derivatives

29.1. The actuarial approach to valuing an option involves calculating the expected payoff using historical data and discounting the payoff at the risk-free rate. The risk-neutral approach involves calculating the expected payoff in a risk-neutral world and discounting at the risk-free rate. The two approaches give the same answer when the market prices of risk for the variabes underlying the option are zero.

29.2. The average temperature each day is 75°. The CDD each day is therefore 10 and the cumulative CDD for the month is $10 \times 31 = 310$. The payoff from the call option is therefore $(310 - 250) \times 5,000 = \$300,000$.

29.3. The CDD is $\max(A - 65, 0)$ where A is the average of the maximum and minimum temperature during the day. This is the payoff from a call option on A with a strike price of 65.

29.4. It would be useful to calculate the cumulative CDD each July each year for the last 50 years. A linear regression relationship

$$\text{CDD} = a + bt + e$$

could then be estimated where a and b are constants, t is the time in years measured from the start of the 50 years, and e is the error. This relationship allows for linear trends in temperature through time. The expected CDD for next year (year 51) is then $a + 51b$. This could be used as an estimate of the forward CDD. Suppose that the estimate is $\hat{F}$ and a long forward contract has a delivery CDD of K. The value of the forward contract is the present value of $\hat{F} - K$.

29.5. The volatility of the three-month forward price will be less than the volatility of the spot price. This is because, when the spot price changes by a certain amount, mean reversion will cause the forward price will change by a lesser amount.

29.6. The price of the energy source will show big changes, but will be pulled back to its long-run average level fast. Electricity is an example of an energy source with these characteristics.

29.7. The gas producer can regress profits against price and temperature. It can then use weather derivatives to hedge temperature (i.e., volume) risk and energy derivatives to hedge price risk.

29.8. A 5×8 contract for May, 2003 is a contract to provide electricity for five days per week during the off-peak period (11pm to 7am). When daily exercise is specified, the holder of the option is able to choose each weekday whether he or she will buy electricity at the strike price at the agreed rate. When there is monthly exercise, he or she chooses once at the beginning of the month whether electricity is to be bought at the strike price at the agreed rate for the whole month. The option with daily exercise is worth more.

29.9. CAT bonds (catastrophe bonds) are an alternative to reinsurance for an insurance company that has taken on a certain catastrophic risk (e.g., the risk of a hurricane or an earthquake) and wants to get rid of it. CAT bonds are issued by the insurance company. They provide a higher rate of interest than government bonds. However, the bondholders agree to forego interest, and possibly principal, to meet any claims against the insurance company that are within a prespecified range.

29.10. The CAT bond has very little systematic risk. Whether a particular type of catastrophe occurs is independent of the return on the market. The risks in the CAT bond are likely to be largely "diversified away" by the other investments in the portfolio. A B-rated bond does have systematic risk that cannot be diversified away. It is likely therefore that the CAT bond is a better addition to the portfolio.